†SECRET† SOCIETIES

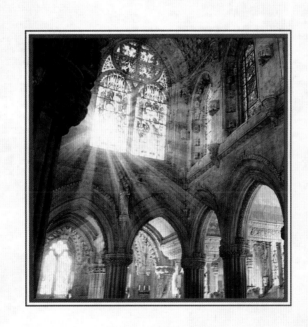

✝ SECRET ✝ SOCIETIES

The truth behind the Templars, Freemasons and other secretive organizations

DAVID V. BARRETT

A GODSFIELD BOOK

Dedicated to all who seek spiritual truths, challenge religious orthodoxy and choose to think for themselves.

An Hachette Livre UK Company
www.hachettelivre.co.uk

First published in Great Britain in 2008
by Godsfield Press
a division of
Octopus Publishing Group Ltd
2–4 Heron Quays,
London E14 4JP
www.octopusbooks.co.uk

ISBN: 978-1-84181-356-1

366
BAR

A CIP catalogue record for this book
is available from the British Library.

Printed and bound in China

2 4 6 8 10 9 7 5 3 1

CONTENTS

Introduction

There have probably been secret societies since the dawn of civilization, and certainly since humankind began to develop religions. Although some secret societies are political or revolutionary in their motivation, and others are criminal, many are religious, at least in their origins, and it is on these that this book mainly focuses.

Where there are religions, there are hierarchies – usually of some form of priests. These are the publicly seen elite, the men (historically, nearly always men) who possess all the teachings of the religion and interpret them for the ordinary people, and who lead the ceremonies and rituals. Often they wear special clothing to set them apart from the congregation, the ordinary people. Sometimes they use a special language that most people do not understand; until the 1960s, for example, Catholic Masses were held in Latin, which the vast majority of ordinary Catholics did not understand, beyond a few taught phrases such as *Ave Maria* and *Pater Noster*.

PRIESTS AS INTERMEDIARIES

In many religions, both thousands of years ago and today, priests were the intermediaries between God and humans. In earlier societies, when the relationship between gods and humans was less codified, this was considered a dangerous role; priests took the risk of propitiating the gods on behalf of the people, and so were highly honoured in society. The priest can also be the middleman between God and the people as effectively the representative of God. This is seen in the title 'the Vicar of Christ' for the Pope; as in the word 'vicarious', he stands in for, or substitutes for, God on Earth.

The Roman Catholic Church believes that Peter was the first Pope – a foundation myth akin to many that we shall encounter in this book. The three main strands of Christianity, the Roman Catholic, Eastern Orthodox and Anglican (or Episcopalian) Churches, all follow the tradition of the laying-on of hands in consecration and ordination to confer spiritual power on bishops and priests. This Apostolic Succession is supposed to go back through a continuous line to Peter (and the other Apostles), and so to Jesus Christ.

As we shall see, there are many priests and bishops in less well-known Churches, some of them linked to secret societies today, who also claim the Apostolic Succession, usually tracing their line back through a renegade Catholic bishop, or sometimes through one of the smaller Orthodox Churches. Claiming a historical lineage (real or imagined) is partly what gives esoteric religions and secret societies their authority.

THE ESOTERIC SPIRITUAL PATH

Throughout history there have always been people whose approach to religion – or, perhaps better, to spirituality – has been outside the confines of established religion. While most believers go to church, synagogue or mosque and participate in exoteric (outer or public) religion, smaller numbers of Christians, Jews and Muslims have for centuries followed a more esoteric (inner or hidden) spiritual path.

This book covers secret societies of all types, around the world, but focuses mainly on those in what is known as the Western Mystery Tradition. This comprises societies, groups of people and individuals who search for a relationship with the Divine outside the structures of established exoteric religion. Because of this, the mainstream religions have often looked on such people with suspicion. Mainstream Judaism and Islam have often had an uneasy relationship over the centuries with the more mystical Kabbalists and Sufis respectively. In Christianity, mystics such as St John of the Cross, Julian of Norwich and Hildegard von Bingen have occasionally been given a position of respect, but more often they have been suspected of heresy, persecuted and sometimes burned at the stake in the name of the God of Love, for claiming a personal, one-to-one relationship with God. By stepping outside the rules of established religious society, they have been seen as setting themselves up against the (supposedly God-given) authority of religious orthodoxy, and so must either be brought under the control of the established religion – by force if necessary – or simply stamped out.

This is one reason why secret societies, whose members follow individual esoteric paths, have carefully maintained their secrecy over the centuries: self-protection. Another is the basic difference between exoteric and esoteric teachings and practices. The former are for everyone, a public expression of religious belief, common to all. The latter are for the select few, initiates who are taught in small groups, sometimes even on a one-to-one basis. While the ritual of, for example, the Catholic Mass is familiar to countless millions, the rituals of secret societies are known to very few.

FEAR OF THE UNKNOWN

It is a sad fact of human character that ignorance often generates fear and suspicion. This applies even to the best-known of all secret societies, so unsecret that they have impressive buildings in the centre

of towns and cities around the world: the Freemasons. They are characterized by stereotypes ('men with funny handshakes') or viewed with distrust because of 'all those stories about corruption – and there's no smoke without fire'. As we shall see, the Roman Catholic Church has long been vehemently opposed to Freemasonry, while some fundamentalist Christians even accuse it of being Satanic, yet this is a society that has

throughout its history had respected pillars of the community among its members.

Unfortunately too many people are prepared to attack others for what they believe – or, rather, for what their critics mistakenly or mendaciously *claim* they believe. In the super-rationalist, scientific, materialist 21st century, it is easy to smile condescendingly at the alchemists and Rosicrucians of the Renaissance as if they

Above Built by the Knights Templar in 1185, the distinctive circular Temple Church in London contains several marble monuments in memory of medieval knights.

were lesser beings than ourselves. But today members of esoteric societies with very similar beliefs, including astrology, alchemy, Tarot, Kabbalah and magical ritual, are all too often accused of being occult, Pagan and Satanic, and so evil or dangerous.

'Occult' simply means 'hidden'; the word is used in astronomy when one body passes in front of another, hiding it, as in an eclipse. 'Pagan' has several meanings, ranging from the religions of ancient Greece and Rome to today's Neo-Pagan religions. As for 'Satanic', almost no one in the various esoteric worlds of secret societies (let alone of Neo-Paganism) has anything to do with Satanism. As will become clear throughout this book, most secret societies have deeply spiritual origins, however they have developed over the centuries. Those within the Western Mystery Tradition are based on the quest for a close personal relationship with God, and on helping to heal society.

Freemasonry is a good example of this. It puts all sectarian divisions – of religion and of politics – to the side; it focuses, through the symbolism of its rituals, on the moral improvement of its members; and it raises large amounts of money around the world for charitable causes. These are similar to the ideals and aspirations outlined by the original Rosicrucians.

AN ENQUIRING MIND

What sort of people join secret societies, and why do they do so? During the Renaissance, and right through to the late 19th century, members would have been men of a certain social status who were well-educated, well-read thinkers. Many of them were natural philosophers, the scientists of their day. (We shall see a link between the Rosicrucians and the Royal Society, the first, and still the most prestigious, scientific society in the world.) Some were doctors, others were clerics – and all had enquiring minds. They were curious, inquisitive; they asked *why?* and *how?* They challenged the authority of 'received wisdom'. They did not want to be told what to believe by other people; they wanted to find out for themselves.

Today members of secret societies are just the same sort of people; however, because of widespread education, they are people of all classes, all occupations and all ages, and, with a few exceptions such as mainstream Freemasonry, most societies now include women as well as men.

Why do people still join secret societies, when so much of the knowledge that was formerly the preserve of a privileged few is now readily available to everyone, and when we enjoy personal freedoms – of expression, of enquiry and much else – undreamed of by our forebears?

For some it is no doubt the desire to belong to a select group, to know things that

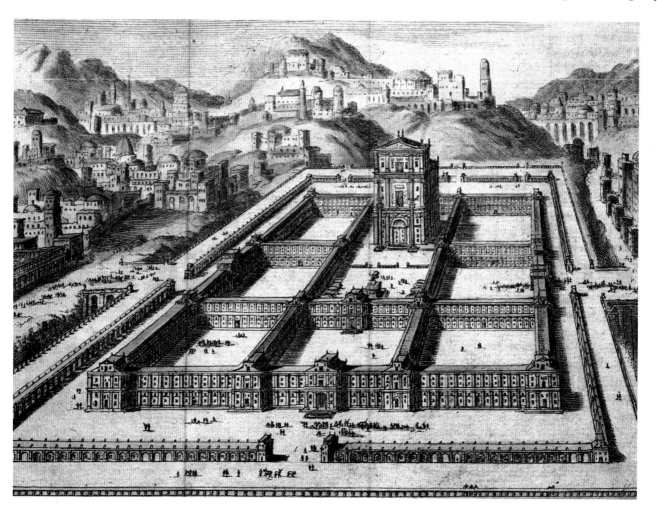

Left *A 1705 Dutch interpretation of how King Solomon's Temple might have looked. Worshippers would make their offerings in the courtyard; the Holy of Holies was reserved for the high priest alone.*

8 INTRODUCTION

Right The ceremonial seal designed for Aleister Crowley's esoteric society, Argenteum Astrum (A∴A∴), or the Order of the Silver Star, by J.F.C. Fuller in 1911.

few other people know, and perhaps to gain some sort of power through this. Similarly, some people undoubtedly join the Freemasons and similar societies for the social contacts and advancement they hope they will gain. These may be selfish reasons, but they are very human ones.

However, for many it is the same curiosity that drove the early natural philosophers – the simple desire to find out more about the universe and our place within it. For many, too, it is a genuine desire for a spiritual depth that they cannot find in established religion. In the 18th and 19th centuries intelligent freethinkers found their spiritual home in Deism, Unitarianism or Quakerism. From the 1960s onwards many have explored a host of new religions, especially new Western

expressions of Eastern philosophies, self-help movements such as *est*, Neuro-Linguistic Programming and Scientology, New Age ideas and Neo-Pagan religions.

THE RIGHT TO CHOOSE

Some of these same people today also join the more esoteric societies that have grown out of, for example, the Hermetic Order of the Golden Dawn, which itself developed from a branch of Freemasonry on the one hand and the 19th-century French esoteric resurgence on the other – and both of these, in reality or in resemblance, can be traced back to the Rosicrucians, and before them to the Hermetic Philosophers of the Renaissance, medieval alchemists, astrologers and Kabbalists, and spiritually

independent and individual people going back to the Gnostics and Neoplatonists, and even the Mystery Religions of the early years of Christianity.

Mainstream religions, which have invested much effort over the centuries in developing their orthodoxy (literally 'straight opinion'), are affronted by such heterodox ('other-thinking') rebels and condemn them as heretics. The word 'heresy', however, comes from a Greek root meaning simply 'choice'.

Those who follow their own spiritual path, whether through esoteric religions or secret societies – which, as this book shows, are often much the same thing – are simply exercising their right to choose, and surely that is something to be admired, not maligned and condemned.

CHAPTER 1

THE ANCIENT MYSTERIES

To understand secret societies through the ages, including those we have today, it is important to look at the development of esoteric spiritual ideas as long ago as the time of Christ, and even earlier. Most of the ancient beliefs that have contributed to what is now known as the Western Mystery Tradition came from around the Mediterranean – Greece, Egypt, Rome and the Holy Land – some two thousand years ago. They included Gnosticism, dualism, Neoplatonism, the Mystery Religions and the teachings attributed to Hermes Trismegistus.

ITALY

Rome

GREECE

BLACK SEA

MEDITERRANEAN SEA

SYRIA

IRAQ

JORDAN

EGYPT

The origins of
secret societies

The countries around the Mediterranean 20 centuries ago were a melting pot of cultures and religious beliefs. As well as the 'official' religions of Greece and Rome, and the temple-centred religion of the Jews, there were many other spiritual philosophies that competed with, overlapped with and influenced each other.

For some there was the belief that divinity can be found within us. For others the emphasis was on having a personal relationship with God, rather than going through the hierarchy of priests in a formal religious structure. All of them focused on individual spiritual experience. These revolutionary ideas have continued to be fundamental to esoteric spirituality and to secret societies.

GNOSTICISM

Two thousand years ago, plus or minus a century or so, a new religious idea gained a lot of ground in the Middle East. Directly and indirectly it has influenced Western religious beliefs ever since. This was Gnosticism.

Gnosticism was not itself a religion, but it lay at the heart of a number of different religious groups. It did not comprise just one set of ideas, like the teachings of the Roman Catholic Church; Gnostic religions varied greatly from each other, with very different teachings, mythologies and moral codes.

However, at the heart of all of them was one deep belief: that individual people, without the need for priests and bishops and all the hierarchies and complexities of more structured religions, can know God. The Greek word *gnosis* means 'knowledge', particularly spiritual knowledge – having a personal knowledge of God, *knowing God.*

A finely balanced debate

Scholars differ on whether Gnosticism was one of the earliest offshoots of Christianity or whether the Gnosticism of the 2nd century CE was just a Christian version of a pre-existing religious philosophy – hence the wording of the opening sentence above. But Christian Gnosticism was so widespread and popular, long before the Christian Church became established in Rome, and even before the content of the New Testament had been decided, that some of the earliest Christian writings we have are attacks on the Gnostics.

In particular, the nature of Jesus – how much he was man and how much he was God – was hotly debated. Bishops battled with

THE GOD-WITHIN AND THE GOD-WITHOUT

Gnostics, in their many forms, believe that there is a spark of divinity within each of us. In searching for, finding and communing with the God-within, we can make personal contact with the God-without. Whether it is labelled Gnostic or not, this fundamental idea of an individual spiritual quest lies at the heart of Jewish Kabbalism, Christian mysticism and Muslim Sufism, as well as the 'self-realization' of many areas of Hinduism and Buddhism, and the esoteric and magical teachings and practices of modern Neo-Pagan religions. It is also at the very heart of many of the world's secret societies throughout history, right up to the present day.

each other, each one arguing vociferously that his beliefs were the true interpretation of the faith and that everyone else's were wrong. This went on around the Mediterranean for more than three centuries after the life and death of Jesus. In the end, one particular version of Christianity became accepted as 'standard', and all the other versions (including Gnosticism) were condemned as heresy. Few Christians today have any idea that the beliefs of their religion could so easily have been very different, had the balance tipped in another direction 1,700 or 1,800 years ago.

Manicheism and its dualist derivations

One very influential Gnostic religion, which was as much Zoroastrian as Christian in origin, was Manicheism, founded by a Persian teacher, Mani (216–76 CE). This maintained a presence in the Middle East for some centuries, probably surviving in some part because Mani set up a hierarchical framework, an organization, from the start. (Without a well-defined structure, new religions often do not survive beyond the first or second generation, with the last members who actually knew the founder, who was often a charismatic personality; and the same applies to secret societies.)

The significance of Manicheism can be judged by the fact that St Augustine of Hippo (354–430 CE) was a Manichean for 12 years in his youth – which probably accounts for his zeal in fighting heresy later in his life.

The best-known Gnostic religion, Catharism, appeared in the Languedoc (now southern France) in the 12th and 13th centuries. The Cathars almost certainly developed from the 10th-century Bogomils of Bulgaria, who can probably be traced back through the 7th-century Paulicians in Armenia, and in turn back to the Manicheans. The beliefs of each religion may not have been identical, but they were all dualist and Gnostic.

The Cathars rejected the wealth and rampant corruption of the medieval Catholic Church; their leaders (unlike many bishops and cardinals) abstained from meat and sex. Unusually for the time, Cathar leaders

included women as well as men. The Cathars became so popular that the Roman Catholic Church declared a crusade against them, killing hundreds of thousands of believers and wiping out not only a peaceful religion, but also an entire culture.

Above Shapur, early 3rd-century king of Persia, speaking with Mani, who dedicated a treatise to him, and is said to have converted his brother.

Above Zoroaster or Zarathustra, founder of Zoroastrianism, the first major monotheistic religion.

by the bad God – which accounts for all the negative things in the world, from lying, stealing and murder in human behaviour to earthquakes, famine, floods, the tsetse fly and the common cold. This is an ingenious answer to perhaps the most difficult question every religion has to answer: if God is good, why is there suffering in the world? (Attempts to answer this question are known by religious scholars as theodicy.)

Zoroastrianism was arguably the first monotheistic religion – that is, having a belief in one God. Most scholars think that Zoroaster (or Zarathustra) probably lived in the 7th century BCE, although he may have lived several centuries earlier. He reformed the complex polytheism (worship of many gods) of Persia (today's Iran) by declaring that there was one God, Ahura Mazda, the Wise Lord; all the other gods were lesser beings, equivalent perhaps to angels, serving the One God.

There was also an evil power, Angra Mainyu, who was not actually a god, but was very skilled at turning men away from the truth of God. It is likely that the more specific dualist beliefs of Gnostics – including those of the medieval Cathars of the Languedoc – stemmed ultimately from versions of the Zoroastrian belief.

The 'Religions of the Book'

Even in the three mainstream monotheistic 'Religions of the Book' – Judaism, Christianity and Islam – a type of dualism lives on in the form of Satan. He may not be a god, but whether he is an agent of God to test humans, or a fallen angel or a jinn, his role is to oppose God. Judaism, Christianity and Islam also inherited from Zoroastrianism the concepts of an afterlife in heaven and hell, resurrection and the final judgement at the end of time.

NEOPLATONISM

As with Gnosticism, there is not just one belief called Neoplatonism. The term applies to the spiritual teachings of a number of Greek philosophers in the first few centuries CE; and, like Gnosticism and dualism, these ideas influenced both exoteric (outer or

DUALISM AND MONOTHEISM

Many Gnostics had a dualist belief: that there was a good God and a bad God (or perhaps a mad God). The good God was the Ultimate, the highest power, but our world was created public) and esoteric (inner or hidden) Christian beliefs.

One of the most important beliefs to come out of Neoplatonism, through the Syrian philosopher Iamblichus (c.250–c.330 CE), is that while there is one supreme God, infinite and incomprehensible, below this are a host of lesser beings, servants of the greater God, known collectively as *dæmons*. (This is similar to the belief in Zoroastrianism.) Depending on the religion, these might include lesser gods, or angels, or the spirits of the heroic dead, but they are not to be confused with the Christian concept of 'demons' meaning evil spirits. When magicians and esotericists throughout the ages have summoned beings, it is *dæmons* they have called, not demons, and certainly not the Devil and his evil spirits.

Neoplatonism rediscovered the importance of the experiential: the pre-Socratic principle that experience is important in all things. So in your spiritual life you should not just believe what you were told to believe (as in most exoteric religion even today), but you should have an individual mystical contact and connection with the power of God and spiritual beings. As with Gnosticism, this emphasis on individual spiritual experience weakened the authority of the priesthood.

Such esoteric spiritual beliefs may be found in many secret societies through the centuries, but have also made their mark on exoteric religion. The rituals within all religions – including, for example, the Catholic Mass – are effectively a symbolic way of drawing people into a relationship with the ineffable.

Far-reaching influences

Some Neoplatonists such as the Greek philosopher Plotinus (204/5–270 CE) were opposed to magic and advocated the mystical contemplation of God. Others, such as Iamblichus, were advocates of magical rites. These two very different attitudes were both to have an effect on secret societies as far ahead as the 20th century (see pages 113 and 116). Iamblichus also taught that the gods of the world's religions are simply human beings' way of trying to approach the

Above The Zoroastrian medieval Takyeh Amir Chakhmagh in Yazd, Iran.

Even in the three mainstream monotheistic 'Religions of the Book' – Judaism, Christianity and Islam – a type of dualism lives on in the form of Satan.

ineffable One God through more accessible lesser gods. This belief can be found, expressed in various ways, in many esoteric religions and in many secret societies today, both mystical and magical.

The term Neoplatonism, as well as including this variety of philosophical beliefs, also generally includes Neo-Pythagorianism. For the Greek philosopher Pythagoras (581–497 BCE), the deep symbolic meanings of numbers and their relationship underlay everything in the world: not just the mathematics for which he is remembered in schools today, but also architecture, music and mysticism. Later reinterpretations of the teachings of Pythagoras are fundamental to the teachings of many secret societies, including Kabbalism, Freemasonry and magical 'correspondences' (see pages 109 and 166).

THE MYSTERY RELIGIONS

In the centuries before and after the time of Jesus, around the Mediterranean there were numerous 'mystery cults', devoted to a variety of gods including Mithras, Orpheus, Dionysus, Isis and Osiris, and Demeter and Persephone. These were esoteric religions, open only to initiated members; the rituals and the beliefs were restricted to those who had passed through initiation ceremonies, which often included a symbolic dying of the old life and rebirth into the new life.

Some of these Mystery Religions, particularly the Orphic movement, taught their members that they had a spark of the Divine deep within themselves – spirit trapped in the gross matter of their bodies. This belief is fundamental to many of the secret societies that are explored in this book.

Mithraism

Perhaps the best known of these religions today is Mithraism, a popular religion among Roman soldiers. Like other 'mystery cults', it had a progressive initiatory structure: members advanced from *Corvus* (Raven) through *Nymphus* (Bride), *Miles* (Soldier), *Leo* (Lion), *Perses* (Persian) and *Heliodromus* (Runner of the Sun) to *Pater* (Father). They held their meetings in secret, either in caves or in buildings symbolizing caves.

In the first few centuries CE, Mithraism was actually a more widespread religion in the Roman Empire – including Britain – than Christianity. Indeed, as Christianity developed, it borrowed several aspects of Mithraism, possibly to boost its own popularity. Mithras was a sun god and a saviour god; Christianity changed its day of worship from the Jewish Sabbath (Saturday) to Sunday, and, as its theology developed, Jesus became a saviour figure. It is also unlikely to be a coincidence that one of Mithraism's main festivals was celebrated on 25 December, around the winter solstice. Like many other religions at the time, Mithraism had a symbolic ritual meal; St Paul's description of the first 'Communion service' (I Corinthians 11:23ff.) would have been familiar to the Greco-Roman Pagan community in his native Tarsus.

The various aspects of Christian belief and practice did not spring fully fledged from nowhere; they came from the historical and geographical context of when and where Christianity developed.

Left *The Egyptian God Osiris. Detail from the grave of Haremhab, Valley of the Kings, Egypt, c.1300 BCE.*

HERMES TRISMEGISTUS

One of the most influential sources of later secret societies, Hermes Trismegistus, never existed – at least not as one person. Hermes was the winged messenger god, the Greek equivalent of the Roman god Mercury and the Egyptian god Thoth. *Trismegistus* means 'thrice greatest'. In the fertile blending of Greek and Egyptian religious philosophies, Thoth/Hermes became the ultimate god of esoteric knowledge, communication and power. Works written in his name were once believed to pre-date Jesus, or even to go back as far as the time of Moses, but are now known to date from the first three or four centuries CE.

The *Corpus Hermeticum*

Though hugely important at the time of their creation, these writings were lost to the West until the late 15th century. Cosimo de' Medici (1389–1464) was one of the wealthiest and most influential men in Renaissance Italy, and a great patron of the Arts. He commissioned the scholar and monk Marsilio Ficino (1433–99) to find obscure manuscripts and translate them into Latin. When the *Corpus Hermeticum* came to his attention, Cosimo de' Medici ordered Ficino to stop his current task of translating the works of Plato in order to translate the writings attributed to Hermes Trismegistus.

The texts in the *Corpus Hermeticum* were a distillation of Greek-Egyptian esoteric teachings of the early centuries CE. They covered philosophy and religion, alchemy and astrology, mysticism and magic. One work, known as *Poimandres* or 'The Shepherd of Men', is a Gnostic text about the *nous*, the inner intellect, reaching out to and gaining direct knowledge of God. The *Perfect Sermon* of Asclepius speaks of a hierarchy of beings below the Divine Unity, and of human beings' divine nature.

A related text, the *Emerald Tablet* or *Tabula Smaragdina*, contains one of the most important esoteric spiritual sayings of all time: 'As above, so below', linking the macrocosm and the microcosm, heaven and Earth, God and humankind.

The writings ascribed to Hermes Trismegistus were crucial to the development of esoteric thinking during the 16th and 17th centuries, particularly the Hermetic Philosophers (see pages 54–55), from whom would develop Rosicrucianism, Freemasonry and the many occult societies of the 19th, 20th and 21st centuries.

Right A 2nd century CE Roman marble statue, depicting Mithras sacrificing the bull. The spilt blood of the bull ensured the fertility of nature.

CHAPTER 2

THE KNIGHTS TEMPLAR

Much that has been written about the Knights Templar over the years is misinformation; some is no doubt misunderstanding; some is wishful thinking; and some may well be deliberate deception. It can be difficult now to disentangle the historically verifiable facts from the tangled web of highly colourful romantic fantasy. What is certain is that the story of the Templars continues to fascinate thousands of people throughout the world.

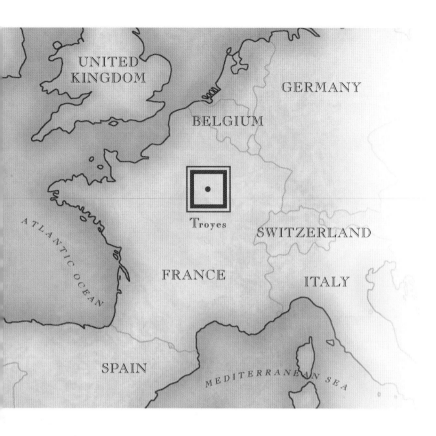

Templar origins

Medieval chronicles show that the Knights Templar were formed around 1119, with the aim of protecting Christian pilgrims travelling to Jerusalem. Jerusalem had been captured by the Crusaders in 1099, and some Christians naturally wanted to go on pilgrimage to the place where Jesus had been crucified. However, the journey was long and hard; as well as the physical problems of travelling over difficult terrain in uncertain weather, there was the ever-present risk of attack.

The Order of Knights Hospitaller already looked after sick pilgrims in Jerusalem, but there was no one to protect pilgrims from being attacked as they made their way there; the Hospitallers did not become a military Order themselves until the 1130s, following the formal recognition of the Knights Templar as such.

FOUNDING OF THE ORDER

The Knights Templar were founded by Hugues de Payen (*c.*1070–1136), a noble from Champagne in north-east France, with Godfroi de St Omer and just seven other knights, mostly of noble families. Their numbers quickly grew; by 1130 there were around three hundred knights in Palestine. They took their name from their quarters in Jerusalem, which were near the al-Aqsa mosque on Temple Mount, supposedly built over the ruins of Solomon's Temple (see pages 92–93). Their full name was the Order of the Poor Knights of Christ and the Temple of Solomon.

Although the Order existed from around 1119, it was not formally created and approved by the Pope until 1128, at the Council of Troyes, south-east of Paris. This was largely at the instigation of the highly influential Cistercian abbot Bernard of Clairvaux (1090–1153), who also drew up the Rule for the new Order; until then they had been under the Augustinian Rule. Bernard was later largely responsible for rallying support in launching the disastrous Second Crusade at Vézelay in France.

Knights of the Order of the Temple took the usual monastic vows of poverty, chastity and obedience; but they were unique in being a religious Order specifically dedicated to fighting. Previously there had been a great moral divide between knights – who were trained to kill and were not squeamish about it, and who took their sexual pleasure where they willed (chivalry being unknown in the harsh real world) – and monks, who had to keep themselves clean from all things worldly (especially killing and sex). The Knights Templar crossed that line.

A Templar knight had to be born in wedlock and unmarried – that is, with no hint of sexual sin. He had to come from a knightly family, so no common riff-raff were allowed. There were four other conditions: he must be adult, not in debt, free of all other obligations, and not a member of any other Order. Some esoteric societies, even today, make these same four demands of their members.

THE TEMPLARS' RULE

All religious Orders live by a Rule; the Templars' Rule, initially strongly influenced by Bernard of Clairvaux, developed during the 12th and 13th centuries. It set out the daily rules and regulations for the way Templar knights must live, their religious obligations, their food, clothing, and so on. In common with other monastic Orders, Templars had to attend a succession of services throughout the day, starting with Matins at 4 a.m.. They ate simply and in silence, although (unlike the Cistercians) they were allowed to eat meat three days a week to keep up their fighting strength; on Fridays they had to eat fish and eggs. The Rule also set out the penalties for any infringements; these ranged from a knight having to eat off the floor to being stripped of his mantle, weapons and horse, and even being expelled from the Order.

The company of women is a dangerous thing, for by it the devil has led many from the straight path to Paradise ...

We believe it to be a dangerous thing for any religious to look too much upon the face of woman. For this reason none of you may presume to kiss a woman, be it widow, young girl, mother, sister, aunt or any other; and henceforth the Knighthood of Jesus Christ should avoid at all costs the embraces of women, by which men have perished many times ...

It was no doubt Bernard of Clairvaux's decision to include these paragraphs in the Rule. Whatever spiritual virtues he may have had, he utterly loathed women.

The vow of poverty, however, was a more flexible concept. Despite the well-known Templar image of two knights sharing one horse, in reality each knight would be expected to have two or three horses, a mounted sergeant, several foot soldiers and other men in support of him.

Above *The Dome of the Rock and al-Aqsa Mosque on Temple Mount, Jerusalem, today. In the early 12th century the original Knights Templar are believed to have been housed near here.*

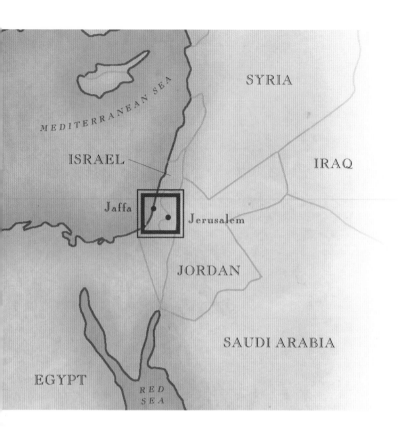

The heyday of the Templars: fighting men

The Knights Templar quickly built up a reputation as very skilled, dedicated and highly disciplined fighting men. The knights themselves were the spearhead of a larger organization that included sergeant brothers and squires, as well as all the infrastructure of lay brothers, infirmary brothers, priests, cooks and other servants.

One estimate is that for each knight there were up to ten other men, so that just before the destruction of the Order in 1307 it numbered some 15,000 men, of whom 1,500 were knights.

Only the knights wore the white mantle (initially plain, but later bearing the famous red cross); sergeants wore a black or dark-brown mantle. One of the most important people on the battlefield, in fact, was not a knight, but one of the sergeant brothers who had the post of standard-bearer. As long as the Templars' black-and-white standard, known as the Beauseant, was still flying, no knight was allowed to leave the battlefield; however dire their plight, they must stay and fight to the death. For the standard to fall or to be captured was a great dishonour, so it might be protected by as many as ten fighting men; and, in case it should somehow be lost, the Templar force would have a second one folded away, ready to be raised as a replacement.

THE ROAD TO JERUSALEM

Although the original purpose of the Knights Templar was the protection of pilgrims en route to Jerusalem from Jaffa on the Mediterranean coast, within a couple of decades they were perceived as an elite fighting force. Their first-known military encounters, in the 1130s, were near Antioch in present-day Turkey, far to the north. Similarly, the first Templar castle was built

some 645 km (400 miles) north of the Jaffa–Jerusalem road.

The Templars came into their own during the ill-fated Second Crusade (1145–49). In part, perhaps, they shone in comparison to the other ill-disciplined fighting forces during that Crusade. By the time Louis VII's

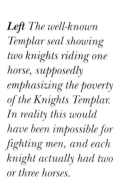

Left The well-known Templar seal showing two knights riding one horse, supposedly emphasizing the poverty of the Knights Templar. In reality this would have been impossible for fighting men, and each knight actually had two or three horses.

French army arrived in the Holy Land (the German army of Conrad, the Holy Roman Emperor, had already given up and returned to Constantinople), they had lost large numbers of people and were utterly demoralized, fragmented and squabbling among themselves. The discipline of the Knights Templar brought them together sufficiently to survive, and then to go on to win some victories.

After the Second Crusade the Knights Templar were involved in most of the military action in the Holy Land, and in Europe; they were in the forefront of the retaking of Spain from the Moors. But not all went well for the Templars, militarily. In the late 12th century they were in regular conflict with the great Muslim leader Saladin (1138–93). His troops were just as disciplined as the Templars, and there were many more of them – and Saladin was a brilliant strategist. Cities, forts and roads were fought over and many of them were taken by Saladin's forces. They had a brilliant skirmishing tactic of firing their

bows at the gallop, easily picking off Christian soldiers who were used to set-piece battles.

THE MASTER'S MISTAKES

The Templars were also caught up in the internecine struggle for the rulership of Jerusalem, between Guy de Lusignan and Raymond of Tripoli. In 1187 the Master of the Knights Templar, Gérard de Ridefort (a close friend of Guy de Lusignan), made a huge miscalculation at Nazareth in attacking one of Saladin's sons, who had been granted permission to cross Raymond's land. The Muslim group had superior numbers and the Templars were thrashed; 60 knights were killed, including the third-highest officer in the Order, the Marshal of the Temple.

The same year the same Master made an even greater mistake. The Horns of Hattin were twin hills guarding an important pass through the mountains west of Tiberias, which had been taken by Saladin. West of the mountains lay the road to Acre, on the Mediterranean coast. Gérard de Ridefort,

against the advice of Raymond, persuaded Guy de Lusignan to move his troops from Acre to engage Saladin's troops. The march, across waterless hills in the heat of July, was disastrous. The Christian soldiers were cut off by Saladin part-way, and were forced to camp overnight with no source of water. The following day, parched and exhausted, they engaged the Muslim force in battle. Despite fighting courageously, they were trounced. Thousands were killed, including 230 Templar knights; thousands more were captured. It was the beginning of the end of Christian – and Templar – influence in the Holy Land.

After Tiberias, Acre fell, then Jaffa and other vital strongholds. In October 1187 Jerusalem was taken by Saladin; the original purpose of the Knights Templar was gone. They were still brilliant and well-disciplined fighting men, and still fought in all the Crusades and campaigns of the next century in the Holy Land; but their talents and influence began to be seen in other areas.

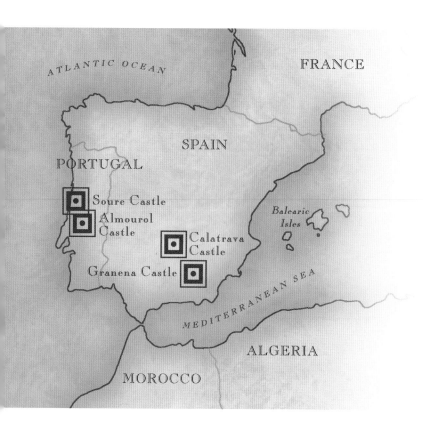

The heyday of the Templars: financiers

The Knights Templar showed their first signs of becoming 'the bankers of Europe' as early as the Second Crusade. Military campaigns are expensive, and it is not uncommon for their leaders to run out of money. Louis VII (1120–80) needed finance in order to continue his campaign; so the Templars gave him a loan, to be repaid when he returned to France.

By then the Order was already beginning to be independently wealthy. Templar knights were fighting the Moors in Spain possibly as early as 1130. Even earlier, in 1128, Queen Teresa of Portugal gave the Templars the castle of Soure on the River Mondego. Count Raymond Bérengar III of Barcelona gave them the castle of Granena in 1130, and King Alfonso VII of Castile gave them the castle of Calatrava, taken from the Moors in 1134. When the Templars took Almourol Castle on the Tagus River from the Moors, it was given to them by Alfonso Henriques, Count of Portugal, as a defensive stronghold (see pages 26–27).

INCREASING WEALTH AND PRIVILEGES

In return for helping to wrest Spain back from the Moors, the Templars were not only given castles, but were granted huge amounts of land – with the revenue that came with it. Additionally, King Alfonso I of Navarre and Aragon exempted the Templars from one-fifth of the tax payable on everything they won from the Moors. He was so impressed by the Templars that, on his

death in 1134, he left one-third of his entire kingdom to the Order, though his will was successfully contested.

The Church also gave the Knights Templar huge privileges that quickly contributed to their wealth. In 1139 Pope Innocent II granted them independence from all secular and ecclesiastical authority, save only for the Pope himself. In 1161 Pope Alexander III exempted them from all tithes, and allowed them to receive tithes themselves.

With the Order so clearly in the high favour of the Church, kings and nobles vied with each other to give the Templars castles and land; lay members who joined the Order often donated large amounts of money. At this time in history, if other commitments meant that you could not dedicate your life to God's service, it was quite normal to give to the Church, perhaps to a specific monastery or to an Order – and to give substantially, effectively to buy a place in heaven. King Henry II of England and Plantagenet France (1133–89) left 5,000 silver marks to the Knights Templar in his will of 1182, and some nobles borrowed money from the Order, perhaps to pay for going on a pilgrimage, in

THE PROMISSORY NOTE

The Templars also set up an efficient way to carry money safely on long journeys. Taking a wagon full of gold and silver coins with you was asking for trouble – not just from bandits, but from other groups who were on pilgrimage or Crusade. Instead, you deposited your money with the Order in London or Paris, or another secure headquarters, and were given a promissory note (the equivalent of today's cheque) to take with you. On arrival at your destination, you took the note to the local Templar house or commandery and exchanged it for money.

exchange for leaving all their property to the Templars on their death.

COMMERCIAL ENTERPRISES

With their wealth, coupled with their military might, the Templars became hugely powerful in late-medieval Europe. They owned large numbers of farms and manors – a few, such as Templecombe in Somerset, England, still exist today – which provided further income. They acquired ports and shipping fleets. They used their ships to transport pilgrims, to provision their own knights in the Holy Land and, increasingly, for commercial purposes.

They not only gained expertise on the seas, in sailing and navigational skills, but they became even more wealthy.

Templar centres were also a safe place to deposit valuables – even the Crown Jewels; in England, both King John (1167–1216) and Henry III (1207–72) found the London Temple a safer place to keep their valuables than their own castles.

The Knights Templar became, effectively, Europe's banker. Kings and nobles, always short of ready cash, would borrow from the Templars. The religious injunction against usury, or charging interest, was fairly easily circumvented by charging a fee for 'expenses' – a fee that tended to be proportionate to the amount being loaned. Although for many years lending money to kings gave the Templars astonishing power and influence, it was eventually to bring about the downfall of the Order.

Below After the Knights Templar left the castle of Calatrava it became the base of the new military Order of Calatrava.

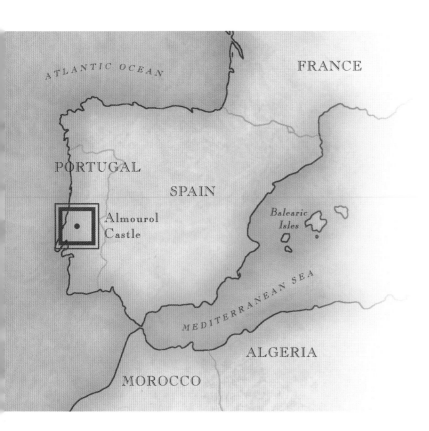

Almourol Castle

At their height the Knights Templar had castles and strongholds throughout Europe. Some were built specifically for them, but many were existing castles donated to the Order. Almourol Castle in Portugal is a good example of how the influence and responsibilities of the Knights Templar extended far beyond their original work of protecting pilgrims in the Holy Land.

Alfonso Henriques (c.1109–85), who gave Almourol Castle to the Knights Templar, technically became Count of Portugal at the age of three in 1112, but he assumed authority in 1128. He used the legendary fighting power of the Knights Templar and the Knights Hospitaller in his battles against both the Moors and the Spanish. Through his many victories he became a figure of legend as well. He was recognized by other Iberian rulers as an independent sovereign in 1143, and was formally acknowledged by the Pope as the first hereditary king of a fully independent Portugal in 1179. He died in 1185 and was succeeded by his son King Sancho I (ruled 1185–1211).

Under several dictatorships in Portugal in the first half of the 20th century, Almourol Castle became an Official Residence of the Republic. It is now owned by the Ministry of Defence, but remains open to the public.

① ROCKY ISLAND

Almourol Castle is built on a small rocky island in the middle of the Tagus River, 20 km (12 miles) south of the city of Tomar in central Portugal. The island has been fortified since at least the 2nd century BCE.

② HIGH ROCK

The rocky outcrop was known as Almorolan ('high rock' in Arabic) when Portugal retook this land from the Moors in 1129 during a lengthy reconquest. Count Alfonso Henriques gave the castle to Gualdim Pais, the fourth Master of the Order of the Knights Templar in Portugal, to strengthen the line of the existing Templar defences of the surrounding area, including the then capital city of Coimbra, to the north.

The Templars' reconstruction of the castle was completed in 1171, two years after another Templar castle at Tomar, the main Templar stronghold in Portugal.

③ QUADRANGULAR DESIGN

The basic quadrangular design of the castle, with its high walls protected by nine equally positioned circular towers, was typical of Templar military architecture of the time. The castle is 310 m (1,000 ft) long, 75 m (250 ft) wide and 18 m (60 ft) high at its highest point.

④ THE GAOL

The castle's walls enclose two communicating courtyards. The gaol tower in the centre of the castle was an unusual feature of castles of the time, although it can also be seen in the Templar castle at Tomar, built at the same time. Known as the Torre de Menagem, it had three levels.

⑤ ACCESS BY BOAT

As the castle is on an island in the river, completely surrounded by water, the only access to it is by boat, which is undoubtedly one of the reasons why it was never taken by force in succeeding centuries. Today, tourists visiting the castle are taken right around the island in a small boat before landing.

⑥ FAIRYTALE APPEARANCE

Following the dissolution of the Knights Templar, the castle at Almourol fell into disrepair over the centuries, until the 19th century when it was rediscovered and 'restored'. The castle's present fairytale appearance owes much to 19th-century romantic ideas of medieval chivalric ideals. Much of the original structure was destroyed during this 'restoration'.

⑦ ROMANTIC LEGENDS

One of several romantic legends associated with Almourol is that the castle is haunted by the ghost of a princess sighing for the love of her Moorish slave. Another is that the daughter of a Moorish lord of the castle fell in love with a Christian knight, and revealed the secret entrance to the castle to him. When the knight used this entrance to invade the castle, the lord and his daughter threw themselves off the highest tower of the castle rather than be captured.

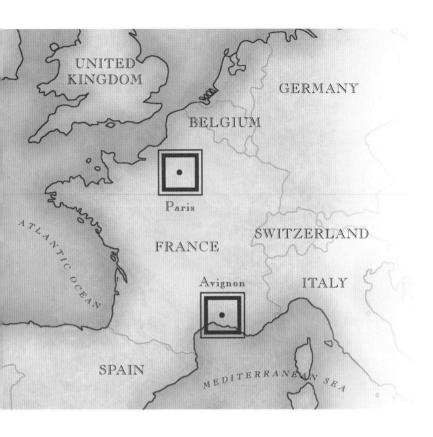

Dissolution of the Order

Early in the morning of Friday 13 October 1307, on the direct orders of Philip IV, King of France (1268–1313), every member of the Order of the Knights Templar in France was arrested on a charge of heresy. The King was known as Philippe le Bel (Philip the Fair), but for his looks, not his character.

As a secular ruler, Philip had no legal right to order these arrests on this charge, but that did not trouble him; he had power on his side. Over the previous decade he had effectively taken control of the Inquisition in France; the Inquisitor-General in Paris was under his thumb. So was Pope Clement V, the first of the Avignon popes, who owed his election as Pope in 1305 to Philip.

Philip's action against the Templars had nothing to do with heresy. They were the French royal bankers, and he was massively in debt to them. By destroying the Order, and incidentally confiscating their assets (including their Paris treasury), he could wipe out his debt.

THE CHARGES AGAINST THE KNIGHTS TEMPLAR

The charges were very serious: the Templars were accused of secret dealings with the Saracens so that the Holy Land would be Muslim, not Christian; of homosexual acts; of blaspheming against Christ; of spitting, trampling or even urinating on the Cross; of worshipping the head of an idol called Baphomet; and more.

Were any of the charges true? The Templars certainly had dealings with the Saracens from time to time; this was inevitable in medieval warfare, when enemy forces were often only a few miles apart, campaigns went on for decades, cities and forts were taken and retaken, and captives and hostages were exchanged or ransomed. However, there is absolutely no evidence that the Knights Templar wanted the Muslims to win the Holy Land.

Sexual debauchery, and especially homosexual acts, were a standard charge if you wanted to bring someone down. Then (just as today) simply an accusation was damaging, without any proof being necessary. The Templar knights swore an oath of chastity – but so did monks, nuns and priests, and it was not unknown for them to misbehave sexually, but there is no evidence the Templars did so.

Blasphemy was the most serious charge of all. For anyone – let alone dedicated members of a Christian Order – to blaspheme against Christ and desecrate the Cross was abhorrent. If there was any truth in these charges, the condemnation of the

Above *A 19th-century image of the demon Baphomet. This image, originally from Éliphas Lévi's* Dogme et Rituel de la Haute Magie, *was adapted by Leo Taxil in his attack on Freemasonry (see pages 90–91).*

Knights Templar would have been fully acceptable, according to the mores of the time – but was there?

THE CASE FOR THE DEFENCE

In addition to Philip the Fair's financial motivations, there are at least four very strong reasons for believing that the charges against the Knights Templar were a complete fabrication. First, the Templars were dedicated men of God who performed their religious obligations faithfully; their Rule shows the degree of commitment they made to the conventional beliefs and practices of a Christian Order. Second, two of the main charges – heresy and sodomy – were expressly listed in their Rule as a cause for immediate expulsion from the Order. Third, before Philip's accusations, there had been no hint of any spiritual impropriety, let alone heresy. If there had been any cause for suspicion, even any gossip against the Templars, the Inquisition would quickly have investigated – but it did not.

Fourth, and perhaps most damning, is that Philip's chief prosecutor against the Templars was his royal Keeper of the Seals, Guillaume de Nogaret. Excommunicated and vehemently anti-clerical, he had previously drawn up a case against the deceased Pope Boniface VIII, accusing him retrospectively of heresy, sodomy and conversing with demons. He also accused the Bishop of Troyes of practising magic, spitting on the Cross and sodomy. In other words, the charges against the Knights Templar were Nogaret's standard set of accusations.

THE VERDICT

A number of experienced lawyers and Dominican heresy-hunters examined the charges against the Templars and found no evidence to substantiate them. Despite this, Philip the Fair pressed ahead with torturing the Templar knights in his custody. The fact that some of them confessed to the charges proves only that people sometimes make confessions under torture. Many of those who did so later retracted them, even though this would lead to their deaths. On 12 May 1310, Philip had 54 Templars burned to death in a field outside Paris, all of them protesting their innocence of the charges against them.

Despite severe misgivings, and under military threat from Philip, a secret meeting of the Council of Vienne under Pope Clement issued a formal suppression of the Order in April 1312. The last Master, Jacques de Molay, was burned at the stake in Paris in March 1314. It is said that, as the flames licked around him, he swore that he would meet both Philip and Clement before the throne of God within a year. Both King and Pope died within the next 12 months.

A number of experienced lawyers and Dominican heresy-hunters examined the charges against the Templars and found no evidence to substantiate them.

Templar myths

There are many myths about the Knights Templar. One is the assumption that they were condemned as heretics by the Catholic Church. This is not so. Despite Philip IV's best efforts at blackening their name and closing the Order down, the Templars were never formally condemned by the Church. Indeed, a recently discovered document in the Vatican archives, the Parchment of Chinon, reveals that Pope Clement V granted absolution to Jacques de Molay and the other Templar leaders in August 1308, thinking he could still save the Order or merge it with the Knights Hospitaller.

Another myth is that because the Templars were accused of being heretics they actually were heretics. This is the 'no smoke without fire' argument, and is just as valid.

THE SUPPOSED MAGDALENE CONNECTION

Speculative writers with their own agendas have forced a number of beliefs and practices on the Templars, which it is unlikely any of them actually held. For example, some writers state as fact that the Templars were devoted to Mary Magdalene. Examination of their Rule, however, shows a special devotion to the Virgin Mary (as was common at the time), but the only mention of the Magdalene is among other saints in the list of feast days to be observed.

Some say (with a complete absence of evidence) that the Templars had a head or skull that they venerated, and that this might have been the head of the Magdalene, of John the Baptist or even of Jesus himself. Alternatively, it was an idol that they

worshipped: Baphomet was either a demon or the Provençal way of pronouncing Muhammad. The 20th-century Jewish scholar Hugh Schonfield believed that Baphomet was a Jewish code representing the Greek name Sophia, the (female) Wisdom persona of God.

Many non-scholarly books about the Templars state as fact that during their early years in Jerusalem, rather than protecting pilgrims on their way to the Holy City, they spent their time digging under Temple Mount. They are supposed to have uncovered tunnels containing both great treasure (thus accounting for the Order's later wealth) and/or some terrible heretical secret: perhaps (depending on the agenda of the authors) the body of Jesus or of Mary Magdalene, or proof that Jesus had been married to the Magdalene. Despite all the assertions of

Left A 19th-century impression of the last Master of the Temple, Jacques de Molay, wearing the distinctive red cross pattée on a white mantle.

the conspiracy theorists there is not a scrap of historical evidence for this; but because it is stated so often, and with such assurance, many readers accept it as fact, some even convincing themselves that scholarly refutations of the theories are all part of some massive cover-up.

ALTERNATIVE THEORIES

Other myths claim that the Templars possessed either the Holy Grail or the secret of what it was. As with practically everything written about the Grail, this is no more than wishful thinking.

There is a recurrent belief that the Templars were secret supporters of the Cathars, the Gnostic sect who were strong in the Languedoc (see page 13) during the 12th and early 13th centuries. It is possible that some individual Templars from that region were Cathar sympathizers; so were many nobles, without necessarily being Cathars themselves; but there is no evidence of any

connection between the Templars and the Cathars, and all the Templar knights who died at the stake protested their loyalty to the Catholic Church.

In Chapter 6 (see pages 74–93) we shall look in some detail at one of the most long-lasting myths: that after the suppression of the Order a group of Templar knights took ship to Scotland, eventually becoming the Freemasons. That myth is tied in with another: that Rosslyn Chapel near Edinburgh is a repository of Templar symbolism and secrets. Once again, this is no more than a romantic fiction. Rosslyn is indeed full of religious symbolism, but it is neither Masonic nor Templar in origin.

At least one popular writer believes that, following the suppression of the Order, Templar knights discovered America nearly a century before Christopher Columbus (1451–1506). Oddly, there is a genuine Templar connection with Columbus: both he and Vasco da Gama (1460–1524) sailed

Above Despite the many claims in popular fiction and speculative history, Rosslyn Chapel near Edinburgh has no connection to the Knights Templar.

under the flag of the Order of Christ, a Portuguese Order that (like the Order of Montesa in Spain) was newly created in 1319 when the Knights Templar were closed down. It took over Templar property, including their castles at Tomar and Almourol, absorbed a number of former Templar knights and adopted the Templar flag of the red cross.

One last popular myth should be dispelled: that the superstition concerning Friday the 13th comes from the arrest of the Templars on that day and date. In fact, this day was not seen as a specifically unlucky one until the early 20th century.

Neo-Templar Orders

Partly as a consequence of some of the myths just described, and partly for other romance-coloured historical reasons, the Knights Templar took hold of the popular imagination over the centuries. Their supposed influence on Freemasonry will be discussed later, but they formed the mythical basis of a number of other organizations – some perhaps laudable, others less so.

It is worth stressing that any links between the original Order of the Knights Templar of the 12th to 14th centuries and later groups claiming descent from them are almost certainly fabricated in every case.

Right *Hermann von Salza, fourth grand master of the Teutonic Knights (founded in 1190) who turned them into a military order, being appointed by Pope Innocent III in 1209.*

During the mid-18th century people began to take a renewed interest in the Templars after four hundred years. Although he did not mention the Templars by name, a Scottish Mason, the Chevalier Andrew Ramsay, made a speech in France in 1736 that mentioned the Crusading knights returning to Europe with secrets and symbolism (see pages 76–77).

LEGENDS OF PERPETUATION

Nearly 20 years later, in 1754, Baron Gotthelf von Hund founded the Rite of the Strict Observance, claiming that in 1742 he had been initiated into an Order of the Temple that had Unknown Superiors – a concept that would become popular in later secret societies – who had authorized him to create his new Order. At the heart of this was a Legend of Perpetuation: that, before he died, Jacques de Molay, the last Master of the Temple (see page 29), appointed a successor, Pierre d'Aumont, the Templar Prior of Auvergne; he and his successors kept their Templar Order going in secret for the next four hundred years, before passing the baton to von Hund.

In 1804 the Charter of Larmenius appeared. It claimed to date back to 1324, saying that de Molay had appointed a different successor, Johannes Marcus Larmenius. The Charter listed 22 other Masters of the Temple, up to Bernard Raymond Fabré-Palaprat in 1804. Although the Charter is provably a fake, it enabled Fabré-Palaprat, a French Freemason, to found his own Order of the Temple.

The Chevalier Ramsay and Baron von Hund started the ball rolling, but the main influence of their Templar myth-making was on Freemasonry. It was Fabré-Palaprat's Order of the Temple that was to have far-reaching effects in the wider esoteric world. He also founded the Johannite Church, an esoteric version of Christianity, whose priests and bishops have a valid (though highly irregular) link to the supposed Apostolic Succession of the bishops of the Catholic, Orthodox and Anglican (Episcopalian) Churches. Similar churches, with their so-called 'Wandering Bishops' or *episcopi*

Above A poster for one of six exhibitions of the Salon Rose-Croix, organised by Joséphin Péladan in Paris in the 1890s.

Right The Chevalier Andrew Michael Ramsay (c.1681–1743) first connected the Freemasons with crusading knights.

vagantes, have also become a standard part of the esoteric scene (see pages 118–119).

During the 19th century several secret societies sprang up in France. One of the most influential esotericists was Joséphin Péladan (see page 71), who was involved in Rosicrucian and Kabbalistic societies; he also became the 'custodian' of Fabré-Palaprat's Order of the Temple. Péladan's Orders led to much else – including, indirectly, the Priory of Sion (see pages 138–139).

OFFSHOOTS OF THE ORDER OF THE TEMPLE

Fabré-Palaprat's Order of the Temple gave birth over the years, directly or indirectly, to the Sovereign and Military Order of the Temple of Jerusalem (founded in 1932 in Belgium), the Sovereign Order of the Solar Temple (founded in the 1950s in France), the Renewed Order of the Temple (c.1970, also in France) and eventually the Order of the Solar Temple (founded in the late 1980s by Luc Jouret and Joseph di Mambro), which

imploded with the murder or suicide of more than 70 members in Switzerland, France and Canada in 1994, 1995 and 1997.

Today there are many different esoteric societies that, in one way or another, have supposedly Templar connections. Some are Rosicrucian in nature, others Masonic. Some, such as the Ordo Templi Orientis (OTO), teach and practise sex-magic (see pages 130–131). Others are highly chivalric in their stated ideals, and their ceremonies involve colourful costumes, regalia and swords. All have either a highly romanticized image of the original Knights Templar or follow an esoteric spiritual path based on what they imagine the heresies of the original Templars to have been. None has any connection in reality with the knights who founded an Order in 1119 to protect Christian pilgrims en route to Jerusalem.

THE NAZI CONNECTION

In the early 20th century German nationalism began to be organized in societies. Old societies, such as the Teutonic Knights, were resurrected in a right-wing incarnation. In 1907 Jorg Lanz von Liebenfels founded the *Ordo Novi Templi* (Order of New Templars); this was followed by the Germanen Order in 1912 and the Thule Society in 1918. These societies believed in the purity of German blood, and were anti-Semitic. They formed the background for the National Socialist or Nazi Party, and for all that followed.

CHAPTER 3

THE ASSASSINS

As with the Knights Templar, there are well-known colourful myths about the Assassins. The truth is just as astonishing: they were a group of deeply believing men who were precise and dedicated killers, prepared to die in utter obedience to their Master. They were a small Muslim sect who killed other Muslims – and who struck deals with the Knights Templar.

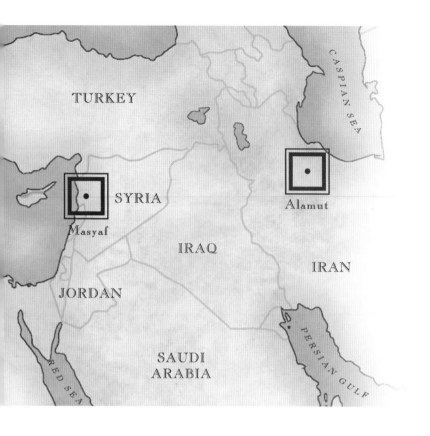

The myths

High in the mountains of northern Persia was a fortress called Alamut, or Eagle's Nest. This was the headquarters of the Assassins, dedicated and ruthless murderers who were feared throughout not only the Christian but also the Muslim world in the 12th and 13th centuries.

According to legend, a traveller stands next to the Assassins' Grand Master, Hasan-i-Sabah. They look across a deep valley to a mountaintop, where a man stands. The Grand Master raises his hand, and the man on the mountaintop flings himself to his inevitable death in the abyss beneath. Although this story is almost certainly apocryphal, its lesson was true: Hasan's followers would obey him implicitly, even if that led to their own death. How did he achieve such dedication?

THE HIDDEN VALLEY OF PARADISE

The best-known story about the Assassins was told by the explorer Marco Polo (1254–1324) in his book *Milione* (literally 'Million') or *The Travels of Marco Polo*. He claims to have visited Alamut in 1273, and to have heard a fabulous tale there.

Hasan would recruit boys as young as 12 whom he thought would become fearless warriors. He drugged them by giving them hashish to drink, and when they slept he took them into a hidden valley near the fortress of Alamut. When they awoke they found the most clement atmosphere,

perfumed flowers, trees heavy with fruit and streams running with wine, milk, honey and pure water; and they were attended by beautiful young women, who played music, sang, danced and obeyed their every desire.

After a few days Hasan would drug the boys again and remove them from the valley. He told them they had been granted a glimpse of Paradise, and that they could return there only by obeying his will unquestioningly. Then he sent them out to kill and to die willingly, knowing they were going back to Paradise. Some also say that the Assassins took hashish to fire them up and make them fearless before going out to kill. The Assassins, then, took their name from *hashshashin*, meaning 'users of hashish'.

The hidden valley of Paradise is a delightful story, but it has several problems. First, Marco Polo's visit to Alamut occurred 150 years after Hasan's death, by which time the Assassins had largely been defeated; Alamut itself was taken by the Mongols in 1256. Second, Marco Polo was a colourful storyteller, and knew that few (if any) would follow in his footsteps to prove him wrong. Third, hashish is rarely taken in liquid form.

Fourth, hashish is far more likely to make someone mellow than to fire them up to kill. And fifth, crucially, Hasan-i-Sabah was a strict ascetic; he would have been unlikely to sanction the use of drugs.

In fact, the supposed derivation of the name Assassins from hashish was unknown until the early 19th century. There are several other possible derivations, including that the name comes from an Arabic word *assasseen* meaning 'guardians'; but the most likely derivation is from their founder: *Hassassin* were followers of Hasan.

THE ASSASSINS VERSUS SALADIN

Another common belief about the Assassins is that they aimed their murderous attentions at the Knights Templar. In fact, they were far more likely to assassinate other Muslims, and it is probable that on several occasions the Syrian Assassins actually cooperated with the Knights Templar against a common Muslim enemy.

In 1175 and 1176, between the Second and Third Crusades, the Syrian Assassins, under their powerful leader Rashid al-din Sinan (known as 'the Old Man of the

Right A Persian miniature, c.11th century, showing Muhammad's Paradise. Scholars disagree on whether Muhammad is the figure in the green turban, or is completely engulfed in the golden flames.

Mountain'), even tried to assassinate the great Muslim leader Saladin – twice. The second time they were nearly successful, causing him minor wounds. Saladin was so angered by these attacks that in the summer of 1176 he laid siege to the Assassins in their stronghold at Masyaf. After a few weeks, however, he withdrew and never threatened the Assassins again.

There are several legends explaining why Saladin should have changed his mind. One is that Sinan sent a messenger to Saladin, insisting on speaking to the great leader in private. Saladin sent all his men out except his two most trusted officers, saying he regarded them as his sons. The messenger turned to the two men and asked if they would kill Saladin, if ordered to do so by Sinan. 'Give us your orders', they said, drawing their swords. The messenger left, taking the two officers with him.

The truth is likely to be more mundane. Many believe that Sinan threatened Saladin's family, and that a measure of the Assassins' strength was that Saladin knew he would not be able to protect his family against them, and so capitulated.

The reality

The Assassins were a small sect known as Nizari Ismailis, part of Shi'ite Islam. In his youth their founder, Hasan-i-Sabah, is said to have studied alongside the astronomer and poet Omar Khayyám (writer of the Rubáiyát) and the future prime minister of Persia, Nizam ul-Mulk – whom Hasan later had murdered. Alamut, the Eagle's Nest, had been a Sunni fortress until Hasan took it over in 1090; it was his main base, though over the years he acquired numerous other fortresses.

For Hasan, as for many Islamic leaders of the time, religion and politics were inextricably linked. The different sects within Islam – just like Catholics and Protestants at certain points in Christian history – often hated each other even more than they hated non-Muslims. Hasan had come from a Twelver family and had converted to the Sevener Ismaili sect (see page 42). With the zeal of a convert, his beliefs developed to the point where it became his religious duty to kill those with different beliefs. However, he did not practise indiscriminate terrorism, but targeted specific leaders, both religious and political.

THE ORDER TO KILL

One tactic used by the Assassins was to plant 'sleepers' in the court of a ruler. These men would stay quiet, sometimes for years, showing no sign of dissent, and might work their way up to positions of great responsibility and trust. At some point they would receive a signal from Hasan or his successors, and would kill the ruler. If they did this publicly, they would almost certainly be slain immediately by the ruler's guards, but their complete loyalty to their leader – and the promise of Paradise awaiting them –

ensured that they did not waver in their duty. A public killing, often in a mosque, was always preferable: it could only increase the reputation of the already-feared sect.

The fourth leader of the Assassins was also called Hasan. He declared himself to be the Mahdi, the Hidden Imam, the One that many Shi'ite Muslims, in different ways, expect to come. Hasan stated that the strict restrictions on the behaviour of Muslims no longer applied: he told his followers to turn their back on Mecca when praying, and said they were allowed to drink wine and eat pork. Such overturning of conventional religious belief, often seen in secret societies, was a powerful binding force in the movement.

THE SYRIAN ASSASSINS AND THE KNIGHTS TEMPLAR

The Assassins began in Persia, and became very powerful in the areas that are now Iran and Iraq, but they are perhaps better known to the Western world for their Syrian branch, which came into close contact with the Crusaders in the Holy Land – including the Knights Templar. The Syrian Assassins were feared for being dedicated, efficient and utterly ruthless killers. They also sometimes extended their remit, taking on commissions

from other people or organizations, making them paid assassins in the modern sense – effectively hit-men.

The Assassins did not see themselves as murderers. One Assassin said of their victims: 'To kill them is more lawful than rainwater.' Emphasizing the point that they targeted

other Muslims, not of their own sect, rather than Christians or Jews, he explained: 'To shed the blood of a heretic is more meritorious than to kill seventy Greek infidels.'

One of the accusations against the Knights Templar was that they had a secret alliance with the Saracens. Local deals were sometimes struck with the Saracens, but the Templars had a far more significant arrangement with the Assassins, who at one point paid the Knights Templar two thousand gold pieces a year in order to avoid direct military conflict with them.

Comparisons have been drawn between the organization of the Knights Templar and the Assassins, but it is likely that any similarities came about simply from the way the organizations were structured. The Assassins had a Grand Master or chief *d'ai*, under whom came senior *d'ais* and ordinary *d'ais* or missionaries; there were also *rafiqs* or companions and *lasiqs* or laymen. These were the various layers of the hierarchy and the support structure for the *fidais* or *fedayeen* ('faithful' or 'devotees'), who were the actual killers out in the field. Similarly, a Templar knight was part of a hierarchy with a Master of the Temple and other masters and priors, and a support structure including lay brothers, sergeants, squires, and so on.

The revolutionary teachings of Hasan were overturned by a new Grand Master, Jalal ad Din, in the early 13th century, and the Assassins returned to traditional Muslim values. The Persian Assassins were defeated by the Mongol leader Hulagu Khan in 1256. The Syrian Assassins, who had become an independent force, were defeated by the Mamluk Sultan Baybars in 1273. However, isolated groups of Assassins continued throughout Europe for some considerable time.

One tactic used by the Assassins was to plant 'sleepers' in the court of a ruler. At some point they would receive a signal from Hasan or his successors, and would kill the ruler.

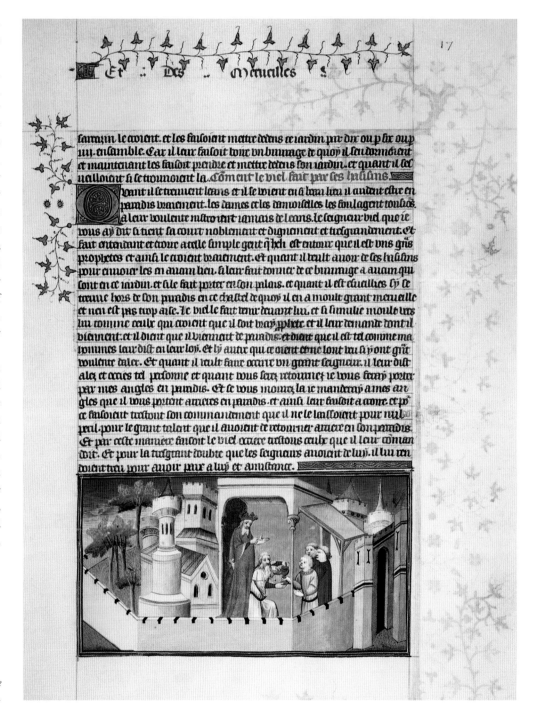

Left *Omar Khayyám (1044–1123), the great Persian poet, scholar, scientist and mathematician, said to have been a student friend of the founder of the Assassins.*

Right *This extract from* The Travels of Marco Polo *(1298/99) is responsible for the myth that the Assassin leader gave young men an intoxicating elixir before sending them out to kill.*

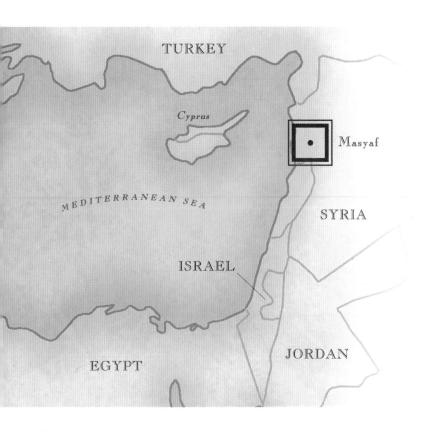

The Assassin castle, Masyaf

The impressive fortress of Masyaf is located in the Hama province of Syria, on the eastern side of the Jabal al-Nusairia mountain range. The original construction of the castle was probably Byzantine, but it came to prominence as one of the most important Ismaili fortresses in the 12th century.

The castle came into the hands of the Nizari Ismaili sect, the Assassins, in 1136, and became effectively the capital of the Ismaili principality of Syria. Much of the castle as it exists today dates from this period; in some places decorative patterns can still be seen on the walls.

THE OLD MAN OF THE MOUNTAIN

The Assassin leader in Syria, Rashid al-din Sinan, a convert to the Ismaili faith, was so powerful that he was effectively independent of the Assassins' Persian leadership at Alamut, though they took tighter control of the Syrian Assassins after his death in 1192–94. A teacher and physician, Sinan was known as the Old Man of the Mountain, or in Latin *vetulus de montanis*, a slightly demeaning translation of the respectful Arabic title *sheikh al-jabal*, which actually means elder (or prince) of the mountain.

One 14th-century historian believed that the Assassins actually took their name from the mountain where the Masyaf fortress is situated. He claimed that it was called Jabal Assikin, or Jabal al-Sikkin, and that, as the word *sikkin* meant dagger or knife, the

mountain was called 'the mountain of the dagger'. However tempting this derivation might be, most historians disagree with it.

TODAY'S CASTLE

Since the year 2000 the castle has undergone considerable conservation work through the Historic Cities Support Programme of the Aga Khan Development Network. Prince Karim al-Hussayni, Aga Khan IV, is the spiritual leader today of the Nizari Ismaili sect of Shi'a Islam, the sect to which the Assassins belonged.

IMPREGNABILITY OF THE CASTLE

The fortress at Masyaf withstood all attacks, including one from the great Muslim leader Saladin. Having nearly been assassinated by the Assassins, Saladin laid siege to Masyaf fortress in 1176. One story claims that, after a series of almost supernatural encounters, the Syrian Assassin leader Rashid al-din Sinan crept into Saladin's tent one night, unseen by his guards, and left some distinctive Ismaili cakes pinned down with a poisoned dagger, and a threatening note, next to the sleeping leader. The usually fearless Saladin decided

to make peace with the Assassins and called off his siege. The story is almost certainly apocryphal, like many others about Sinan, but illustrates the power of the Assassins in Syria. The fortress was not taken until 1270, when the Assassins lost their power in Syria to Sultan Baybars of the Mamluk dynasty of Egypt.

① EAGLE'S NEST

The fortress surmounts a natural limestone platform, raising it to a commanding position 20 m (65 ft) above the surrounding boulder-strewn plain. This enabled it to protect not just the town below it, but the whole area. Like the famous Assassin fortress at Alamut, the castle at Masyaf, on its rocky outcrop, has been described as an eagle's nest for its inaccessibility.

② WALL AND TOWERS

The fortress has an outer curtain wall and imposing towers, providing a strong defence against attackers. Within its fortified stone walls were two interior strongholds around a large gatehouse. The Masyaf fortress was almost impregnable.

The 12th-century Ismaili reconstruction of the fortress made use of earlier building materials, including stonework and columns from the original Byzantine castle. These can still be seen in the ruins.

③ THRONE ROOM AND APARTMENTS

Rashid al-din Sinan's throne room was situated at the highest point of the fortress. The remains of a series of four rooms, which are thought to have been his private apartments, can still be seen today.

④ WATER CISTERNS

Carved deep into the natural limestone foundations of the castle were three huge water cisterns fed from rainwater carried down through a series of channels; this meant that the fortress was not dependent on outside sources for its water and could thus withstand a long siege. The water was brought to the surface from the underground cisterns through ceramic pipes. Excavations in the 21st century have also revealed that the fortress contained a traditional bathhouse.

⑤ CAVES AND TUNNELS

Natural fissures in the limestone outcrop were widened and carved into a series of caves and tunnels beneath the fortress, providing even greater security to the occupants. Recent excavations have discovered what are thought to be secret escape passages.

Background and beliefs

Why should a group of devout Muslims become professional killers – and mainly of other Muslims? It is a long and complicated story that goes right back to the beginnings of Islam in the 7th century CE, and it involves politics and ruling dynasties just as much as the spiritual aspects of religion.

Shortly after the death of the Prophet Muhammad there was a split among his followers, between those who saw the elected caliphs of Baghdad as their leaders and those who believed that the leadership should come only from the descendants of Muhammad's daughter Fatima and her husband Ali, who was the fourth caliph (ruled 656–661 CE). The former group became the Sunni Muslims, and the latter group the Shi'ite Muslims; both these major strands of Islam still exist today and are sometimes still bitter enemies. Both Sunni and Shi'ite Islam have subdivided further over the centuries.

THE SEVENERS AND THE TWELVERS

In Sunni Islam, an imam or leader is anyone who leads prayers in a mosque; in Shi'ite Islam, the imam is the divinely inspired appointed successor to the previous imam. The main division among the Shi'ites is between the Seveners and the Twelvers. The Seveners date back to 762 CE, when Isma'il (who would have been the seventh Shi'ite imam) died before his father, creating a crisis of succession. One group, who would go on to become the majority Twelvers, appointed Isma'il's younger brother Musa as imam, with the line continuing from him. A smaller group disagreed with this, some claiming that Isma'il had gone into hiding and

would reappear as the Mahdi, the Chosen One foretold in the Koran, who would return to right all wrongs and restore Islamic purity. They are known as Seveners, or Ismailis, and set up a new line of succession called the Fatimid dynasty, after the Prophet Muhammad's daughter.

***Above** An early 19th-century etching of 'Grand Cairo' by Samuel Rawle, based on a watercolour by Henry Salt.*

The Twelvers – the majority of Shi'ites – believe that the 'hidden' twelfth imam will one day return as the Mahdi.

The Twelvers – the majority of Shi'ites – believe that the 'hidden' twelfth imam, who disappeared as a child around 878 CE, will one day return as the Mahdi. Today the Twelvers are by far the largest group in Iran, and are also strong in parts of Iraq.

The Ismailites developed a complex esoteric version of Islam. They gave great significance to the number seven: there were seven emanations of God, seven legislating prophets, and they initially expected the seventh Fatimid imam either to be the Mahdi or to start a new dynasty of seven imams, of whom the seventh would be the Mahdi.

Their teachings were mystical and metaphysical, with considerable Neoplatonic and Gnostic influence (see pages 12–15), and borrowings from esoteric Judaism and Christianity as well as from Babylonian astrology. They were also radical, challenging the religious, social, political and intellectual establishments. Some taught that it was permissible to drink wine, and that the strict *shari'ah* law could be broken in other ways. They also taught that only their own imams understood the inner meaning of the Koran and the law. This inevitably brought them into conflict with the far more conservative 'establishment' of both Sunni and (Twelver) Shi'ite Islam.

THE RISE AND FALL OF THE FATIMID DYNASTY

To survive, at times the Seveners effectively went underground, becoming a secret society with initiatory rites, and carrying out guerrilla activity against their oppressors, particularly against the Seljuk Turks who were uncompromisingly orthodox Sunni Muslims. Sometimes they disguised themselves as Christians or Jews, because it was actually safer to be a Christian or a Jew than what was judged a heretical Muslim. They grew in strength and eventually took control in Egypt.

The Fatimids became the leading dynasty in Egypt, Syria and North Africa from 909 CE, and were generally less hostile towards the Christians of western Europe than the (Sunni) Abbasid caliphate of Baghdad. They championed culture and intellectual enquiry, and established the Al-Azhar University, one of the first in the world, in Cairo around 975 CE.

Another schism occurred in 1094 on the death of the imam al-Mustansir; the Ismailis split into two groups, followers of his sons Nizar and al-Must'ali. Most Ismailis followed al-Must'ali. The followers of Nizar were known as Nizari; they were led by Hasan-i-Sabah, and they became the Assassins.

In 1171 Saladin overthrew the Fatimid dynasty in Cairo, and the Ismailites resumed their guerrilla activities against other Muslims, particularly in Syria – thus coming to the attention of the Crusaders, and of the Knights Templar – and the colourful myths began to be born.

Right *The courtyard of the mosque at Al-Azhar University in Cairo, founded by the Fatimid dynasty c.975 CE.*

CHAPTER 4

ALCHEMISTS AND HERMETIC PHILOSOPHERS

In the 15th to 17th centuries there was a small but remarkably influential group of men whose interest in astrology, alchemy, Kabbalah and the study of magic and mysticism would affect the thinking of generations that followed them. Both scientists and seers, they would have thought of themselves as natural philosophers, but today we call them the Hermetic Philosophers.

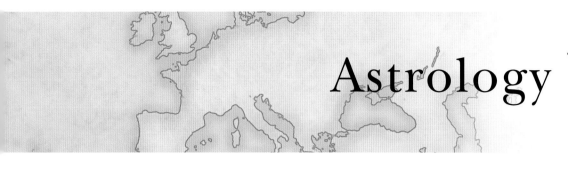

Astrology

Astrology is perhaps the most explicit example of the famous Hermetic maxim 'As above, so below', in that human beings are affected by the stars in the heavens. However, this is not the astrology of newspaper horoscopes, which are no more than a bit of fun. This is the astrology that says that everything in the universe is connected, though not in a deterministic way.

Just because particular planets are seen travelling across particular constellations from the viewpoint of a location on Earth at a certain time, it does not mean that a person born at that moment must have a specific personality, or be 'fated' to have a happy or unhappy, rich or poor, exciting or dull, long or short life. And it most certainly does not mean that because the planets will be seen in a different configuration against the backdrop of the stars next Wednesday you will inherit money, or have an accident or meet a tall, dark, handsome stranger.

NATURAL PHILOSOPHY
Until two or three hundred years ago, astrologers and astronomers were essentially the same thing. Today's astronomers, who are scornful of astrology, depend on the

meticulous record-keeping of centuries of astrologers for their knowledge of past comets, eclipses and nova. The astrologers studied the heavens, and then interpreted what they saw in a symbolic way.

It is only quite recently that we have separated science and poetry and spiritual belief so far that we insist that, if something is a scientific fact, then it has no other meaning. In the 15th, 16th and 17th centuries, and even up to the mid-18th century, a scientist was a natural philosopher, and the purpose of scientific study of the world was to gain a greater knowledge of the Creation of God, and hence of God himself.

Even the great scientist Sir Isaac Newton (1642–1727) studied astrology – among much else; he wrote far more on esoteric subjects than he ever did on the science for which he is renowned. He may have been one of the last true Renaissance men: a scholar who was both a brilliant scientist and deeply absorbed in studies of the Bible, the pyramids, astrology and alchemy. The 18th-century Age of Reason brought an end to such scholarly eclecticism until very recently.

ASTROLOGY AND THE CHURCH

Although today the Christian Churches would distance themselves from astrology (and fundamentalist Christians would see it as 'occult' and a dangerous work of Satan), in the medieval and Renaissance periods many astrologers were priests or monks, and even popes would consult them. After all, the stars are mentioned favourably in the Bible: 'The heavens declare the glory of God; and the firmament sheweth his handiwork' (Psalm 19:1). The psalmist also speaks of 'thy heavens, the work of thy fingers, the moon and the stars, which thou hast ordained' (Psalm 8:3).

Opposite A calendar dial with astrological images below the Astronomical Clock on the Old Town Hall, Prague. Original 1490, repainted 1865.

Left A 16th-century portrait of John Dee aged around 67. Dee was a mathematician, astronomer and astrologer, cartographer and much else.

Pope Alexander VI, Rodrigo Borgia, even had a full zodiac painted on the ceiling of his apartment in the Vatican, and many historical churches have zodiacal and other astrological symbols carved in wood or stone.

Astrology, if used to the greater glory of God, was seen as one way that humans could discern the will of God and order their lives in a manner most pleasing to Him. Astrologers had to be careful. If they were thought to be using astrology for any other purpose, such as gaining hidden knowledge or power for themselves, they might be accused of heresy, or of trafficking with demons.

THE ART AND SCIENCE OF HOROSCOPE-READING

Kings and nobles would also call on astrologers, often to find the most propitious time for taking a major action. For example, on the death of Queen Mary in November 1558, the young Queen Elizabeth I called John Dee to her court, to ask him to determine the most auspicious date for her coronation. He cast a horoscope and advised her to choose 15 January 1559. Her long and largely successful reign of more than 40 years (she died in 1603) was seen by many as a testimony to Dee's skill as an astrologer (see pages 56–57).

Astrologers view their work as a mixture of science and art. Drawing up a horoscope involves complex and time-consuming computations; however, the true skill is not in the mathematics, but in the interpretation of the resultant horoscope. This is as much poetry as it is science. The astrologer looks for patterns in the horoscope and opens himself up to a symbolic interpretation of them, just as a Tarot reader does with the pattern of cards. So, although the most basic information to be drawn from a horoscope should be the same whoever reads it, the fuller interpretation depends on discernment – and this is what made (and still makes) some astrologers keenly sought-after.

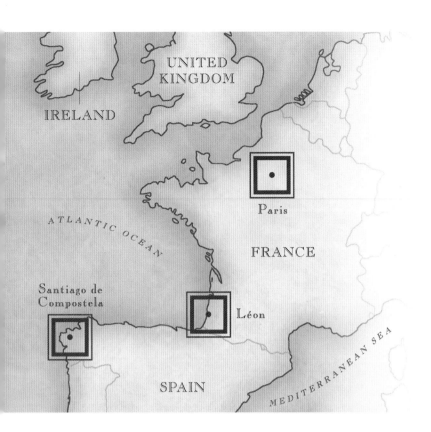

Alchemy

Alchemy is sometimes known as the Royal Art – not because it was practised by kings (though sometimes it was), but because of its prestige as the highest of esoteric endeavours. Even more than astrology, alchemy was a fusion of the scientific and the spiritual. On one level, just as astrology laid the foundations for the later scientific (in the modern sense) astronomy, so alchemy was the forerunner of today's science of chemistry.

FLAMEL THE PHILANTHROPIST

One of the best-known early alchemists in the Western world was Nicholas Flamel (*c*.1330–1418). His story, which first appeared in print in French in 1612, is probably more fable than fact, but illustrates several facets of alchemy.

Flamel was a scrivener (a copyist) living in Paris. One day he bought for two florins a very old, large and beautiful gilded book written by 'Abraham the Jew'. The 21 pages contained Latin text, with illustrations. The final page mentioned the transmutation of metals, but Flamel was unable to interpret the meaning of most of the book. He decided to go on a pilgrimage to Santiago de Compostela in north-west Spain, in the hope of meeting a wise Jew on his way. During his return journey he met at Léon one

Master Canches, a Jewish-born Christian, who was able to decipher some of the book, but became ill and died at Orléans. However, Flamel had learned enough that, on arriving back at Paris, after three years' experimentation he was able, in 1382, to transmute 0.2 kg (½ lb) of mercury into pure silver, and a few months later mercury into gold, and became very wealthy.

By 1413 Flamel and his wife Perenelle had endowed 14 hospitals in Paris, had built three chapels, given gifts to seven churches and provided aid to numerous widows and orphans. The moral lesson, of course, is that esoteric learning should be used for the good of humankind. Through his wise use of the Philosopher's Stone, Flamel has indeed achieved a form of immortality.

In physical terms, alchemy was the search for the Philosopher's Stone, which had two astonishing properties. As the Elixir of Life, it held the secret of eternal youth – or at least kept the alchemist living to a ripe old age, but the main reason why kings and nobles were prepared to be patrons to alchemists is that it was claimed the Philosopher's Stone could turn base metals such as lead into gold.

THE PROCESS OF DISTILLATION
In woodcut illustrations, alchemists are often pictured, in their laboratories, surrounded by alembics and retorts, with jars of different powders and liquids and a stove, or the Renaissance equivalent of a Bunsen burner. They became highly skilled at sublimation and distillation, and at producing a wide variety of chemical reactions – some of them learning the hard way: explosions in alchemical laboratories were by no means unknown – but they persevered.

Alchemical texts were always shrouded in mystery. Instead of naming the various chemicals, texts referred to them by the names of animals or birds, dragons, lions, salamanders, kings and queens. They used

Left *This illustration to an early 17th century German poem on alchemy shows an alchemist's laboratory with its typical tools and vessels.*

terms such as the 'alchymical marriage' and the 'androgyne', the fusion of the male and the female. (Much of the symbolism could be interpreted in a sexual way, suggesting links between medieval and Renaissance alchemists and the sex-magic of 20th-century organizations such as the Ordo Templi Orientis, see pages 130–131.)

MYSTICAL TEXTS

Often the texts were richly illustrated with glorious symbolic images, sometimes with text 'explaining' the illustrations, as in this example of 1617 by Michael Maier:

Therefore they have poured these volatile birds with solar and lunar feathers over the python; then the python has again melted into these birds. Then they have poured out the clear solution and once more thrown it over a new python and so obtained a fat and heavy liquor. Then they have united the king and queen and poured them together.

Another very long text, *Cantilena* by Sir George Ripley (1415–90), includes verses such as this:

A Lyon Greene did in her Lapp reside
(The which an Eagle fed), and from his side
The Blood gush'd out: The Virgin drunck it upp,
While Mercuries Hand did th'Office of a Cupp.

The multi-layered symbolic language is indicative of the multiple layers of alchemy itself. As well as being a search for a physical Philosopher's Stone (actually not a stone at all, but either a tincture or a powder) that could turn base metal into gold, alchemy was about spiritual transformation: the purification of the soul. This was the true quest of the alchemist; but individual spiritual advancement outside the hierarchical structures of the Church was always viewed with suspicion. Although some priests and monks did practise alchemy, they had to be careful to avoid the taint of heresy. Other alchemists were more open (at least within their own circles) about their scientific and spiritual quest.

As well as being a search for a physical Philosopher's Stone that could turn base metal into gold, alchemy was about spiritual transformation.

Kabbalah

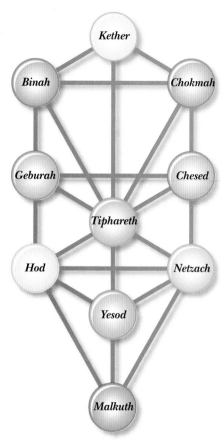

Kabbalah (also spelt Cabala or Qabalah) is a complex system of mystical Judaism. The word comes from Hebrew, the variant transliterated spellings (starting with a K, C or Q, with one or two Bs, and with or without the final H) reflecting different tastes at different times, and different methods of interpretation. As a rough rule, Kabbalah is the medieval Jewish mystical system, Cabala is the Renaissance Christian variant and Qabalah is its modern Hermetic or occult usage. However, many Kabbalists, and writers about Kabbalah, simply choose one spelling and stick with it, whichever variant they are speaking of.

Kabbalah means 'receiving' or 'received tradition' or even 'mouth to ear', reflecting the fact that originally the teachings were passed on orally, one to one. These teachings include: long and detailed speculations on the Creation; explorations of the nature of divinity – aspects or attributes of God; the nature of the human soul; and, crucially, how God and humans can communicate, interact and work together. In some ways it is deeply theoretical; in others it is a powerful practical system of mysticism, even of magic.

THE TREE OF LIFE

The best-known symbol of Kabbalism is the Tree of Life, which is often described as being both very simple and very profound. The Tree is composed of ten Sephiroth (singular: Sephira), meaning 'enumerations', each one representing an attribute of God manifest in the physical universe and together symbolizing the ten rays of light of God's creation. Above and beyond the Sephiroth is the ultimate concept of divinity, the Ain Sof (literally 'Without End'): both

transcendent and immanent, the utter inexpressible Oneness of God.

The ten Sephiroth are connected to each other by 22 paths (there are 22 letters in the Hebrew alphabet, and numbers are also represented by these letters). Although the sacred name of God, represented by the tetragrammaton, cannot be uttered by any Jew, the ten attributes of God – such as Understanding, Wisdom, Judgement and Mercy – and the relationships (paths) between them can be used by the Kabbalist to relate mystically to God.

The Tree represents the nature of God, the way that the universe came into being and the interrelationship of God and his creation, including humankind. As well as the intricate relationships shown by the paths between the Sephiroth, the Tree can be divided in many ways. The right and left sides represent active and passive principles respectively. Different groups of Sephiroth can represent Root, Trunk, Branch and Fruit, or Will, Intellect, Emotion and Action. Because it is a symbolic map, the Tree can be adapted and extended to symbolize different patterns of teachings.

THE POWER OF GEMATRIA

Another aspect of Kabbalah is gematria, which is the study, manipulation and interpretation of letters and numbers. The letters of a Hebrew word become their numerical equivalents, which are then added together. (A popular version of this is Numerology, in which adding up the consonants and vowels of your name is supposed to give an insight into your personality; this is about as far from mystical Jewish gematria as newspaper horoscopes are from serious astrology.) Kabbalists find it significant when different words or phrases result in the same numerical equivalent, suggesting that they have a connection in their inner meaning.

Part of the significance of gematria comes from the belief, expressed in Genesis 1, that it was through God's spoken words that the world came into being; a more philosophical rendering of this occurs in the opening of the Gospel of John. Words, then, have power in themselves. Many religions have 'words of

Opposite *The basic structure of the Kabbalistic Tree of Life.*

Right *Original symbolic sketch of the 'Garden of Eden Before the Fall of Man', showing the Tree of Life, by Elizabeth Burnett, wife of William Wynn Westcott, co-founder of the Hermetic Order of the Golden Dawn, c.1892 (see page 115).*

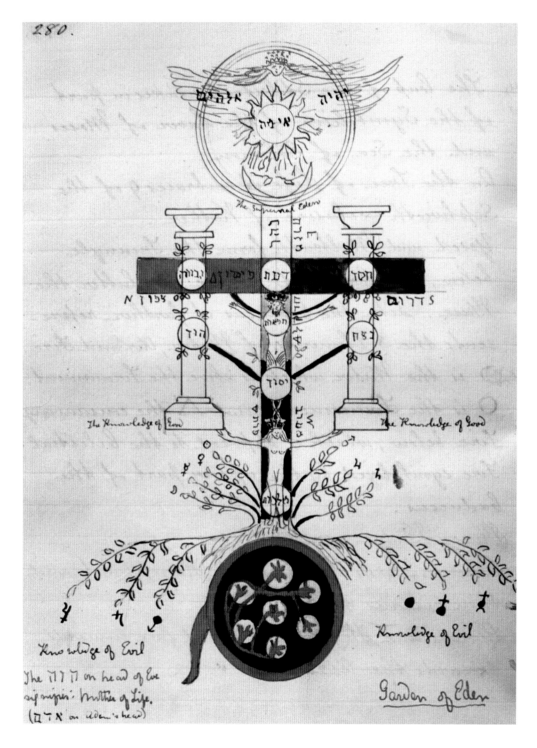

power' (in Eastern religions they are often called *mantras*) – words, phrases, entire prayers or invocations that are chanted or uttered in a special way. In Kabbalah, these words can include the names of angels or archangels and secret names (or attributes) of God. The meanings of the names of angels (or of *dæmons*, see page 15) are determined through gematria, which can also reveal magical correspondences (see page 109).

Kabbalah, like many other esoteric spiritual systems, is a way of achieving harmony between God and humans, of human beings *knowing* God deeply and personally, without the need for mediation by a priest; in that sense (though not in others) it could be called Gnostic (see page 12). At the heart of Kabbalism for many who practise it is the belief that the Creation is damaged and imperfect, and that by their own spiritual improvement they can not only make a real difference for good in the world, but can also help to heal Creation. A similar belief was expressed in the Rosicrucian Manifestos (see pages 62–63).

Kabbalah is a way of achieving harmony between God and humans, of human beings knowing God, without the need for mediation by a priest.

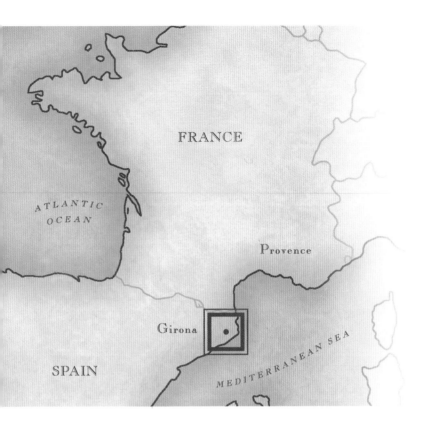

History of Kabbalah

Like many aspects of the esoteric world, Kabbalah has a 'traditional history'; it is said to have originated with Moses – secret mystical teachings that he was given by God, which were oral, not written down as the Law was, and were passed on from mouth to ear for many centuries. Others believe that Kabbalah in its written form dates back around two thousand years.

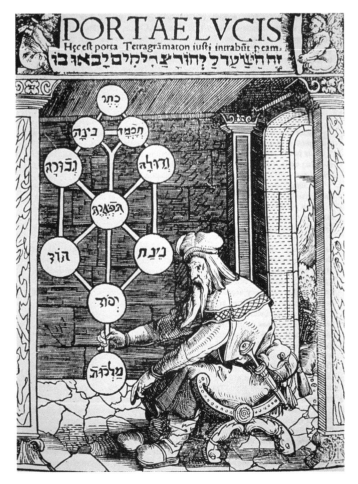

Left *The earliest known representation of the Kabbalistic Tree of Life in print: the cover of* Portae Lucis, *a Latin translation by Paulus Riccius in 1516 of* Sha'arei Orah *by Joseph Gikatilla, a friend of Moses de Léon.*

In fact Kabbalah in any sort of systemized written form originated in late-12th-century Provence (now southern France) with the writing of the *Sefer ha-Bahir* (Book of Brilliance or Enlightenment) around 1174, in the School of Girona in 13th-century Catalonia (northern Spain), and in the writing of the *Sefer ha-Zohar* (Book of Splendour) in central Spain around 1280–86. Mystical Jewish beliefs had certainly existed before then, but in just over a century these teachings formalized them.

ISAAC THE BLIND AND HIS LEGACY
Many scholars believe that the *Sefer ha-Bahir* was written (or perhaps compiled) by the great Kabbalistic teacher Isaac the Blind (1160–1235), who is sometimes known as 'Father of the Kabbalah'. Others dispute this, in part because Isaac was critical of some of his students for writing down Kabbalistic teachings. Whether he authored the *Sefer ha-Bahir* or not, he is credited with giving names to the ten Sephiroth, and even with giving the name Kabbalah to Jewish mysticism. Isaac also, unusually, taught the idea of metempsychosis, the transmigration of souls

after death or reincarnation – a Platonic and Neoplatonic belief, very much against the prevailing Aristotelian ethos of the time.

Two of Isaac's students, Rabbi Ezra ben Solomon and Rabbi Azriel, took his teachings to the small Catalan city of Girona and founded a School of Kabbalah there. Among other works, Azriel is thought to have written the influential *Explanation of the Ten Sephiroth*.

The great Jewish philosopher and teacher of the Talmud, Moses ben Nachman Girondi, usually known as Nahmanides (1194–1270), was born in Girona. He studied Kabbalah under Azriel and later went on to teach it in Barcelona, emphasizing once again its oral transmission. He became the leading Jewish teacher in all of Spain, stressing a mystical interpretation of the Torah (the Pentateuch, or first five books of the Old Testament) through personal enlightenment; again, he and his students were proponents of Neoplatonic mysticism (see pages 14–15) rather than the more rationalist and materialist Aristotelian philosophy that had taken hold in medieval Europe.

Much Kabbalistic thought since the 13th century can be traced back to the influence of the Girona school of Ezra, Azriel and Nahmanides, following in the footsteps of Isaac the Blind, but in 1492 all Jews were thrown out of Spain, and their former influence was swiftly forgotten. Nearly five hundred years later the long-buried School of Kabbalah in Girona was physically unearthed by the local poet Josep Tarrés in the mid-1970s, as strikingly described by the English writer Patrice Chaplin in her autobiographical work *City of Secrets*.

THE QUEST
FOR SPIRITUAL TRUTH

When the Jews were expelled from Spain, they travelled wherever they were able to throughout Europe, taking both their exoteric and esoteric teachings with them. The alchemists and Hermetic Philosophers who pursued heterodox spiritual wisdom were aware of the hidden teachings within Judaism and began to study them. At around the same time that Marsilio Ficino (1433–99) was translating the *Corpus Hermeticum* (see

THE BOOK OF SPLENDOUR

The *Sefer ha-Zohar*, a huge collection of mystical commentaries on the Torah, is probably the best-known Kabbalistic work. Although some Kabbalists apparently still believe the tradition that the *Zohar* is of 1st-century origin and was found in a cave in the Holy Land by Moses de Léon, the majority of scholarly opinion for many years states that it was largely written by Moses de Léon of Guadalajara, Spain, around 1280–86. Many commentators describe the work as complex, if not incomprehensible, but it contains perhaps the most complete exposition of Kabbalistic thought, and is still the central text of Kabbalah more than seven hundred years later.

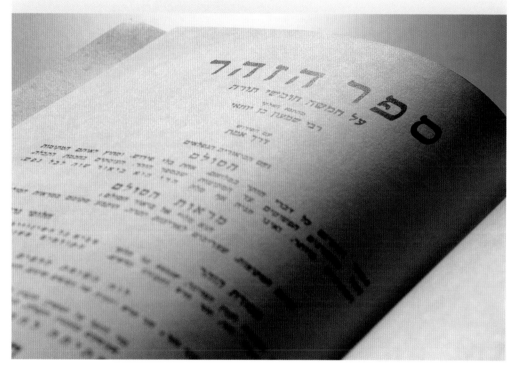

page 17), two other scholars – Giovanni Pico della Mirandola (1463–94) and Francesco Giorgi (1466–1540) – were immersing themselves in Kabbalah and 'proving' that Kabbalah supported Christianity.

These and other scholars who were questing for hidden spiritual truths throughout the 16th and 17th centuries made Kabbalah an essential part of their studies. The French occultists of the late 19th century, especially Éliphas Lévi, drew correspondences between the 22 paths linking the Sephiroth and the 22 cards of the Major Arcana of the Tarot. These ideas were developed further by the Hermetic Order of the Golden Dawn (see pages 103–119), and

Above The Sefer ha-Zohar, *one of the central texts of the Kabbalah, probably written or compiled by Moses de Léon c.1280–86.*

are now an integral part of the teachings of many present-day esoteric Orders and schools of occult science.

There are many different interpretations of Kabbalah today, and many different groups promoting them, beyond the recent high-profile organizations known for their celebrity members.

Hermetic Philosophers

The early Renaissance involved a revolution in thinking as well as in art, and in both cases it was largely dependent on the direction and support of wealthy patrons. One of these was the Florentine banker Cosimo de' Medici (1389–1464), who became the first Medici ruler of Florence. Influenced by Neoplatonist ideas (see pages 14–15), he established a new version of Plato's Academy in Florence, and chose the scholar Marsilio Ficino to head it.

Right *Hermes Trismegistus, the mythical author of the* Corpus Hermeticum, *one of the most influential collections of esoteric spiritual writings of all time. Artist: Johann Theodor de Bry, c.1580.*

Cosimo had commissioned Ficino to translate the works of Plato from Greek to Latin, but directed him to interrupt this endeavour when in 1460 the *Corpus Hermeticum* surfaced in Italy. This consisted of a number of works attributed to Hermes Trismegistus, the mythical ancient Greek/Egyptian god/philosopher (see page 17). In 1471 Ficino's translation of the *Corpus Hermeticum* was published in Latin, sparking a new wave of esoteric philosophical thought in Europe. Ficino also translated a number of Neoplatonist texts into Latin. Aristotelian philosophy had long been at the heart of Western academe, and the greater flexibility of Neoplatonism was of considerable appeal to natural philosophers, the scientists and thinkers of the day.

KABBALAH AND CHRISTIANITY

Kabbalah spread from Judaism into esoteric Christianity, largely through Giovanni Pico della Mirandola (1463–94), a pupil and friend of Ficino. He used certain Kabbalistic techniques, such as the manipulation of letters and the concentration on names of God, to demonstrate that Kabbalah proved the truth of Christianity.

Pico's ideas were built on by Francesco Giorgi (1466–1540), who 'proved' that the sacred Jewish name for God, the tetragrammaton (four-letter) YHWH, could be manipulated into the name Jesus, and that Jesus was therefore the Messiah expected by the Jews. Giorgi was one of the earliest and most influential Hermetic Philosophers, who effectively developed into the Rosicrucians; they in turn developed into the many 19th- to 21st-century occult societies, many of which study Kabbalah, along with astrology and alchemy, theoretical and practical magic, and mystical spirituality.

Henry Cornelius Agrippa von Nettesheim (1486–1535) was another major influence on the Hermetic movement, with his encyclopedia of magic *De Occulta Philosophia Libri Tres*; although this was written around 1510, it was not published until three years before his death. He lectured on Hermes Trismegistus, and drew together Christianity, Neoplatonism and Kabbalah.

PARACELSUS AND BRUNO

Hermetic teachings were not purely theoretical. Theophrastus Bombastus von Hohenheim (1493–1541) was a physician and surgeon who condemned most others in his profession for not having developed their skills since the Roman physician Galen, well over a millennium earlier. A Neoplatonist, he took the name Paracelsus in tribute to the Pagan teacher Celsus, who lived at the end of the 2nd century CE. As a physician Paracelsus was unusual in actually examining his patients, and he not only developed a number of medicines based on minerals and chemicals, but also initiated the use of ether as an anaesthetic. He believed in treating 'the whole man', teaching that 'if the spirit suffers, the body suffers also'. He saw humans in relation to the cosmos, the microcosm and the macrocosm.

Giordano Bruno (1548–1600) originally trained as a Dominican monk, was later a Lutheran, then a Calvinist, and was eventually burned at the stake for heresy. Among other teachings at variance with religious authority were his belief that the Earth orbited the Sun rather than vice versa, and that therefore each star in the sky might be a sun with planets around it. This pushed God out of the picture, which was not the wisest thing to do.

Bruno also taught a complex version of the Art of Memory, which was a method of classifying and categorizing all knowledge. Originally he taught a development of the Lullian Art, a system devised by the Spanish-born mystic Ramon Lull (c.1235–1315), with several concentric circles divided into segments. In later years Bruno taught a version of the Memory Palace, where items of knowledge would be positioned in specific places in 'memory rooms', each room symbolizing a branch of knowledge. Other teachers used an imaginary Theatre of Memory for the same purpose. Because of the detailed classification system, items of knowledge could be filed and retrieved, and interrelated to each other – effectively a Renaissance precursor of hyperlinks on the Internet, but all stored neatly in the practitioner's mind.

ALTERIVS NON SIT, QVI SVVS ESSE POTEST.

LAVS DEO, PAX VIVIS, REQVIES ÆTERNA SEPVLTIS.

OMNE DONVM PERFECTVM À DEO, IMPERFE À DIABO.

AVREOLVS PHILIPPVS THEOPHRASTVS

FREETHINKERS

It is unlikely that any of these people thought of themselves as Hermetic Philosophers; they and others like them were thinkers, teachers, scientists, doctors, monks, but above all *enquirers*. In today's phrasing, they thought outside the box. They were not constrained by the rigid structures imposed by the Church. They were prepared to work with forbidden knowledge.

In one way or another each one of these men was a heretic, in the true sense of the term: someone who thinks for himself, who *chooses* what to believe, rather than being told by a hierarchical establishment. Above all they were freethinkers, in an age when that was a very dangerous thing to be.

***Above** Theophrastus Bombastus von Hohenheim (Paracelsus) surrounded by philosophical symbols, from a work of 1567.*

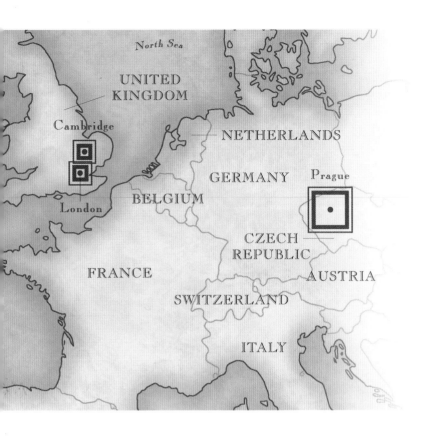

John Dee

John Dee (1527–1608) was a mathematician, a doctor, a cartographer, an astrologer and astronomer, an alchemist, a theologian, a philosopher ... He was Queen Elizabeth I's astrologer and adviser – and, no doubt, her spy. He was one of the most brilliant men of his day, with a wealth of knowledge and a sharp intellect. Yet he died in poverty, leaving behind a very mixed reputation.

Dee studied a range of subjects at Cambridge, including Greek, Latin and philosophy, but it was mathematics and astronomy that most fascinated him. He graduated in 1546, becoming a Fellow of St John's College and then a founding Fellow of Trinity College. He spent a few years travelling in Europe, studying and lecturing, and turned down the offer of a professorship in mathematics in Paris in 1551.

MIXED FORTUNES, ECLECTIC INTERESTS

During the reign of Queen Mary, both Dee and his father were arrested – his father for being a Protestant, and John Dee for 'calculating', probably for casting horoscopes of Mary and her sister Elizabeth. Dee lost his inheritance; he was never to have financial security throughout his long life. In contrast, when Mary died in 1558, the young Queen Elizabeth asked Dee to cast a horoscope to choose the most propitious date for her coronation. Some years later he even gave the Queen mathematics lessons.

Dee was fascinated by maps (he was a close friend of the famous mapmaker Mercator) and by instruments of navigation. He was enthusiastic about the exploration of America and the establishment of a British Empire around the world. Elizabeth sent him on some foreign trips, probably in the role of spy. Over many years he built up a massive library and an impressive collection of scientific instruments, globes and clocks. He suggested setting up a national library as a repository of knowledge as early as 1556, but the forward-thinking idea was not taken up.

As well as many scientific works, Dee wrote a major esoteric text on symbolic language, *Monas Hieroglyphica*, in 1564. This was heavily influenced by Hermetic ideas and explained the meaning of his own glyph (see far right). Always a mathematician, Dee took from Kabbalism, Neoplatonism and Neo-Pythagorianism a deep belief in the esoteric power of numbers, which had also been propounded by Marsilio Ficino (see pages 17 and 54). Indeed, the great historian of the Renaissance occult movement, Dame Frances Yates, wrote: 'The sensational angel-summoning side of Dee's activities was intimately related to his real success as a mathematician.'

DEE'S ASSOCIATION WITH EDWARD KELLEY

Whatever his other achievements, Dee will forever be known for the seven years of his involvement with Edward Kelley (1555–97). Kelley may or may not have had powers as a mystic, but he was undoubtedly a fraud and a con man as well. Dee was taken in by him, as were many others.

Dee was a great scholar of the esoteric, but he had no mystical abilities himself; he had to depend on others to be his seer. Kelley was not the first to perform this task for Dee. Kelley claimed to be able to see angels in Dee's scrying glass (an obsidian mirror now on display in the British Museum, London), taking messages from them in the angelic language he called Enochian. An indication of the power that the unscrupulous Kelley had over Dee was when he passed on the angels' instruction that Dee and Kelley should share everything in common – including their wives. (Dee's third wife Jane was much younger than him, the same age as Kelley, and reportedly very attractive.)

Looking for patronage to fund their research, Dee and Kelley went to Prague,

where for a while they worked at Hradcany Castle for King Rudolf II (see pages 58–59); later they received patronage from the Bohemian count Vilem Rosenberg. Kelley had a red powder that he claimed was the Philosopher's Stone, with which he could turn base metals to gold – no doubt the promise that gained them their funding.

Dee returned to England in 1589, to find that his marvellous library at his home in Mortlake, by the River Thames, had been ransacked and much of it stolen. (He had left Kelley in Bohemia, where he was to die in 1597, probably while trying to escape from imprisonment.) Dee, now an old man, was still poor. Queen Elizabeth eventually gave

him the post of Warden of Christ's College, Manchester, but Dee did not fit in well there and was mocked by the Fellows. While in Manchester, Dee's wife Jane and several of their children died of the plague. Dee returned to Mortlake, where he had to sell off many of his instruments; he even told fortunes in order to survive. His daughter Katherine cared for him until his death.

Dee's eldest son Arthur (1579–1651) was also a well-respected esoteric author and alchemist and a Paracelsian physician. He managed to win the royal appointments that had eluded his father, becoming personal physician to James I's queen, and physician extraordinary to Charles I.

Above A map of the Americas by Gerardus Mercator, a friend of John Dee, 1595.

Right In Monas Hieroglyphica *John Dee explained this glyph as revealing the unity underlying the universe.*

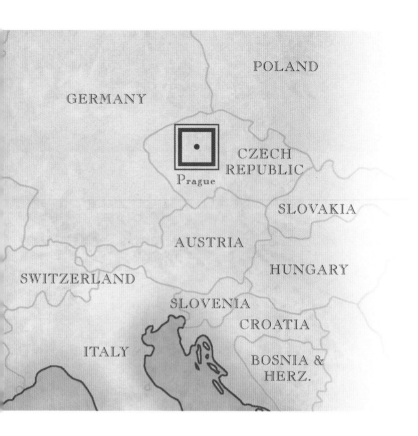

POLAND

GERMANY

CZECH
REPUBLIC

Prague

SLOVAKIA

AUSTRIA

SWITZERLAND

HUNGARY

SLOVENIA

CROATIA

ITALY

BOSNIA &
HERZ.

Hradcany Castle, Prague

The great Elizabethan mathematician, astronomer, cartographer, occultist and (probably) spy John Dee moved to Prague in August 1584 with his family and associate Edward Kelley. There he met the Holy Roman Emperor, Rudolf II (1552–1612), a devotee of occult arts and learning. In particular Rudolf was fascinated by alchemy, a discipline in which Kelley specialized.

Kelley stayed on in Europe and enjoyed great wealth and success, claiming results as an alchemist. Rudolf II made him a baron and established him in a house close to the palace. However, as time passed and Kelley failed to succeed in turning base metal into gold, Rudolf's patience wore thin. In 1591 he had Kelley arrested and imprisoned in a castle outside Prague, where Kelley died in 1597.

Prague Castle (or Hradcany Castle) is the largest medieval castle complex in Europe, containing not just several palaces, but also a cathedral, monastery, art galleries and many towers. It was in its heyday during the reign of Rudolf II, but dates back to the 9th century. A Romanesque palace constructed in the 12th century was rebuilt in the Gothic style in the 14th century; further major reconstruction took place in the late 15th century, and also after a massive fire in 1541.

THE DEFENESTRATION OF PRAGUE

The famous Defenestration of Prague, on 23 May 1618, sparked off the Thirty Years War. An assembly of Protestant nobles, defending their right to freedom of religion granted by Rudolf II, threw two imperial governors and their scribe out of a window of the council room in the castle. The fall was only about 4.5 m (15 ft) and they survived. According to Protestants, they fell into a heap of manure; according to Catholics, the Virgin Mary spread her cloak to catch them and carried them safely to the ground.

ROYAL GARDEN AND SINGING FOUNTAIN

The extensive Royal Garden lies to the west of the Summer Palace, north of the castle itself. It was laid out by Rudolf II's grandfather Ferdinand I in 1534. The garden contains the Singing Fountain, built by Tomas Jaros between 1564 and 1568. Water flowing from the carvings of animals falls into a great bronze bowl, causing it to 'sing'.

① OLD ROYAL PALACE

The Old Royal Palace, halfway along the southern side of the Castle complex, dates back to the late 9th century, but was rebuilt in Romanesque style in the early 12th century. Just to the east of it is the Church of All Saints, which was consecrated in 1185. It was used for formal ceremonial occasions, including coronations.

② CATHEDRAL OF ST VITUS

The castle's most prominent feature, visible for miles around, is the cathedral of St Vitus. The cathedral contains the tombs of many Bohemian kings and the relics of several patron saints of the country, including St Vitus himself, St Adalbert, and St Wenceslaus (the 'good king' of the Christmas carol).

③ POWDER BRIDGE AND SPANISH STABLES

Entrance to the castle is through the Powder Bridge at the north-west of the castle, leading to the Pacassi Gate. Rudolf II built extensive stables, sometimes called the Spanish Stables, alongside the gate. These housed around 300 horses, reputedly the best from all the countries of the world.

④ NEW HALL (SPANISH HALL)

West of the cathedral is a group of buildings, now majestic state rooms. The northern wing of these, above the imperial stables, is known as the New Hall (or Spanish Hall), and was built by Rudolf II to house his paintings and statues. Rudolf was the greatest art collector of his time; any visiting dignitary knew that, however important he might be, he would not gain an audience with Rudolf unless he gave the Emperor a gift of artwork.

⑤ LONG CORRIDOR

Rudolf II built a 100-metre Long Corridor to connect the North Wing to a Summer Palace he had built at the south of the castle complex. The Corridor contained more of his extensive art collection: rare saddles and horse harnesses on the ground floor; his famous Chamber of Art on the next floor, and further sculptures and paintings on the top floor.

⑥ POWDER TOWER

The Powder Tower, built by King Vladislav II at the end of the 15th century, is the largest of all the defensive cannon towers, though it was never used as such. It is next to the Foundry, and at one point in the 16th century the bell founder and gunsmith Tomas Jaros, who created the famous Singing Fountain in the Royal Garden, lived and worked here. He also built Prague's largest bell,

Zikmund, which is in the bell tower of St Vitus's Cathedral. Rudolf II used the tower as his alchemy workshop, where visiting alchemists, including Edward Kelley – and sometimes Rudolf himself – would perform their alchemical experiments. The tower was later used to store gunpowder, hence its name. In later centuries the sacristans of St Vitus's Cathedral lived in the Powder Tower.

CHAPTER 5

THE ROSICRUCIANS

The Rosicrucian Brotherhood has had a remarkable effect on esoteric groups – secret societies – for the last 350 years. As is so often the case with secret societies, it is important to search for the symbolic truth in the alleged history of the original Rosicrucians. Did the brotherhood literally arise as described in the Rosicrucian Manifestos, or are its origins even more mysterious and complex?

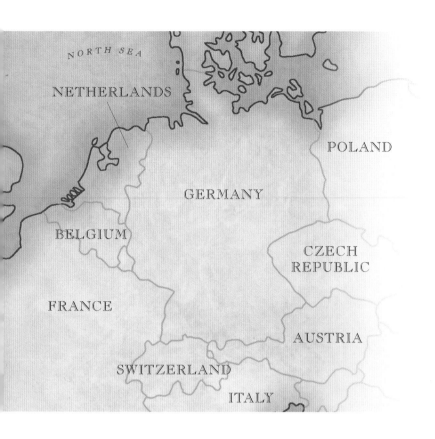

The Rosicrucian Manifestos

In the early 17th century three intriguing documents were published in Germany. Collectively known as the Rosicrucian Manifestos, these were the Fama Fraternitatis *in 1614, the* Confessio Fraternitatis *in 1615 and the* Chymische Hockzeit *or* The Chemical Wedding of Christian Rosenkreuz *in 1616. They were the first that anyone had heard of the Rosicrucians. All three documents were anonymous.*

The *Fama Fraternitatis* tells the story of how the Rosicrucian Brotherhood came into being. It relates how the tomb of Father C.R.C., or Christian Rosenkreuz (literally 'Rosy Cross'), was discovered in 1604, 120 years after his death at the age of 106. Born in Germany in 1378, he had travelled to the Holy Land, Turkey and Arabia. In the city of Damcar (possibly Damascus) he was taught by Muslim sages and mystics. Now a man of great esoteric learning, he returned home to Germany, where he gathered together a few like-minded men and founded the Order or Brotherhood of the Rosy Cross. They would become an Invisible College of enlightened men.

THE BROTHERHOOD IS REVEALED

The brothers agreed that they would cure the sick, without charge; that they should not wear any sort of habit, but the normal clothing of the country they were in; that they should meet once a year; that each of them should find someone to succeed him; that their 'seal, mark and character' should be the words Rosy Cross; and that they should remain secret for a hundred years.

Left 'The Rose Gives Honey to the Bee' from Robert Fludd's Clavis Philosophiae et Alchymiae *1633. The seven-petalled red rose above the thorny cross is one of the most potent Rosicrucian symbols. The bee represents both industry and wisdom.*

When Rosenkreuz's tomb was discovered by one of the brothers, just over a century later, it was in a seven-sided vault lit by a Sun in the ceiling; it contained a round altar beneath which lay the uncorrupted body of Christian Rosy Cross. 'In his hand he held a parchment, called T., the which next unto the Bible is our greatest treasure', the account reads. The tomb was resealed and the Brotherhood revealed to the world.

THE SECOND MANIFESTO

The *Confessio Fraternitatis* appeared in the following year. This document affirmed that the Brotherhood was Christian, and very clearly Protestant, for it condemned not only 'Mahomet' (that is, Islam) but also the Pope for 'their blasphemies'. It said that the members of the Brotherhood were skilled in learning and in medicine, and brought good to the world through their teachings and their work, even though it was hidden. It strongly condemned charlatans who brought alchemy and astrology into disrepute.

The document invited people of like mind to join them, but warned: 'Therefore it must not be expected that newcomers shall attain at once all our mighty secrets. They must proceed step by step from the smaller to the greater, and must not be retarded by difficulties.' This is a basic characteristic of all secret societies: that members proceed slowly but surely through the mysteries.

Above left A classic late-19th century interpretation of the rose cross imagery from the Hermetic Order of the Golden Dawn: Westcott's lamen or the Rose Cross lamen.

Left An unusual interpretation of 'The Temple of the Rose Cross', by Theophilus Schweighardt Constantiens, 1618.

THE THIRD MANIFESTO

The *Chemical Wedding of Christian Rosenkreuz* is very different from the first two manifestos, although it contains much symbolism of red roses and crosses and is clearly connected to the earlier documents in some way. It is a long, complex, highly symbolic tale in prose and poetry, an allegorical romance of a personal spiritual journey, told in much the same way as John Bunyan's *Pilgrim's Progress*. The story is divided into seven chapters, telling of Christian Rosenkreuz's journey over seven days.

While praying on Easter eve, Christian has a vision in which he is given an invitation to a wedding between a king and queen. On his journey he has to pass through a number of gates, which are obstacles in his way, to progress from each stage to the next. With each success he receives new insight. On the fourth day he witnesses the wedding, as well as a funeral and a resurrection, in a wonderful castle full of marvels, after which his journey and his testing continue, in order to bring about 'the work'.

The fable can be interpreted in many ways – one of which is that it relates, in symbolic form, the alchemical process. (The sixth day actually describes alchemical work in some detail.) This can be divided into seven stages, including such processes as sublimation and distillation. The 'uniting' of the king and queen, or bridegroom and bride, in the alchemical wedding is only one step along the way; but the entire 'journey' is one of personal transformation.

The members of the Brotherhood were skilled in learning and in medicine, and brought good to the world.

The purpose of the manifestos

Who wrote the Rosicrucian Manifestos? What was their purpose in doing so? Where did their ideas spring from? Who actually were the Rosicrucians? There are no clear answers to any of these questions, but a few things can be stated with some certainty.

First, the Brotherhood of the Rosy Cross, or Rosicrucian Fraternity, did not exist prior to the publication of the manifestos, or even for some time afterwards. Prospective members could have searched Europe high and low; the manifestos invited people to join, but did not include an application form or any address.

Second, although the organization did not exist, its 'members' certainly did. All over Europe there were individuals pursuing the sort of work that the manifestos spoke of: alchemists, astrologers, Hermetic Philosophers, and people who were following a Neoplatonic search for their individual path of enlightenment, for their personal spiritual transformation, outside the structures and strictures of the Church. These were the Rosicrucians – though without that name.

A CALL TO ARMS

The three Rosicrucian Manifestos were, in a sense, a call to arms. They were the esoteric community identifying itself to itself, and to the outside world. They were also calling for a distinction to be made between genuine enquirers into the Hermetic mysteries and charlatans who faked the making of small quantities of gold in order to gain the patronage of a king or wealthy noble (see page 48). The manifestos were making the point, very strongly, that the search for individual enlightenment should not be a selfish quest for knowledge or influence, or power or wealth, but that personal transformation should benefit the world. The purpose of the Rosicrucians was to be healers – not necessarily just of physical complaints, but of the ills of the world. Time-wasters, the immature and the selfish need not apply.

POTENTIAL AUTHORS

Who wrote the Rosicrucian Manifestos? Who issued this call to arms? It is probable that the third manifesto, the dramatic allegory of *The Chemical Wedding*, was written by a Lutheran minister called Johann Valentin Andreae (1586–1654). In his autobiography, which was not discovered until 1799, he claimed to have written a version of it when he was a student at the age of 17 (around 1603) as a *ludibrium* or academic jest, though throughout his life he denied any connection with it. If he did write it, Andreae's original has never been found, so historians cannot tell how similar it was to the 1616 version.

Some people think Andreae wrote all three manifestos, but this is unlikely; they are very different in style. The *Fama* and the *Confessio* were both published bound with other documents. The *Fama*, though first published in 1614, had been in circulation for at least two years before then, and probably longer, because published alongside it was the first of many 'replies' to the manifestos, written by one Adam Haselmayer in 1612. There was also an extract from a German translation of a recent Italian satirical work about liberal thinkers in a reactionary world; the chapter is about the need for a new reformation, because all previous attempts have failed.

The *Confessio* was published with a work called *A Brief Consideration of the More Secret Philosophy* by one Philip à Gabella, who is otherwise unknown to history and is probably a pseudonym; both works were in Latin. The *Consideratio Brevis* was based on John Dee's most important esoteric work, *Monas Hieroglyphica*, written in 1564. It is also undoubtedly significant that on the first page of *The Chemical Wedding* is John Dee's personal glyph (see page 57), which he explains at length in *Monas Hieroglyphica*.

Historian Dame Frances Yates argued persuasively in her classic work *The Rosicrucian Enlightenment* that John Dee was the 'father' of Rosicrucianism. He did not write the manifestos, but they would not have existed without his prior work.

Many have argued that the Rose and Cross symbolism derives from Andreae's own coat of arms, thus 'proving' his authorship, but it should be said that they are also in the coat of arms of Martin Luther, founder of the Protestant revolution – and the first Rosicrucians were very firmly Protestant.

Some esotericists believe that the symbolism of the Rosicrucians does not in fact derive from the Latin *rosa* meaning 'rose', but from *ros* meaning 'dew' – and that dew is the alkahest, or universal solvent, of alchemy.

Opposite *German theologian Johann Valentin Andreae (1586–1654), the probable author of the third Rosicrucian manifesto.*

Right *'Martin Luther Translating the Bible, Wartburg Castle, 1521', by Eugene Siberdt, 1898. The early Rosicrucians clearly had a Protestant agenda, but it is highly unlikely that their symbolism was linked to Luther's family coat of arms.*

Responses to the manifestos

Responses to the Rosicrucian Manifestos began immediately; as we have seen, the Fama *was published alongside a reply to it. Both supporters and detractors were quick to take up their pens. A number of writers – philosophers, scientists, doctors, mystics – expressed their solidarity with the ideas expressed in the manifestos, or expanded on them, fitting them into their own world-view. However, there were some who were vehemently opposed to the ideas within the manifestos, on religious or political grounds.*

THE SUPPORTERS

Robert Fludd (1574–1637) was one of the most innovative thinkers of his day, a Fellow of the Royal College of Physicians, despite being Paracelsian in his beliefs and drawing on Kabbalistic, Neoplatonist and Neo-Pythagorian ideas. His solution to the perennial problem of good versus evil was not the Good God/Bad God dualism of the Gnostics (see page 14), but the even more radical belief that YHWH encompasses both good and evil, both sides of the coin in one deity. (In this he was anticipating by centuries the ideas of thinkers like Carl Jung that archetypes contain their opposites within them, so that the strong, firm leader can also be the dictatorial tyrant.) Fludd wrote an influential defence of Rosicrucianism as early as 1616, responding to an attack on it by the alchemist Andreas Libavius.

Fludd's friend Michael Maier (1568–1622) was also a strong defender of Rosicrucianism. He was physician to Rudolf II of Prague, who was fascinated by esoteric studies, including alchemy. Maier was a prolific author at much the same time as the manifestos were published, producing *Arcana Arcanissima* (*Secret of Secrets*) in 1614 and at least three further books by 1618, including his

renowned and beautifully illustrated *Atalanta Fugiens* (*Fleeing Atalanta*), the images being accompanied by alchemical philosophical commentaries. Although Maier said in his writings that he was not himself a member of the Brotherhood of the Rosy Cross, he wrote of it as if it actually existed. He defended it in *Silentium post Clamorem* (*The Silence after the Shouting*), explaining why the Brotherhood had not responded to all those who were trying to contact them: they had done their bit by publishing the manifestos.

The English mystic Thomas Vaughan (1621–65), brother of the metaphysical poet Henry Vaughan, taught a belief developed from Kabbalism that 'the spirit of man is itself the spirit of the living God' – that is, that God is immanent, within us. Vaughan published the *Fama* and the *Confessio* in one volume in an English translation in 1652, under the pseudonym Eugenius Philalethes. The great

scientist Isaac Newton owned a copy of Vaughan's edition of the manifestos. Vaughan's patron was Sir Robert Moray (see pages 69 and 81).

THE DETRACTORS

Some found the idea of the Rosicrucians a threat. In 1623 it was believed that there were Rosicrucians in Paris, both visibly and invisibly – the term 'Invisible College' (see page 62) being taken literally. Rumours spread rapidly, and soon there was a pamphlet entitled 'Horrible Pacts Made Between the Devil and the Pretended Invisible Ones'. The pamphlet claimed – in an intriguing echo of the charges made against the Knights Templar by Philip the Fair three hundred years earlier (see pages 28–29) – that Rosicrucians prostrated themselves before a demonic figure, swearing to deny Christianity and the Church's rites and sacraments. Only in the sense that the Rosicrucian Manifestos were clearly anti-Catholic could the last charge be seen to have any validity; as for the first charge, the manifestos demonstrate that the Rosicrucians were devout Christians.

Similar defamatory charges are still levelled today by fundamentalist Evangelical Christians against Rosicrucians, Freemasons and members of other esoteric or 'occult' organizations. They are as valid now as they were four hundred years ago.

Opposite The Rosicrucians were natural philosophers, the experimental scientists of their day. This engraving from Michael Maier's Atalanta Fugiens *(1618) shows the mathematical problem of squaring the circle.*

Right Heidelberg Castle, Germany, the home of Frederick V, Elector Palatine, whose wedding to Elizabeth Stuart is probably linked to the third Rosicrucian manifesto.

THE WINTER KING'S ENLIGHTENED ERA

As well as the religious controversy, the manifestos must be seen in the political landscape of Europe at the time they were published. The alchemical wedding is often compared to the spectacular wedding in 1613 between Frederick V, Elector Palatine, and Elizabeth Stuart, granddaughter of Mary, Queen of Scots, and its Protestant implications for central Europe. (There is no doubt that some of the illustrations in Rosicrucian literature show Heidelberg Castle, Frederick's home.) This argues against the third manifesto having been written by Johann Valentin Andreae in 1603 (see page 64), though the published version may have been substantially different from Andreae's original.

Frederick ('the Winter King') and Elizabeth were briefly King and Queen of Bohemia in 1619–20, reigning in what had been Rudolf II's Hradcany Castle (see pages 58–59); but the spiritual Renaissance anticipated in the Rosicrucian Manifestos was destroyed when the Catholic Habsburgs defeated Frederick at Prague and then Heidelberg, in the process literally scattering the artistic heritage of Heidelberg – its library – to the wind. Frederick was driven into exile in The Hague. Soon the disastrous Thirty Years War (1618–48) would lay waste to Germany. Many of the Catholic pamphlets attacking the Rosicrucians also attacked Frederick's enlightened, but short-lived, Protestant reign.

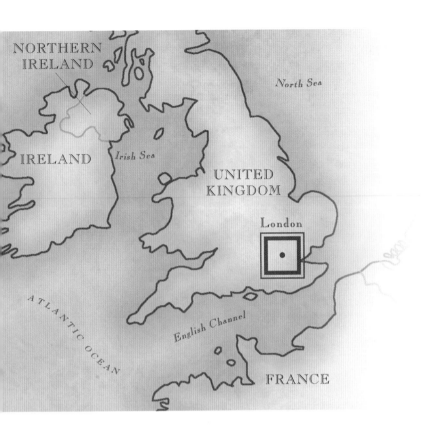

From the Invisible College to the Royal Society

Though the Rosicrucian society described in the first two manifestos almost certainly did not exist, within a short time Rosicrucian groups were created in response to the manifestos – perhaps exactly as their authors intended.

Germany and France saw their greatest resurgence of Rosicrucian-type societies in the 18th and 19th centuries (see pages 70–71), but England took a different route, or perhaps two different routes, in the 17th century.

Just as the Thirty Years War was limping to its ignominious end in Germany, England had its own problems, leading to the execution of King Charles I in 1649 and the establishment of Oliver Cromwell's Protectorate or Commonwealth. During that time, and immediately before and after, Royalist and Parliamentarian supporters were at daggers drawn.

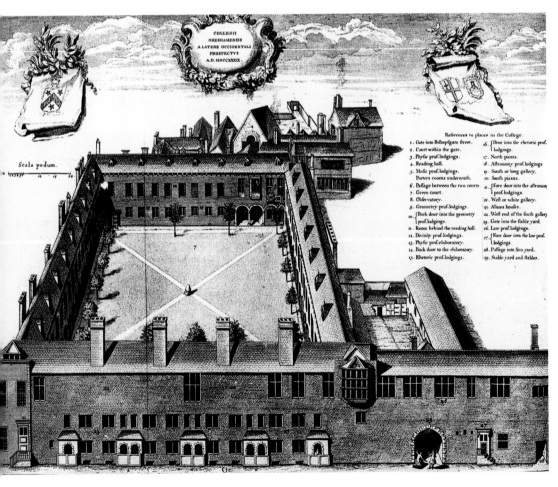

Left The home of
Thomas Gresham in
Bishopsgate, London,
left in his will of 1575
to become the first
buildings of Gresham
College – and which
became the first home
of the Royal Society.

Left *Isaac Newton presiding at a meeting of the Royal Society in its second home at Crane Court, off Fleet Street, London, where the Royal Society was housed in 1710–80.*

GRESHAM COLLEGE

However, a group of natural philosophers (including supporters of both sides) met regularly at Gresham College in Bishopsgate, near what is now the financial centre of the City of London. Gresham College was founded in 1597 and was named after Sir Thomas Gresham, who had endowed it in his will. It was effectively the first university college in London, though it is independent of the University of London, has no students and does not grant degrees. It still exists today, based in an ancient hall near Holborn in central London, where its eight professors continue to give free lectures to the public.

In the mid-17th century the scholars who met for lectures and discussions at Gresham College included Sir Christopher Wren (who became Gresham Professor of Astronomy in 1657), Dr William Petty (Professor of Music), Dr Jonathan Goddard (Professor of Physic, or medicine), the scientist Robert Boyle, Sir Robert Moray and others. At the time of the Civil War, some of these – such as Moray – were fervent Royalists, while Goddard was Cromwell's personal physician.

They did not meet just to hear lectures. According to an account by John Wallis, a Professor of Geometry at Oxford, they would continue to meet out of term time – sometimes at Goddard's lodgings, sometimes in a local hostelry – 'to discourse and consider of Philosophical Enquiries'. During the Protectorate (1648–59) some met in Oxford rather than London; among these were Robert Boyle, Sir Christopher Wren and William Petty. They met in the Wadham College rooms of John Wilkins, author of *Mathematicall Magick* (1648), who was chaplain to the Elector Palatine (son of the Winter King; see page 67).

BIRTH OF THE ROYAL SOCIETY

A few months after the restoration of the monarchy, in November 1660, a dozen men attended a lecture at Gresham College, then went on to a meeting where they agreed to set up a formal society for the study and promotion of experimental science – or, in their words, 'a Colledge for the Promoting of Physico-Mathematicall Experimentall Learning'. In 1661 Sir Robert Moray petitioned King Charles II for a Royal Charter for their society, and in 1662 the Royal Society was officially born – the oldest and most prestigious such institution in the world. Many of its earliest members, including Isaac Newton (see page 47), who was President of the Royal Society from 1703 until his death in 1727, studied alchemy and astrology and other disciplines familiar to Hermetic Philosophers.

Significantly, Robert Boyle (later to formulate Boyle's Law about the properties of gases) described their meetings as 'the Invisible (or as they term themselves the Philosophical) College'. The Invisible College of the Rosicrucians had thus been reified, made real – and visible.

MORAY AND BACON

Who was Sir Robert Moray (1608–73)? He helped prepare for the return of Charles II to England. Among his friends were the diarist Samuel Pepys and the metaphysical poet Andrew Marvell. As well as being the patron of Thomas Vaughan, who first published the Rosicrucian Manifestos in English, Moray is the first person of whom there is a record of membership of a Freemasons' lodge, in 1641 (see page 81).

One other figure must be mentioned: the essayist and statesman Sir Francis Bacon (1561–1626). Despite the claims of some of today's Rosicrucian Orders, especially in the USA, that Bacon was one of their illustrious forebears, there is absolutely no evidence that he ever had any connection with Rosicrucianism or with Freemasonry, which he has also been credited with founding. However, it is clear that Bacon knew of the *Fama Fraternitatis* because of references to aspects of it in a work unfinished at his death, *New Atlantis*, an allegorical romance of a mythical Utopian society in which science and religion work together. In this society, the House of Salomon is 'dedicated to the study of the works and creatures of God... whereby God might have the more glory in the workmanship of them, and men the more fruit in the use of them'. This is the Rosicrucian ideal, and some have seen the Royal Society as the realization of the House of Salomon.

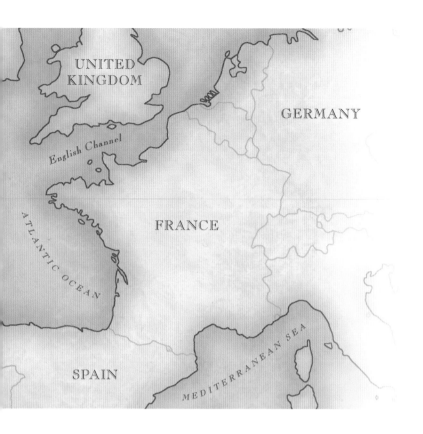

European movements in the 18th and 19th centuries

Elias Ashmole (1617–92) was a writer, an antiquarian, a loyal royalist and a scholar of alchemy and astrology. The Ashmolean Museum in Oxford began with his donation of books, engravings and scientific specimens to Oxford University in 1677.

The first building of the Ashmolean Museum is said to have been designed by Sir Christopher Wren. In a sense Ashmole succeeded, where John Dee had failed, in setting up a national library.

Many sources claim that in 1646 Ashmole and the astrologer William Lilly (who in 1647 published a major book entitled *Christian Astrology*, still highly regarded today), with others, founded a Rosicrucian Society in London. Its aim was apparently to put into action the ideals of Sir Francis Bacon's Utopian Society. Others assert that this was actually the foundation of the Freemasons. Looking back from over 350 years later, it is difficult to say definitively what it was that Ashmole and Lilly founded. It was perhaps more likely to have been the Gresham College group rather than Freemasonry, but these different interpretations of the past show how much these bodies – the Rosicrucians, the Freemasons, the Gresham College group, the Royal Society – were all linked to each other, if only because the same people were members of several of them.

Above *Antoine Court de Gébelin (c.1719–84), who first suggested that Tarot had Egyptian origins.*

FROM GERMANY TO FRANCE

In 1710 in Germany the laws of the alchemical Brotherhood of the Golden and Rosy Cross were published. In a document of 1777 the Brotherhood claimed a special relationship with Freemasonry (see page 81). This otherwise obscure 18th-century German Order was to have a major influence on two late 19th-century organizations and, through one of them, on 20th- and 21st-century occult groups (see pages 105, 106 and 139).

In the late 18th and 19th centuries the esoteric focus in Europe shifted from Germany to France, and with a new fascination: Tarot. In 1781 Antoine Court de Gébelin wrote a huge multi-volume work, *Le Monde Primitif*, a highly speculative examination of myths, legends and beliefs. In one volume he claimed that Tarot was an ancient Egyptian work, which contained all the wisdom of the ancients. Court de Gébelin had been a member of a French branch of Freemasonry called the Rite of the Philalethes, which focused on, among other things, alchemy, magic and esoteric Christianity. (It is worth remembering that over a century earlier, when Thomas Vaughan published the *Fama* and the *Confessio* in one volume in English, he used the pseudonym Eugenius Philalethes. The word *philalethes* comes from the Greek for 'lover of truth', and has been used by several Rosicrucian and Masonic individuals and organizations over the centuries.)

Court de Gébelin's pronouncements on the origin of Tarot were very wide of the mark, but contained a deeper truth: the Hermetic origins of many of the beliefs of Rosicrucians and other esotericists. His account was swiftly followed by an even more wildly speculative interpretation of Tarot from a Paris wigmaker called Alliette, better known as Etteilla, the fortune teller. His thoughts on Tarot being *The Book of Thoth* were later to influence Aleister Crowley (see pages 126–127).

LÉVI AND HIS FOLLOWERS

In the mid-19th century a hugely important French esotericist appeared: Alphonse Louis Constant, who adopted the name Éliphas Lévi. His *Dogme et Rituel de la Haute Magie* was published in 1855–56. Among a great deal else, it drew connections between the 22 cards of the Major Arcana of Tarot and the 22 letters of the Hebrew alphabet, and was thus a Kabbalistic interpretation of Tarot, which was to influence many others, including the Hermetic Order of the Golden Dawn (see page 117). Lévi was a theoretician rather than a practitioner of magic, but his effect on the wide variety of modern esoteric groups cannot be overestimated.

In 1888 two followers of Lévi, Joséphin Péladan (see page 33) and the Marquis Stanislas de Guaita, founded the Kabbalistic Order of the Rosy Cross, which still exists today. Its emphasis was on restoring the esoteric spiritual element, which they believed had been lost in many of the Masonic groups that had sprung up across the continent, with their focus on colourful ritual and regalia. Although Péladan shortly left the Order to found the Catholic Order of the Rose+Cross, both he and the Kabbalistic Order of the Rosy Cross were influential on many Rosicrucian-type groups today.

Above 'Reading the Tarot', from Le Petit Journal *(a Parisian daily newspaper), 4 June 1892.*

In the late 18th and 19th centuries the esoteric focus in Europe shifted from Germany to France, and with a new fascination: Tarot.

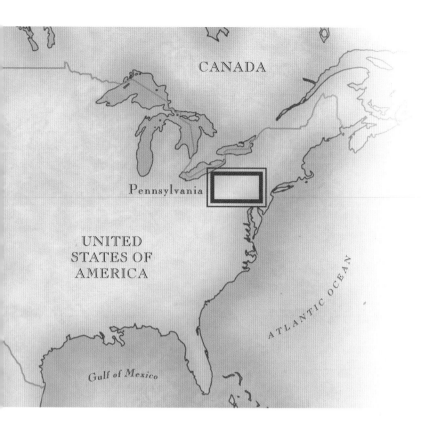

Rosicrucian Orders today

Today there are many competing Rosicrucian Orders both in Europe, where Rosicrucianism originated, and especially in America. From the writings of some American Rosicrucian groups it would almost appear that the United States was founded and nurtured by Rosicrucians, and that it represented the establishment of the Rosicrucian dream; but in reading the literature from any esoteric organization it is wise to treat accounts of their historical lineage as at best symbolic.

It is not unfair to say that many esoteric organizations, from the 17th century till today, have made up their history in an attempt to claim authenticity – that they, and they alone, are the true successors to the Brotherhood of Christian Rosenkreuz, the original Knights Templar or some other early organization. A lineage, however spurious, is like the false provenance of an antique chair that was made last week; it grants authenticity for those who do not enquire too deeply.

The following represent a selection of some of the more prominent Rosicrucian Orders today. There are many others, some with the word Rosicrucian in their name, and others not (see pages 114–119); some large, others small; some with impressive websites, others keeping themselves more private, if not secret. All, in one way or another, owe a debt to those who went before.

AMERICAN-BASED GROUPS

The Fraternitas Rosae Crucis or Rosicrucian Fraternity, based in Pennsylvania, was founded in 1922 by Reuben Swinburne Clymer (1878–1966). It was based on an earlier organization, the Brotherhood of Eulis, a sex-magic group founded by Paschal Beverly Randolph (1825–75) in the year before his death. The Brotherhood of Eulis continued as a small organization under Randolph's successors until Clymer joined it and turned it into the Fraternitas Rosae Crucis, dropping the emphasis on sex-magic. The FRC claims today that it was founded by Randolph, who had been given his authority in 1856 by Éliphas Lévi in France (see page 71), becoming 'Supreme Master of the Western World'.

The Rosicrucian Fellowship was founded by former Theosophist Max Heindel, born Carl Louis von Grasshoff (1865–1919). According to the group, Heindel, having been found fit to receive esoteric teachings, was 'given instructions as to how to reach the Temple of the Rose Cross, which was near the border between Bohemia and Germany', and there he was given teachings by 'Elder Brothers'. In fact when Heindel went to Germany from the United States in 1907, he met and was greatly impressed by the then German leader of Theosophy, Rudolf Steiner (see page 115). A century later there is still controversy – both without and within the

Rosicrucian Fellowship – about whether Heindel took some of the teachings in his foundational work *The Rosicrucian Cosmo-Conception* (1909) from Steiner. The Rosicrucian Fellowship sees its purpose as disseminating the esoteric doctrines of Christianity; in line with the original Rosicrucian precepts, today it concentrates greatly on healing, through what it calls 'Invisible Helpers'.

The Societas Rosicruciana in America is an offshoot of the American branch of the Societas Rosicruciana in Anglia or 'Soc Ros', an English Masonic Order immensely important for what it engendered (see pages 104–105). Also called the Society of Rosicrucians, Inc. and the Rosicrucian Society of America, the American SRIA was set up by George Wilmslow Plummer in 1909 specifically to open up its esoteric teachings to non-Freemasons. It is by no means alone in claiming to be 'a lineal descendant and, in America, the branch of the Society first formulated by Christian Rosenkreuz, the esoteric pseudonym of a spiritual Leader and Adept who was born AD 1378 and died in 1484'.

Above The interior of the New York temple of the Societas Rosicruciana in America, c.1913.

Below The Rosy Cross with other mystical symbols, from the front cover of Max Heindel's The Rosicrucian Cosmo-Conception.

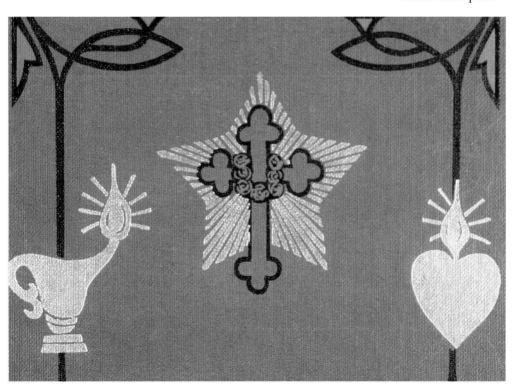

THE CLASH BETWEEN AMORC AND THE FRC

Probably the best-known Rosicrucian Order is AMORC, the Ancient Mystical Order Rosae Crucis, sometimes called the Rosicrucian Order. AMORC was founded by Harvey Spencer Lewis (1883–1939), who was given his authority to set up an Order by Theodor Reuss, founder of the Ordo Templi Orientis (see pages 130–131) in 1915. AMORC itself was set up in 1925. Lewis was taken to court by R. Swinburne Clymer in 1928 over his use of the word 'Rosicrucian'; Clymer claimed that only his Order, the Fraternitas Rosae Crucis, was entitled to use it. The court decided that the name Rosicrucian was in the public domain and could be used by anyone. Each side accused the other of being fake, with Clymer rounding on Lewis (because of the OTO origins of AMORC) as 'the boastful pilfering Imperator with his black-magic, sex-magic connections', ignoring the sex-magic teachings of Paschal Beverly Randolph, the supposed founder of the FRC.

It may seem strange that organizations claiming to hold deeply spiritual secrets should be so litigious. Furthermore, both FRC and AMORC have suffered from schisms and defections over the years. Today's Rosicrucians are no longer small, secretive groups; now they are large corporations openly recruiting their members through advertising. The authors of the Rosicrucian Manifestos would probably be both baffled and horrified at what they had unleashed on the Western world.

CHAPTER 6

THE FREEMASONS

For an organization only around 350 years old, and as well known as the Freemasons, it is surprising that its origins and early history are so shrouded in mystery. Much of the fault lies with Freemasonry itself. Especially in the 18th century, Freemasons delighted in creating a vast number of new Orders and degrees (graded levels of attainment), each with its own regalia and ritual, and its own symbolic history to explain where it came from and to give a background to the moral lessons taught in its rituals. The problem comes when non-Masons read these histories and assume they are supposed to be taken literally – or, worse, mix together the symbolic 'histories' of several different Orders into one quite spurious 'history'.

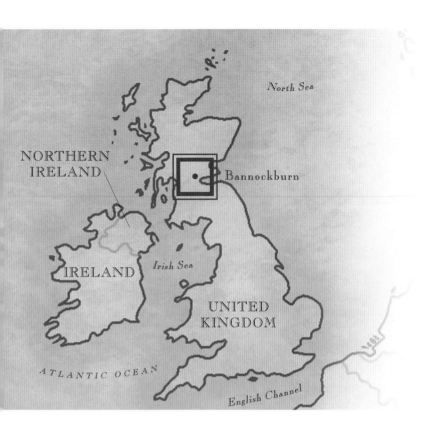

Origins in the Templars

There are three main theories concerning the origins of Freemasonry: that it developed from the Knights Templar, from the Rosicrucians or from the building trade – from stonemasons. The first theory is the most romantic, and by far the least likely (see pages 31–33).

The person responsible for setting the ball rolling on the Templar origins of Freemasonry was the Chevalier Andrew Ramsay, a Jacobite Scot involved in French Freemasonry, who made a speech in 1736 that became known as Ramsay's Oration. Although he did not mention the Templars by name, he spoke of brotherhood, symbolism and secret signs that had come down to Freemasonry from the Crusading knights, who, on returning to Europe, set up lodges where they could continue to study and teach the secrets of architecture, including the rebuilding of Solomon's Temple.

THE SCOTTISH CONNECTION

The Rite of the Strict Observance, founded by Baron Gotthelf von Hund in 1754 (see page 32), was based in part on a Legend of Perpetuation. It claimed that the last Master of the Temple, Jacques de Molay, had appointed Pierre d'Aumont, the Templar Prior of Auvergne, as his successor. D'Aumont took the Order to Scotland, where his own successors kept it and themselves secret for four hundred years, before resurfacing as the Freemasons.

A similar story appeared in *A Sketch of the History of the Knights Templars* (1837) by James Burnes, who had been asked to write a symbolic traditional history for the Scottish Masonic Order of the Knights Templar, founded around 30 years earlier. He wrote of the Knights Templar:

> *we are told by a learned French writer, that having deserted the Temple, they had ranged themselves under the banners of Robert Bruce, by whom they were formed into a new Order, the observances of which were based on those of the Templars, and became, according to him, the source of Scottish Free Masonry.*

Burnes did not expect this story to be believed as historical fact (he casts doubt on it elsewhere in his book), but the ideas of these Templars lying low in Scotland for four hundred years and then springing up again as the Freemasons, and that Masonic rituals and teachings are based on those of the Knights Templar, are now an established part of 'speculative history'.

A colourful addition to this myth is that in June 1314 Robert the Bruce was in desperate trouble at the battle of Bannockburn, when over the hill appeared a group of soldiers waving the Templar standard, who routed the greater forces of the English king Edward II. In gratitude for their assistance, Robert the Bruce allowed them to stay in Scotland, giving them land.

Although there is absolutely no evidence for this story, it continues to appear in the more fanciful books on the Knights Templar and their legacy. It has even been claimed that Rosslyn Chapel (see pages 31, 78–79 and 140–141), which is supposedly overflowing with Templar symbolism, was built to commemorate the Templars' intervention at Bannockburn .

THE FRENCH CONNECTION

Most of these stories clearly date from the 19th and 20th centuries, but their origins lie in the early 18th century, when Scotland was allied much more closely to France than it was to England. The Jacobites, supported by the French, aimed to restore the Stuart monarchy by placing Bonnie Prince Charlie on the throne of Scotland. The Chevalier Andrew Ramsay, who had been tutor to the

Young Pretender, delivered his Oration to French Masons midway between the two Jacobite armed rebellions of 1715 and 1745. To draw on the idea of chivalry in an idealized pseudo-history was a natural way of raising support for 'the King across the water'. The Jacobite cause was a romantic one, and Ramsay's Oration was a romantic vision. The Ancient and Accepted Scottish Rite of Freemasonry, which is very popular in the USA, is a direct successor of *Écossaise*, Scottish Freemasonry that developed and was practised in France.

KNIGHTS OF MALTA

One of the side-degrees of English Freemasonry has the impressive title of the 'United Religious, Military and Masonic Orders of the Temple and of St John of Jerusalem, Palestine, Rhodes and Malta, in England and Wales and Provinces Overseas'. It is usually known more simply as Knights Templar and Knights of Malta, and was founded, as was so much in Freemasonry, in the late 18th century. Although its history concerns the Templars, this Order has no connection to the historical Knights Templar.

Left The Battle of Bannockburn (1314), from the Holkham Bible, 1327–35. There is no evidence that Knights Templar suddenly arrived to save the day for Robert the Bruce.

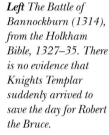

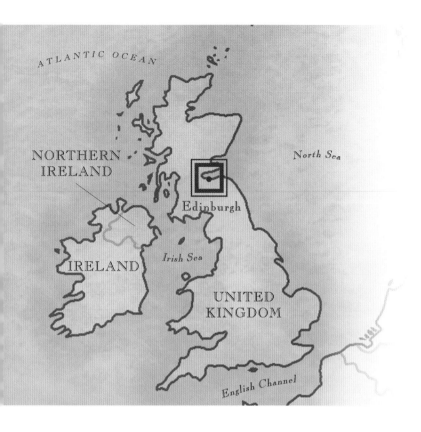

St Clairs, Templars and Freemasons

How do Rosslyn Chapel and its builders, the St Clairs, fit into the overall narrative of the Templars, the Masons and the secrets they were said to guard? This family proves to be intimately connected with the alternative history of the Templars and the Freemasons, with St Clairs as key players in the most significant parts of the speculative tale.

The St Clairs were among the most powerful families in Scotland. They were descended from the Viking kings of the Orkneys, where they were earls, until becoming the Earls of Caithness (in addition to being Barons of Roslin).

The St Clairs' family tree entwines with the kings of Scotland and later of Britain. Throughout history many St Clairs have been called William, which can make it difficult to keep track of which one is being referred to in a historical discussion, either about Rosslyn Chapel or the Freemasons in Scotland.

THE TEMPLAR–MASONIC CONNECTION

It is often written that the St Clairs were involved with the Knights Templar, giving sanctuary to the order when it was dissolved on the continent in 1307, and that they were instrumental in getting the Templars to fight alongside Robert the Bruce, aiding him when he gained independence for Scotland. It has also been claimed that the 14th century Henry St Clair was a Templar or Templar sympathizer, who voyaged to North America a hundred years before Columbus.

Above A tomb effigy of a Templar knight. Such effigies often feature a range of intriguing symbolism including crosses and animals.

One of the most persistent myths regarding the Templars is that, contrary to recorded history, the organization survived its dissolution and continued to practise its supposedly strange rites (see pages 30–33).

Since the Templars were not actively suppressed in England or Scotland, as occurred in other parts of Europe, it is often claimed that it was to Scotland that they transferred their treasure and their fleet of ships, and that it was here that they made their new (undercover) base. As Scotland and England were the birthplaces of Freemasonry, which has been so extensively linked to the Knights Templar (see pages 76–77), the supposed chain of transmission of tradition, knowledge and influence from Templars to Freemasons has also been located in Britain.

SECRET ST CLAIRS

The St Clairs (or Sinclairs) prove to be absolutely central to all these claims. On the basis of his tombstone, which bears a Templar rose, William St Clair of the early 14th century is said to have been a Templar, and his son Henry St Clair's supposed transatlantic explorations are often said to have involved Templar fleets, and to have made use of the Templars' advanced navigational and geographical knowledge. (Some writers have even claimed that this knowledge was proof of a Templar–Masonic link with the lost civilization of Atlantis.) The Templar–Masonic theory holds that the Freemasons were secretly founded in the 14th century as a continuation of the Templars, and that the William St Clair who was then head of the family was the first Grand Master. Into his hands was given the great treasure of the Templars, and one legend has it that when Roslin Castle burned down he conspicuously rescued several large chests containing the treasure, before looking to his own family.

In this telling, the 15th-century William St Clair was part of this Templar–Masonic tradition and constructed Rosslyn Chapel according to Templar precepts and symbolism; it was deliberately left unfinished because it was intended as a re-creation of the ruins of Solomon's Temple (see pages 92–93 and 140–141). He also housed within it – probably in the crypt – the Templar treasure.

One of William St Clair's 18th-century descendants, again called William St Clair, was a major figure in the 'official' birth of Scottish Freemasonry; he was the first Grand Master of the Scottish Grand Lodge. According to the alternative version of history, however, this was a front to cover the fact that the Freemasons had existed for centuries by this point and that the St Clairs had been Grand Masters all along.

FAULTY CONNECTIONS

Unfortunately the evidence does not support any of these exciting contentions. Rosslyn chapel was constructed more than a century after the dissolution of the Templars, and rather than the St Clairs being friends to the Templars, the evidence shows that some of William's ancestors actually testified against them in the trials in 1309. There is also no evidence that any Templars fought alongside Robert the Bruce.

The claims about Henry St Clair are based on a particular interpretation of supposedly 14th-century documents called the Zeno letters and map, which are assumed by most historians to be fakes or a hoax. The Masonic connection is similarly shaky. While the St Clairs may have been associated with stonemasons' guilds (as in the skilled workmen who, for instance, built Rosslyn Chapel), this is not the same as saying that they founded Freemasonry. Freemasonry as a society did not emerge until the 17th century.

Below The Apprentice Pillar of Rosslyn Chapel. According to legend, the chapel's master mason was so enraged by the brilliance of his apprentice's work on the pillar that he struck him with a mallet and killed him.

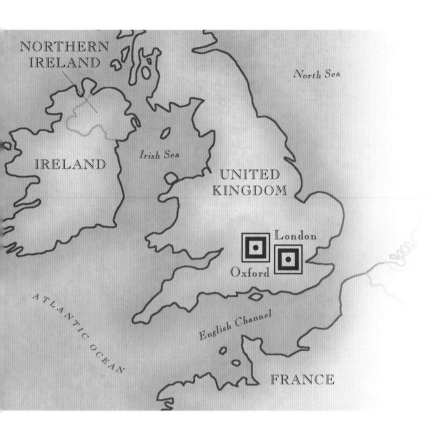

Origins in the Rosicrucians

Are today's Freemasons simply yesterday's Rosicrucians? In several ways the answer is a qualified yes, but not in the sense of one organization becoming the other. There are certainly Rosicrucian groups within Freemasonry, such as the Societas Rosicruciana in Anglia (see pages 104–105). There are also many degrees and some Orders with Rosicrucian-sounding names.

One of the best-known Orders in Freemasonry in England and Wales, for example, with more than 800 Chapters, is the Ancient and Accepted Rite, usually known as the *Rose Croix*. The second degree of the Royal Order of Scotland is Knight of the Rosy Cross; in the Order's traditional history this was instituted by Robert the Bruce after the battle of Bannockburn, thus tying in with the myths about the Templars (see page 76). One of the degrees of the Holy Royal Arch Knight Templar Priests is Knight of the Red Cross of Roseae Crucis. The highest degree of the Rite of Baldwyn, a Masonic Order based in Bristol, is Knights of the Rose Croix of Mount Carmel.

These are just a selection of Rosicrucian names of degrees in Freemasonry. It is likely in most cases that Freemasons creating a new Order or series of degrees borrowed names reminiscent of Rosicrucianism because of shared ideas and ideals – or, more simply, because they sounded suitably mysterious and romantic.

HISTORICAL CONNECTIONS

Historically there are certainly links between Rosicrucianism and Freemasonry, in that the same names of people crop up in both, and in other groups. We have already seen (see pages 64–65) how the Hermetic Philosophers of the 16th and 17th centuries effectively 'became' the first Rosicrucians, following the publication of the Rosicrucian Manifestos in

Above The new Masonic Temple, Boston, Massachusetts, USA; 1865 engraving.

Right The front
entrance of the Scottish
Rite Masonic Temple in
Miami, Florida, USA,
built in 1922–24.

1614, 1615 and 1616. Similarly, some of these same people – enquirers into heterodox spirituality, alchemists, astrologers, philosophers and scientists – met at Wadham College in Oxford and Gresham College in London in the mid-17th century and became the founders of the Royal Society in 1660 (see page 69).

Two of these, Sir Robert Moray and Elias Ashmole, are the very first people of whom there is a record of their being initiated into the lodges of Freemasons: Moray into the Lodge of Edinburgh (the actual initiation occurred south of the border in Newcastle) in 1641 and Ashmole into the Lodge at Warrington, Lancashire, in 1646. The links between the Royal Society and Freemasonry continued well into the next century; at least 89 of the first 250 Fellows of the Royal Society were definitely Freemasons.

In this sense, then, the late Rosicrucians and the early Freemasons, overlapping in the Gresham College group and the Royal Society, in part comprised the same people. So Freemasonry (assuming a 17th-century origin to be rather more likely than the

foundation legends dating back thousands of years) could in a very real sense be said to have developed, at least in part, out of Rosicrucianism.

THE BROTHERHOOD OF THE GOLDEN AND ROSY CROSS

Could Freemasonry have been created as a more open and social 'Outer Court' of a more closed and spiritual Rosicrucian 'Inner Court'? This is considered by most scholars to be unlikely – but this is precisely what one 18th-century Rosicrucian group claimed. The Brotherhood of the Golden and Rosy Cross was first known of in 1710 in Germany. With the full title of the 'Most Laudable Order and the Sublime, Most Ancient, Genuine and Honourable Society of the Golden Rosy Cross, abiding in the Providence of God', nothing more is known of this organization until a document of 1777, which claimed:

> *That the better to conceal their real purpose
> the Superiors of the Order established those
> lower Degrees which pass under the name of
> Freemasonry. That they [the lower Degrees]
> served, moreover, as a seminary or
> preparation for the higher curriculum of the
> Rosicrucian Order and as a kind of spiritual
> prolegomenon [introductory study]...*

The document describes Freemasonry as 'the preparatory school of the Rosy Cross'. This is probably no more than esoteric posturing. The reality is much more likely to be that the Brotherhood of the Golden and Rosy Cross was simply an early example of the many Masonic side-degrees, and that you had to have passed through the basic degrees of Freemasonry in order to join it. Whatever the truth, the Brotherhood of the Golden and Rosy Cross was to have an influence on some later, very important organizations (see pages 70, 105 and 106).

It should be recalled that at the heart of Rosicrucian philosophy is the concept of scholars bringing good to the world through their study, their teachings and – by means of their own inner transformation – their subtle influence on others; this is very much the same as the goals of Freemasonry.

Origins in the stonemasons

The standard explanation within Freemasonry today of its origin is that the movement simply grew out of the medieval stonemasons' guilds – a cross between a present-day professional association and a trade union for skilled craftsmen who worked with freestone, a soft stone that could be carved. 'Freemason' is thus a contraction of 'freestone mason'. The earliest-known reference to them as 'ffremasons' dates from 1376.

Right *Stonemasons from* Traite d'Arpentage *(Treatise on Surveying) by Arnaud de Villeneuve (1240–1312); illustration by Bertrand Boysset (1355–1415).*

THE CATHEDRAL-BUILDERS

The stonemasons who built the great cathedrals of Europe between 1050 and 1350 are said to have jealously guarded the secrets of their trade, and to have had secret signs, recognition signals, and questions and answers so that they could be recognized as properly trained and experienced masons when they moved on from one job to another. They lived, ate, slept, did some of their finer stone carving and had discussions about their work in lodges – temporary buildings against the cathedral walls. Living and working so closely together for years at a time, a bond grew between these men; they became a fraternity.

They were the physical creators of magnificent edifices to the glory of God, buildings whose proportions, patterns and carvings embodied within them deep symbolism. They were craftsmen, not just rough labourers who had not served an apprenticeship and who were capable of building no more than a hut; the latter became known as 'cowans' in Scotland, and the term passed into Freemasonry for those who must be kept out of the lodge. In

contrast, true masons knew how to use the tools of architecture and building – compasses, set-squares, plumb-lines; they understood the mathematics of how to measure an angle, how to construct a square with half or twice the area of another one, how to go from a two-dimensional plan to a three-dimensional building; they knew how to build high, absolutely vertical walls and soaring arches; they understood the mysteries of the pleasing proportions of the Golden Section.

When cathedral-building on a large scale came to an end, the stonemasons dispersed to their home towns and countries. Those who remained found that their lodges now had very few members, so (the story goes) they recruited new members from other professions, later calling them 'speculative masons' as opposed to 'operative masons'. Although something like this may have occurred, the explanation smacks of *ex post facto* argument. Also, just as with the fable of the Templar knights fleeing to Scotland and then, centuries later, resurfacing as the Freemasons, there is rather too long a gap between the medieval stonemasons and the appearance of the Freemasons in the 17th century – a gap containing no evidence whatsoever of continuation.

A NEW JERUSALEM?

An alternative explanation is that after the Great Fire of London, which in 1666 destroyed 13,000 houses and 90 churches, including St Paul's Cathedral, a massive rebuilding project began under the direction of Sir Christopher Wren – who was both a member of the brand-new Royal Society and a Freemason. There has been much speculation about Wren redesigning London as a new Jerusalem, with esoteric symbolism in the street patterns, the positioning and layout of the new St Paul's Cathedral, and the monument to the fire, which still stands today. Whether this is so or not, the rebuilding project led to a huge number of builders – masons – working in London in the late 17th century. As with the medieval cathedral-builders, these were not rough labourers; a master mason was a craftsman and was knowledgeable about the mysteries of architecture, which had embodied esoteric principles for thousands of years.

One theory claims that the English Grand Lodge was established in 1717 because the building work had been completed by then and many craftsmen had left London. The lodges were keen to recruit gentlemen members, not just to maintain numbers, but for their fees, which were twice those of

Above After the Great Fire of London in 1666 destroyed the previous, more conventional, cathedral, Sir Christopher Wren designed St Paul's Cathedral as we know it today.

craftsmen. There may be some truth in this theory, but it should be remembered that Sir Robert Moray and Elias Ashmole (see pages 69, 70 and 81) became speculative Masons 25 and 20 years before the Great Fire of London, and hundreds of miles north.

Despite all the theories there is still no definitive answer as to why middle-class professional men in the mid-17th century should start to get together in clubs, using the tools and language of stonemasonry to symbolize spirituality and morality. In actuality, the Freemasons were not unique. There were similar social organizations with spiritual and moral lessons based on the language of other crafts, including the Free Carpenters, the Free Fishermen and the Free Gardeners, the last of which also date back to the 17th century and had lodges, rituals and 'signs, secrets and grips'.

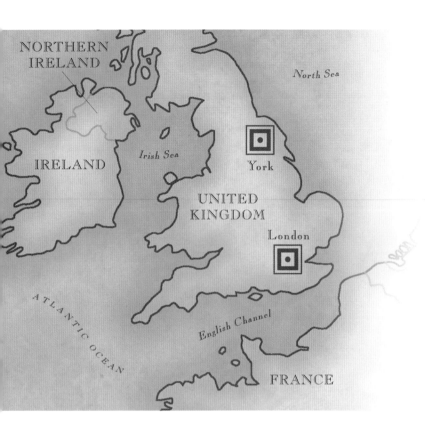

Myth and history

The period from the late 17th century through the 18th century into the 19th century was awash with made-up histories and faked documents, including 'Legends of Perpetuation' from long-distant groups such as the Knights Templar. We have already seen the Charter of Larmenius (see page 32), which the French Freemason Bernard Raymond Fabré-Palaprat used to found his own Order of the Temple in 1804.

Freemasonry was riddled with false histories, though in fairness most were not meant to be taken literally.

Part of the problem for modern historians of Freemasonry is sifting through these 'histories'. For example, although much of Freemasonry is based on the building of Solomon's Temple, Masons today treat this as the teaching story or parable that it is.

However, some major Masonic writers in the past have claimed as fact that Freemasonry goes back to Moses, or even further back to Adam. Only slightly less fanciful, William Preston, author of the highly influential *Illustrations of Masonry* (1772), traced the Masons in Britain back to the Druids; he had Masonry flourishing under the early 7th-century Augustine, Archbishop of Canterbury, and under the late 9th-century King Alfred; he also included a list of questions and answers about Freemasonry, supposedly written by King Henry VI. Preston wrote: 'Ever since symmetry began, and harmony displayed her charms, our Order has had a being.' This was the quality of much of the official Masonic history.

THE YORK LODGE

From the start, centralized Freemasonry had problems both of precedence – the lodges that claimed to be oldest wanting this to be acknowledged – and of uniformity. As lodges had developed around the country, some had variations in their rituals. Most of these were minor and could readily be accommodated, but others were more significant. The York Lodge in particular claimed an authority older than the Grand Lodge of London; it had a legend of a lodge founded by King Athelstan and his son Prince Edwin in 926 CE. Apocryphal though that might be, the York Lodge was one of the oldest in the country, and had different customs from those of London.

Above *The Masonic Arms banner of the Grand Lodge of All England at York, c.1776. Varieties of this design have since been used by many different Masonic organizations.*

Left The Goose and Gridiron Alehouse in St Paul's Churchyard, meeting place of one of the four London lodges which founded the Grand Lodge there on 24 June , 1717. This sketch was made shortly before the building was demolished in 1894.

establishment to wrest any claim to Freemasonry from the Scots, just two years after the first Jacobite Rebellion. This theory is perhaps boosted by the fact that one early Grand Master (1722–23), Philip, Duke of Wharton (a Jacobite supporter), left not only his position but Freemasonry itself when the first *Book of Constitutions* was published, committing Masons to obey the government and banning the discussion of religion and politics in the lodges. Wharton (who had earlier founded the original Hell-Fire Club, see pages 144–145) established a Jacobite alternative to the Freemasons, the Antient Noble Order of Gormogons, but it died with him in 1731.

THE ANTIENTS VS. THE MODERNS

In 1751, barely 35 years after the establishment of the Grand Lodge, a group of reformers accused it of laxness, poor administration and, worst of all, changing (modernizing) the rituals. In consequence they dubbed Grand Lodge the Moderns, and called themselves the Antients. By 1771, after just 20 years, the Antients had 74 lodges in London, 83 elsewhere in the country and 43 abroad; the Moderns had 157, 164 and 100 respectively. The two rival Grand Lodges remained separate until 1813.

There were two other much smaller Grand Lodges in England in the 18th century: the Grand Lodge of All England, based in York, which lasted (with gaps) from 1725 to around 1792; and its southern counterpart, the Grand Lodge of England South of the River Trent, founded in 1779, but lasting just ten years. The Grand Lodge of All England at York was revived once more in 2005, with the King Athelstan story and the Henry VI questions and answers proudly claimed as part of its heritage. It remains small.

However, the major split in Freemasonry in England and Wales, between the Antients and the Moderns, continued for more than 60 years. In December 1813, after prolonged negotiations, the two Grand Lodges – each with a royal prince as its Grand Master – merged as the United Grand Lodge of England and Wales, under the Grand Mastership of HRH the Duke of Sussex.

THE GRAND LODGES ARE ESTABLISHED

We do not know precisely why, when or where Freemasonry began, but from the few genuine historical references we have we can say with a strong degree of certainty that it began in Scotland, not England, possibly as early as 1600.

We know that English Freemasonry existed before 1717, because in June of that year four London lodges met at the Goose and Gridiron alehouse in St Paul's Churchyard and set up a Grand Lodge. By 1730 there were more than a hundred lodges around England and Wales under this Grand Lodge, and Ireland and Scotland followed suit, setting up their own Grand Lodges in the mid-1720s and 1736 respectively.

Why was the Grand Lodge set up in 1717? A theory currently gaining acceptance is that it was a deliberate move by the newly established (and London-based) Hanoverian

The degrees of the Craft

It is important to distinguish between basic Freemasonry, which is often known as the Craft, and all the additional Orders and degrees that have developed over the last two or three hundred years. Freemasonry, like most esoteric organizations, is an initiatory society, in which members progress step by step up a ladder of advancement – a sort of esoteric spiritual career path. At each stage they are given new knowledge, which could be called secrets. They are required to take a vow not to repeat these secrets outside the society, or to anyone who has not reached that specific level.

Craft Freemasonry consists of the three degrees of Entered Apprentice, Fellow Craft and Master Mason. In the early years of Freemasonry there were initially only the first two Craft degrees, the third degree probably being added in the 1720s. Craft lodges are known as Blue lodges in the USA. The three basic degrees of Craft Freemasonry are open to any man who professes a belief in God. He can be of any religion or none; it is actually forbidden to discuss religion (or politics) within the lodge. Many of the additional Orders and degrees, however, are specifically Christian in their symbolism, and are only open to Christian Masons.

INITIATION RITUALS

At each level the initiate is blindfolded to symbolize his state of darkness – and to demonstrate his trust in those who are initiating him. This, like everything in the ritual, is symbolic, though, as a sword point is held to the initiate's naked chest at one stage, he is displaying very real trust as well.

In the rituals the candidate is led, blindfold, through a sequence of steps around the lodge; he is presented to certain officers; he is asked questions, and prompted with the correct answers. When the blindfold is removed, he is shown the symbolic Masonic tools of that degree, and is given secret signs and words.

MASONIC SYMBOLISM

The lodge room itself is full of symbolism. The chequered floor shows that life consists of light and darkness, day and night, joy and sorrow; it can also illustrate that all the individuals within a lodge form a whole.

The letter G, prominently displayed, refers to God (especially when surrounded by rays of light representing the glory of the Shekhinah, the presence of God), or to the Grand Geometrician, and thence to Geometry, 'which contains the determination, definition and proof of the order, beauty and wonderful wisdom of the power of God in his creation'. God is never referred to directly, usually being called the Great Architect of the Universe.

Opposite A late 19th-century reconstruction of a Masonic initiation, showing the precise foot positions of the candidate.

Above This 1740 engraving shows a blindfolded initiate being led into a Masonic lodge in Paris.

On a table in front of the Master of the lodge is the Volume of the Sacred Law; this is usually the Bible, but can be the Torah or the Koran, or 'whatever is understood to contain the will or law of God'. On the same table are the square and compasses, the most common Masonic symbols.

THE TRACING BOARDS

The symbolism is often shown on 'tracing boards', which are used both to transform a lodge from being open in the first to the second to the third degree, and for instruction. The first-degree tracing board shows three classical pillars – Doric, Ionic and Corinthian – representing Wisdom, Strength and Beauty. A 'rough ashlar', or unfinished block of stone, represents the candidate's unfinished moral and spiritual state, and a smooth or 'perfect ashlar' the state to which the newly admitted Mason should aspire. Among much other symbolism are Masonic tools, and an image of Jacob's Ladder reaching up to heaven, sometimes with angels ascending and descending it.

The second-degree tracing board has two pillars, Jachin and Boaz (meaning 'He establishes' and 'In strength'), representing the entrance to Solomon's Temple (see pages 92–93 and I Kings 7:21). Jacob's Ladder has now become a winding stair of seven steps, leading up to the interior of the Temple.

In addition to a large number of Masonic tools, the third-degree tracing board, in different versions, shows a grave or more likely a coffin. In the ritual the candidate is told the story of Hiram Abiff, the Master Mason who built Solomon's Temple and was slain by those trying to steal the secrets of Masonry. He is laid on the floor, or sometimes within a symbolic coffin, and is then raised up by the Master of the Lodge, symbolizing rising from death into a new life. This is why Masons always speak of the Raising of a new Master Mason.

In the lectures about each degree, the symbolism of each action of the ritual, each component of the lodge and each detail of the tracing boards (particularly the Masonic tools) is explained to the new initiate. Once he has understood the meaning of each degree he may progress to the next.

Other Orders and degrees

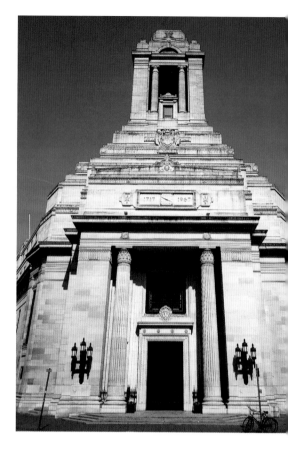

There are many other Orders and degrees within Freemasonry – and, indeed, many different versions of Freemasonry, which often do not accept each other's validity. Because of its age and general acceptance that it was the first Grand Lodge, the United Grand Lodge (UGL) of England and Wales is often taken by non-Masons to be authoritative on Freemasonry. However, each Grand Lodge is independent of the others; even in the British Isles, the Grand Lodge of Scotland and the Grand Lodge of Ireland are quite separate from the UGL of England and Wales. UGL is in amity with some other Grand Lodges around the world, but not with all.

In UGL Freemasonry in England and Wales, following the three degrees of the Craft (see pages 86–87) comes the Holy Royal Arch, which is administered separately; although this is a distinct Order, it is often said to be the fulfilment of the third degree.

THE ROYAL ARCH DEGREE

Like much else in Craft Freemasonry, especially the third degree, the Royal Arch degree is based on Solomon's Temple, but in this case *after* the reign of Solomon when the temple had been destroyed and the tribes of Israel taken into captivity; on their return they commenced rebuilding the temple – and it was here that certain secrets of the Master Mason were discovered.

Part of the legend concerns the Mason's word or 'lost word'; in the Royal Arch degree masons are given a 'substitute' word, 'Jahbulon', which in the past has caused some critics (particularly fundamentalist Christians) to accuse Freemasonry of being blasphemous or even Satanic. Suffice it to say that the word is simply used as a 'test word', as in other degrees, and that the lecture

following the revelation of the word to the new initiate makes it clear that it refers to the God of Judeo-Christianity: 'I am and shall be; Lord in Heaven or on High; Father of All.' Perhaps because of the controversy surrounding the word, English Freemasonry dropped its use in 1989, replacing it with the tetragrammaton YHWH, the sacred name of God in the Bible.

In England and Wales around one-third of Master Masons progress to the Royal Arch. Most American Orders follow the Scottish and Irish practice: that entrants to the Royal Arch must first be Mark Masons. Just as Royal Arch is the 'completion' of the third degree, so Mark Masonry is seen as the 'completion' of the second degree of Fellow Craft. Mark Masonry bases its symbolism on the marks that stonemasons used to identify their work. The moral lesson is that education is the reward of labour, and that fraud does not pay.

THE SCOTTISH RITE AND THE YORK RITE

In the USA, Freemasonry beyond the Craft or Blue Lodges is divided into two broad groups, known as the Scottish Rite and the York Rite. The Ancient and Accepted Scottish Rite of Freemasonry confers 30 degrees beyond the three Craft degrees; usually those up to the 18th are conferred together, with only the 18th-degree ritual (Knight of the Rose Croix) being worked in full. Similarly, the 19th to 29th degrees are conferred in name only in the ritual for the 30th, Knight Kadosh. The 31st, 32nd and 33rd degrees are strictly limited in their numbers and are considered a great honour by Masons.

The York Rite in America consists of a number of different degrees, which in other jurisdictions are usually conferred by separate bodies. These include Mark Mason, Holy Royal Arch, the Cryptic Masons (in the UK called the Council of Royal and Select Masters) and the Knights Templar.

In addition there are many more very selective Orders and degrees, often with fine titles and splendid regalia. Many Freemasons only take the first three degrees of the Craft, but a substantial number go on to the Royal Arch and/or Mark Masonry, both of which are prerequisites for any higher degrees.

There have been female lodges since the 1880s in France and 1903 in the USA. Such lodges are judged 'irregular' by mainstream Freemasonry.

TRADITIONAL EXCLUSIONS

Despite Freemasonry's claims of 'universal brotherhood', American Masonry of the 18th and 19th centuries was white-only; black Americans, whether slave or free, were not welcome. This led to the formation of Prince Hall Freemasonry (named after its founder), which was specifically for black Americans. It is a rather disturbing comment on American Freemasonry that Prince Hall only started to be recognized as legitimate by other American Grand Lodges as late as 1989.

Traditional Grand Lodge Freemasonry, around the world, is strictly men-only. Masons have attempted to justify this over the years. One argument was that women were born naturally virtuous; therefore they were in no need of the rituals' morality and teachings that were so necessary to save 'corruptible' men. The British esoteric historian A.E. Waite, renowned for his acerbic comments, wrote: 'Freemasonry as an institution is not suited to women any more than is cricket as a sport, but they have occasionally wished to play at it.' Indeed they have, and there have been female lodges (known as co-Masonry) since the 1880s in France and 1903 in the USA. Such lodges are judged 'irregular' by mainstream Freemasonry.

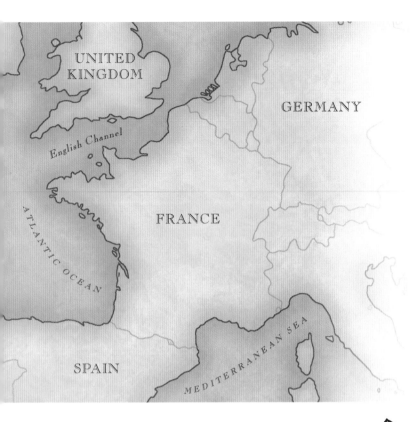

Palladism and Luciferian Masonry

Many of the fundamentalist Christian anti-Masonic books that try to paint Freemasonry as Satanic cite 'Palladism' as evidence for this. In the 1890s, Europe – especially France – was rocked by a scandal. Freemasonry, it seemed, not only had mixed male and female lodges (shocking in itself), but worshipped the Devil, performed black magic and indulged in orgiastic practices.

Furthermore, the whole of worldwide Freemasonry was run by the senior American Freemason Albert Pike (1809–91), who had written that Lucifer was God. These startling revelations came first from a French ex-Mason, Leo Taxil (1854–1907), and then from the high priestess of 'Palladian Masonry' herself, who had turned back to the true (Roman Catholic) Church, had repented of her sinful ways and was now making a full kiss-and-tell, lurid public confession.

DIANA VAUGHAN'S ACCOUNT

Miss Diana Vaughan's stories followed on the heels of an astonishing series of magazines published in France by Leo Taxil. First, in 1891, *Are There Women in Freemasonry?* described the Order of New and Reformed Palladium, which included Satanism and sex-magic. Then in 1893–95 a weekly magazine entitled *The Devil in the 19th Century* said that Pike was 'Sovereign Pontiff of World Freemasonry', that there was 'another and most secret Masonry' behind the socially respectable public face of Freemasonry, that it was anti-Christian, devoted to Lucifer and the occult, and politically revolutionary.

Left *A caricature of Leo Taxil by André Gill in* Les Hommes d'Aujourd'hui, *late 19th century.*

Left *Esoteric historian Arthur Edward Waite (1857–1942), who unmasked Leo Taxil's Palladism hoax in 1896.*

THE LUCIFERIAN MYTH IS PERPETUATED

Some anti-Masonic writers today still quote Taxil's inventions as being true – both the sexual debauchery of the Palladists and the Luciferian sentiments of Albert Pike. The latter is perhaps the more insidious, if only because Palladism was so clearly over-the-top that it is surprising anyone ever fell for the deception. But Pike had been a hugely important Freemason, the Grand Commander of the Supreme Council of the Scottish Rite in America, and widely respected. To destroy his reputation (and hence the reputation of Freemasonry) with accusations of Luciferianism played right into the hands of Christian fundamentalists. (In fact, biblical scholars agree that the word Lucifer, which appears only once in the entire Bible, has nothing to do with Satan, the Devil or demons; it is not even a proper name, but simply means 'the light-bringer' or 'the morning star'.)

Leo Taxil made up a set of 'Instructions' supposedly issued by Pike in July 1889, which included the statement that 'Lucifer is God'. Taxil published these in *The Devil in the 19th Century* in 1893, a safe two years after Pike had died. If these fictions had remained only in Taxil's own works, they might have been forgotten once Taxil owned up to his deception in 1897, but by then the 'Instructions' had been reprinted in a book, *La Femme et L'Enfant dans le Franc-Maçonnerie universelle, d'après les documents de la secte (1739–1893)* by A.C. de la Rive, published in 1894. They have been quoted as fact by anti-Masonic writers ever since; today they are even included in one of the popular fundamentalist Christian comics by Jack Chick, *The Curse of Baphomet*, with an attribution to de la Rive's book.

In 1895–97 Diana Vaughan told her own incredible story in another serial magazine, *Memoirs of an ex-Palladist*. This was dynamite. Now safely returned to the Catholic fold, she recounted her time as 'the wealthy, beautiful and highly placed Palladian Grand Mistress' who took part in sexual and Satanic rituals in this Masonic group. Anti-Masonic literature, especially from the Catholic Church, mushroomed. Taxil was even invited to a private audience with Pope Leo XIII. However, Miss Diana Vaughan, former Palladian high priestess, made no public appearances herself.

In 1896 an English scholar of the esoteric, A.E. Waite, published a book entitled *Devil-Worship in France*, which carefully and efficiently pulled apart the supposedly scandalous revelations. He showed that the entire story of Diana Vaughan was the fabulation of Leo Taxil (pen name of Gabriel Jogand-Pagès), formerly the author of various pornographic and blasphemous satires; Diana Vaughan was actually a typist in his employ.

The following year Taxil called a public meeting, ostensibly to unveil the Palladian grand mistress Diana Vaughan, but instead he confessed that the entire Palladism story had been an elaborate hoax. He was no friend of Freemasonry, true, but his main aim had been to prove how utterly credulous the Catholic Church could be – an aim that clearly succeeded.

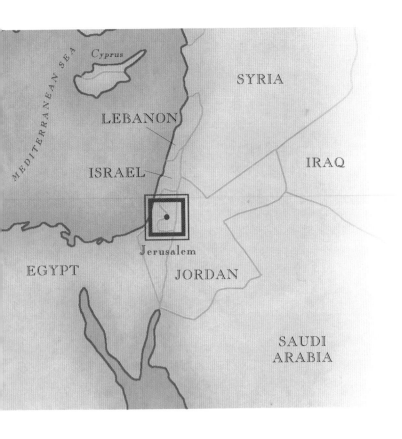

Solomon's Temple

King Solomon's Temple holds an important place in both the history of the Knights Templar and the rituals of the Freemasons. The Templars' very name derives from the fact that they were originally housed in part of the royal palace of King Baldwin (died 1131) in Jerusalem, which was supposedly built over the remains of Solomon's Temple. At the heart of Craft ritual in Freemasonry is the legendary story of the building of Solomon's Temple and the slaying of its architect Hiram Abiff.

The first temple of the Israelite people was built by King Solomon, the son of King David, who was not allowed by God to build it himself because he was too warlike. Solomon built the temple in Jerusalem in the 10th century BCE, and it survived until the kingdom of Judah was conquered by the Babylonians in 586 BCE.

Nothing now remains of that temple. The Second Temple was begun in 516 BCE and was greatly extended by Herod from around 19 BCE. The famous 'Wailing Wall' is part of the surrounding structure of the platform on which Herod built the extended temple, which was destroyed by the Romans in 70 CE.

TEMPLE FACTS

All the reconstructions of Solomon's Temple are based on its description in the Bible (I Kings 5–7), and on the remains of other temples in Syria. There are some differences, but they agree on many points.

At the very heart of the Temple was the Holy of Holies, a 9 m (30 ft) cube, with no windows. Within it was the Ark of the Covenant, a splendid box containing the tablet with the Ten Commandments; this had been the Israelite God's 'home' before the temple was built. Above the Ark were two huge cherubim, with outstretched wings. Only the High Priest was allowed to enter the Holy of Holies, and only on one day of the year: the Day of Atonement. There, with his attention completely focused on God, he would utter the sacred name of God, usually written as YHWH.

Around the temple on the northern, southern and western sides were storerooms, three storeys high. These contained the temple's treasure. This, along with the Ark of the Covenant, the seraphim and cherubim and everything else, vanished when the temple was destroyed by the Babylonians.

The temple was linked to the city via a causeway on the western side of the Temple. Today one of the arches of the causeway has been incorporated into a synagogue built in a section of the men's prayer area of the Western or Wailing Wall.

① THE OUTER COURTYARD

The temple was built by thousands of slave labourers, under the direction of skilled masons and craftsmen; 55 x 27.5 m (180 x 90 ft), and 15 m (50 ft) high at its highest point, it was built from the finest hewn stone and stood on a platform within two courtyards. The outer courtyard was where the people would come to worship God and present their offerings.

② THE INNER COURTYARD

The inner courtyard was the court of the priests. This contained the sacrificial altar, where people brought animals to be burned as offerings to God. The altar was massive: 9 m (30 ft) square and 4.5 m (15 ft) high.

③ BRONZE BASIN

The inner courtyard contained a huge bronze basin 4.5 m (15 ft) in diameter and over 2 m (6½ ft) deep, supported on the backs of twelve bronze oxen. This was for ritual purification of the priests by immersion.

④ STONES

The enormous stones of the temple walls were fitted together without mortar. The wood that lined the rooms, the famous cedar of Lebanon, was purchased from King Hiram of Tyre, and the master builders of the temple also came from Tyre. This has been modified into one of the central legends of Freemasonry: that the Master Mason who built Solomon's Temple was Hiram Abiff, who was killed by a blow to the head when he would not give up the secrets of Masonry.

⑤ THE PILLARS

At the entrance to the temple, on either side of the porch or portico, were two 12 m (40 ft) high bronze pillars, named Jachin (meaning 'He establishes') on the right and Boaz (meaning 'In strength') on the left. These, among many other details of the temple, have been incorporated into Masonic symbolism.

⑥ THE HOLY PLACE

Inside the porch was the main room, the Holy Place or Hekhal, lit by windows high in the walls. Some 21 m (70 ft) long, its walls were panelled in cedar covered in gold leaf. The floor was also covered in gold. Along its length were ten lamps standing in two rows of five, a table and an incense altar, all covered in gold, and a Menorah, or seven-branched candelabrum. Guarding the entrance to the oracle or sanctuary, the Holy of Holies, were two seraphim. The entrance was a two-leaved door with a thick curtain of blue, purple and crimson – the 'veil of the temple' referred to in Mark 15:38. Some descriptions say that it was 18 m (60 ft) high and 7.5 cm (3 in) thick.

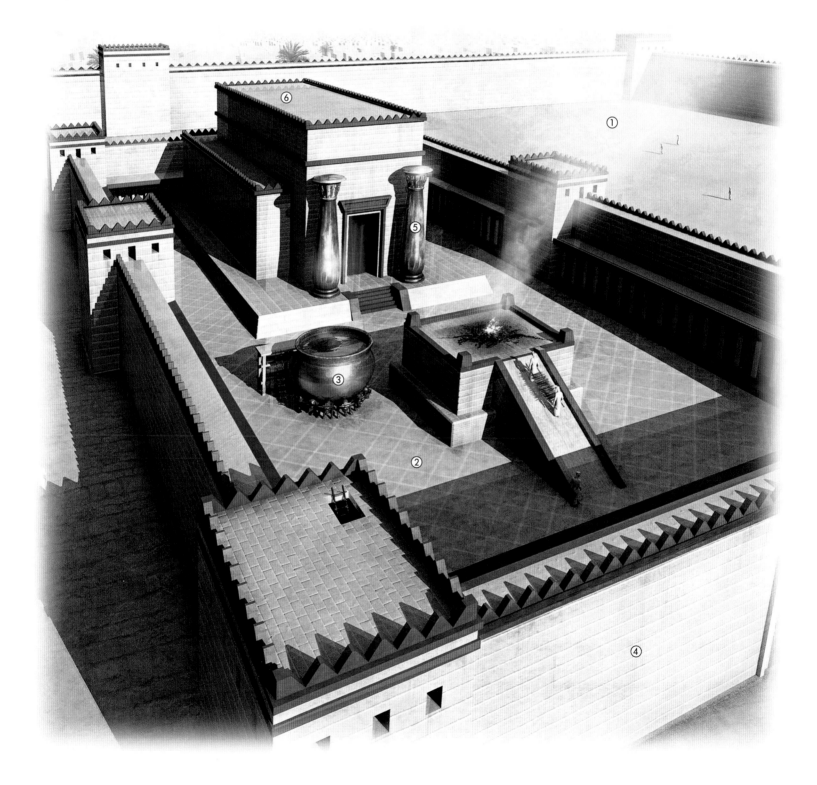

CHAPTER 7

THE ILLUMINATI

The story of the Illuminati begins in Bavaria in 1776 with the founding of a society by Adam Weishaupt. His aim was to perfect both society and the individual, yet centuries later the Illuminati have been at the centre of extraordinary allegations of conspiracy. This chapter unpicks the true story of who the Illuminati were and their continuing influence today.

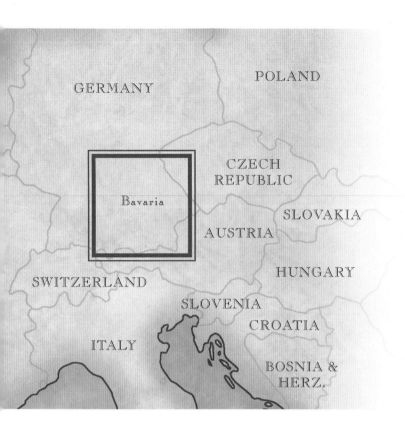

GERMANY POLAND

CZECH REPUBLIC

Bavaria

SLOVAKIA

AUSTRIA

SWITZERLAND

HUNGARY

SLOVENIA

CROATIA

ITALY

BOSNIA & HERZ.

History of the Illuminati

Several very different groups throughout history have been known as the Illuminati, or Illuminated Ones, including early Christians who were thought to receive enlightenment on their baptism; followers of the Swedish philosopher Emmanuel Swedenborg were also sometimes called Illuminati. However, the famous organization usually known as the Illuminati – or the Ancient Illuminated Seers of Bavaria – was initially called the Order of Perfectibilists.

It was founded by a young professor of Natural and Canon Law at the University of Ingoldstat in Bavaria on 1 May 1776. He was Adam Weishaupt (1748–1811 or 1830) – a Jew brought up as a Catholic, who converted to Protestantism; he was the first non-cleric to hold this post at the university and soon found himself in conflict with Catholic priests and academics. He had become fascinated by the Pagan mysteries (see page 16) and the work of Pythagoras. He joined the Freemasons in 1774, but was not impressed by their commitment to esoteric enquiry.

WEISHAUPT, PROGRESSIVE FREETHINKER

His aim was to perfect both the world and the individual, hence the original name of his Order. Their usual name came from his aim of 'illumination, enlightening the understanding by the sun of reason, which will dispel the clouds of superstition and of prejudice'. He could be said to have been at the forefront of the Age of Reason, or the

Above *The Great Seal of the USA, designed in 1782. The All-Seeing Eye of God above a truncated pyramid is widely, but incorrectly, believed to be an Illuminati symbol.*

Enlightenment; as his ideas developed, he became a radical freethinker.

Weishaupt believed that the world could be perfected if nations and religions were abolished; he was opposed to monarchies in particular. Ultimately his intent was to do away with all social structures, including private property and marriage. With such a stance, it is perhaps surprising that the Illuminati lasted for as long as they did.

It has been said that Weishaupt, who had been educated by Jesuits, organized the Illuminati as a deliberate copy of them; much as he came to loathe their beliefs, he was deeply impressed by their strict discipline. Certainly the Illuminati were founded as a society to promote liberal and progressive beliefs, in direct contrast to the Jesuits.

THE ORGANIZATION

Members of the Illuminati were organized into cells who reported to an Unknown Superior (see page 32), thus preserving secrecy, but also (fitting oddly with such an avowedly egalitarian society) maintaining a distance between lower-grade and higher-grade members or, in the phraseology of some Rosicrucian groups, those in the Outer and Inner Courts.

Indeed, although he had found no deep spirituality in the Masonic lodge he joined earlier, Weishaupt was a firm believer in the secret doctrines, the ancient wisdom teachings, which he believed lay at the heart of both Freemasonry and Rosicrucianism. The organized Churches, he believed, had lost the original, deeply esoteric spiritual teachings of Christianity.

The Illuminati began with Weishaupt and four friends in 1776. By 1779 there were 54 members in five lodges (known as colonies) around Bavaria. At that point it began to expand outside Bavaria, largely by infiltrating and taking over existing Masonic lodges. Five years later it had some 650 members in lodges around Germany, Austria, Hungary, Bohemia, Switzerland and northern Italy.

FAILURE OF A COUP, AND END OF THE ORDER

The policy of taking over Masonic lodges seems to have extended to an attempt to take over an entire Order, the Rite of the Strict Observance, founded by Baron Karl Gotthelf von Hund in 1754 (see page 32). By the time von Hund died in 1776 – the year the Illuminati were founded – his Order was in decline, largely because his Unknown Superiors had never made themselves (or their secrets) known. (Weishaupt himself joined the Strict Observance in 1777.) Von Hund's successor as head of the Order, Ferdinand, Duke of Brunswick, called the Congress of Wilhelmsbad in 1782 to rule on whether there had ever been any Unknown Superiors – that is, genuine links to the Knights Templar (see pages 19–33). There were delegates from many different Masonic Orders – and from the Illuminati. By then, however, it seems that the Illuminati policy of taking over Masonic lodges had become known, and their attempt to control the Rite of the Strict Observance failed.

The revolutionary beliefs of the Illuminati were also becoming rather too well known, despite its structure as a secret society.

ADAM WEISHAVPT.

Church and State were united against them. In 1784 Karl Theodor, Elector of Bavaria, banned all secret societies; in 1785 the Illuminati were specifically named as a seditious group. Weishaupt lost his post at the university and was banished from Bavaria. In 1786 the Bavarian authorities seized a great deal of Illuminati documentation, and clamped down on its members, most of whom fled the country.

Weishaupt settled in Gotha in Saxony, where he received a pension from Duke Ernst II; he taught philosophy at the University of Gottingen and wrote books. Without his leadership, the Illuminati quickly died out, despite a couple of attempts by members to rekindle it. It had lasted a mere ten years – although its reputation continues to this day.

Above Adam Weishaupt (1748–1811 or 1830), founder of the Bavarian Illuminati.

Illuminati myths

Much of the misinformation (if not deliberate disinformation) about the Illuminati appeared only a decade after the demise of the Order, from two writers, John Robison and Augustin de Barruel, each of whom had an agenda of his own. Without the attacks in their books, this small, short-lived 18th century society would probably have been long forgotten by now.

In 1797 John Robison, Professor of Natural Philosophy at the University of Edinburgh, wrote a book with the all-embracing (though hardly snappy) title, *Proofs of a Conspiracy Against All the Religions and Governments of Europe, carried on in the secret Meetings of Free Masons, Illuminati, and Reading Societies, collected from good authorities.*

A Freemason himself, Robison's aim was actually to distance good, healthy, socially respectable British Freemasonry from some of the more dubious (in his eyes) continental varieties. After saying that the Illuminati were in favour of abolishing all religions and governments, he wrote that 'the leaders would rule the World with uncontrollable power, while all the rest would be employed as tools of the ambition of their unknown superiors'. Robison's book is full of basic factual errors, such as quoting speeches made at lodges that would not exist for several more years, and describing a ruler's fear of the Illuminati in 1772 – four years before they existed.

THE ABBÉ'S ACCUSATIONS

Abbé Augustin de Barruel, a former Jesuit, was the author of *Mémoires pour servir à l'histoire du Jacobinisme*, a four-volume work published in 1797 and 1798, which was equally full of factual errors.

Among much else, Augustin de Barruel was largely responsible for promulgating a

Left John Robison (1739–1805), who was responsible for launching generations of conspiracy theorists.

later much-cited story that the downfall of the Illuminati began when one of their couriers, Franz Lang or Jacob Lanz, was struck by lightning and killed. Sewn into secret pockets in his clothes, it was said, were coded messages from Adam Weishaupt; these were discovered by the Bavarian police, and

led directly to the ban on the Order by the Elector of Bavaria.

In an echo of accusations against other groups, de Barruel said the Illuminati 'had sworn hatred to the altar and the throne, had sworn to crush the God of the Christians, and utterly to extirpate the Kings of the Earth'.

Left Although Eugene
Delacroix's painting
'Liberty Leading the
People' originally
commemorated the July
Revolution of 1830, it
has become a striking
symbol of the French
Revolution.

FREEMASONRY VS. THE CATHOLIC CHURCH

The Illuminati could, with some justification, be assigned at least part of the blame for the rift between the Catholic Church and Freemasonry that still exists today. Although the Society of Jesus (the Jesuits) had been closed down by Pope Clement XIV in 1773 (they were restored by Pope Pius VII in 1814), their influence was still strong at the University of Ingoldstat where Weishaupt had studied from the age of 15, and where he taught from 1772, becoming a professor in 1773. With Weishaupt's liberal views, he was in constant battle with powerful ex-Jesuits at the university.

The Illuminati, with their revolutionary political beliefs and their campaign against organized religion, were clearly the enemies of both conservatism and Catholicism, and Jesuits (even ex-Jesuits) were ultra-loyal Catholics. Even though the Illuminati involvement with more mainstream Freemasonry was more fiction than fact,

Masonry was tarred with the same revolutionary and anti-Catholic brush as far as the Roman Catholic Church was concerned.

The Catholic Church first pronounced against Freemasonry in 1738, and again in 1751, but that was on the grounds of its secrecy. Full-blown opposition on the grounds of anti-clericalism and radical political views exploded in the early 19th century, with papal pronouncements in 1821, 1825, 1829, 1830 and 1832, and then continuing with a dozen more through the century. The 1829 Bull showed the focus of the Church's opposition, calling on Roman Catholics to 'eradicate those secret societies of factious men who, completely opposed to God and to princes, are wholly dedicated to bringing about the fall of the Church, the destruction of kingdoms, and disorder in the whole world'.

The United Grand Lodge of England and Wales, among others, has protested in vain that this view is a parody of mainstream Freemasonry. Such Catholic antagonism is one of the legacies of the Illuminati.

THE FRENCH REVOLUTION MYTH

The influence of Robison and de Barruel on future conspiracy theories concerning the Illuminati cannot be overemphasized. Although the Illuminati's attempts to infiltrate and recruit from the delegates at the 1782 Congress of Wilhelmsbad failed almost completely, Robison and de Barruel claimed the exact opposite. According to both writers, the revolutionary Illuminati persuaded most of the other delegates of the worth of their cause – resulting, just seven years later, in the French Revolution. Although there undoubtedly were some Freemasons among the many individuals and groups behind the French Revolution (it would have been very strange if there had been none), there has never been any evidence to suggest that the French Revolution was the result of a Masonic or Illuminati plot.

Illuminati conspiracy theories

Is it just coincidence, conspiracy theorists ask, that 1776 – the year that the Illuminati began – was the year of the American Revolution? Or that the first of the influential American 'Greek letter' college fraternities, Phi Beta Kappa, also began in the same year? The Illuminati's tendrils were so widespread, we are told, that they have been behind almost everything that has happened since.

***Left** Licio Gelli, founder of the secret society P2. He spent most of the years after the revelation of the P2 scandal on the run in various countries.*

The conspiracists believe that the Illuminati did not die out in 1786, when they were closed down in Bavaria. Instead, groups around the world went underground, resurfacing as a number of different influential societies today. The Illuminati are already the Secret Rulers of the World, we are told, and are plotting towards a New World Order, a world government under their control. Organizations that it is claimed they run include the Freemasons, the US Council on Foreign Relations, the Trilateral Commission and the World Bank. The real Illuminati are said to be the Bilderberg Group, founded in 1954 as an annual meeting of top politicians, financiers and businessmen; and Bohemian Grove, a rich-and-powerful-men's summer camp, held each July in California.

Effectively, almost any organization containing powerful or influential people is, according to the conspiracy theorists, a front for the Illuminati.

UNCONVINCING CLAIMS

The Illuminati have been given far more importance and influence than they ever merited. The truth about these conspiracy theories is that they rely on assertion rather than evidence, on very poor reasoning, on confusing fiction and fact, and on quoting each other as 'proof' of their validity. The theorists are often ultra-right-wing, and many are white supremacist, promoting the anti-Semitic *Protocols of the Elders of Zion* (proven to be a forgery decades ago) as true.

Of many questions that could be asked by anyone with a critical mind, here are just two. First, if the Illuminati and their offshoots are so all-powerful, why have they been so singularly ineffective in achieving their aims over the last two centuries? And second, if they are so secretive, how is it that their members, aims, motives, plots and plans are so easy for conspiracy theorists to uncover? If the Secret Rulers of the World are so inept, perhaps we don't need to worry too much about them.

However, in 1981 a genuine secret society was discovered in Italy that puts most conspiracy theories in the shade.

P2

P2 (Propaganda Due) was founded by Licio Gelli (born 1919) around 1966. Gelli fought for Franco in the Spanish Civil War, and during the Second World War was the liaison officer between the Fascists in Italy and the Nazis in Germany. He also worked with other extreme right-wing governments, including Argentina's General Perón. With such a background he knew many influential people and their interconnections.

Gelli joined a Grand Orient Masonic lodge in Italy in 1963. By law, Italian Masonic lodges had to give their membership lists to the government. When Gelli set up P2 (named after a 19th-century lodge called Propaganda), it was with the deliberate intention that its membership list would be known only to him. He recruited people who were in other lodges or societies; sometimes he offered inducements to join, while at other times he used blackmail.

P2 was organized in the classic cell structure, where for security reasons members knew only the other members of their own cell. Its members included everyone who was anyone in a position of power in Italy: senior politicians (including former prime ministers), generals and other

senior military personnel, top policemen, top civil servants, newspaper editors, bankers, judges, university professors and the heads of international companies. It even had close connections with the Vatican through senior clergy, including Archbishop Paul Marcinkus, president of the Vatican Bank from 1971 to 1989. With such powerful contacts Gelli was able to manipulate the Italian government and to arrange international deals that benefited both himself and other members of P2.

It all began to unravel in 1981 when police investigating the banker Michele Sindona, who had known Mafia connections and was an adviser to the Vatican, raided Gelli's Tuscany villa. There they found a

membership list containing 962 names, many of them well known (it is thought there were at least a thousand other members); they also found a document entitled 'Democratic Rebirth Plan', about the installation of an authoritarian government in Italy.

Among the casualties from the group's exposure was Roberto Calvi, head of the collapsed Banco Ambrosiano and a member of P2, who was found hanging beneath Blackfriars Bridge in London in 1982.

P2 was not the Illuminati, but its genuine high-level involvement in politics, religion, banking and industry (and much else) is reminiscent of the conspiracy theories about the two-centuries-disbanded organization still being powerful today.

CHAPTER 8

THE HERMETIC ORDER OF THE GOLDEN DAWN

The Hermetic Order of the Golden Dawn is undoubtedly the most significant occult society of the last century or so. In the Victorian era it was way ahead of its time in opening up esoteric teaching to women as well as men. It may only have lasted for about 15 years in its original form, but without the Golden Dawn today's esoteric world would be very different.

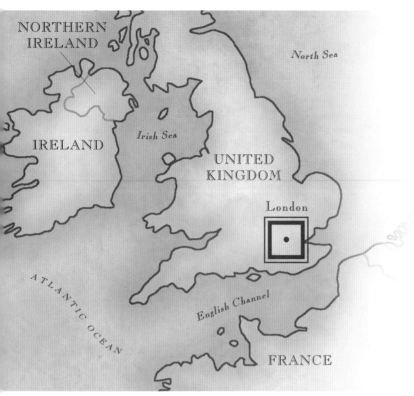

Origins of the Golden Dawn

The Golden Dawn did not spring fully fledged out of nowhere. Its ideas, teachings and practices, and even its organization, drew on those of earlier esoteric societies. Its immediate ancestor – in reality, rather than in its own fabricated history – was the Societas Rosicruciana in Anglia, often known as Soc Ros.

It has been mentioned previously that many, if not most, esoteric societies have a certain degree of fiction in their lineage. This applies to both the Golden Dawn and the Soc Ros – but both seem also to draw on a genuine forebear as well.

THE FOUNDING OF SOC ROS

The Societas Rosicruciana in Anglia was set up in Britain in 1866 as an Order open only to Master Masons. It is arguable whether it is one of the many side-degrees of Freemasonry, or whether it is actually a Rosicrucian Order for which Freemasonry is the necessary 'preparatory school'.

Right *The seal of the second level of the Hermetic Order of the Golden Dawn, Ordo Rosae Rubeae et Aureae Crucis (RR et AC).*

The founder, Robert Wentworth Little (1840–78), worked as a clerk in Freemasons' Hall in London. He claimed to have found some documents containing 'ritual information' in the Library of United Grand Lodge; he had first been shown these by William Henry White, who was Grand Secretary of English Freemasonry until 1857. White had told Little that he was the last surviving member of a Rosicrucian Order set up by an 18th-century Venetian ambassador to England, who had conferred degrees on various people in England. There may or may not be any truth in Little's story, as it was later related by Dr William Wynn Westcott (see page 106), who was not always the most reliable of witnesses.

Little asked for help in deciphering the old ritual documents from the esoteric writer Kenneth R.H. Mackenzie (1833–86), author of the *Royal Masonic Cyclopaedia* (1877). Mackenzie claimed that he had been initiated by some German adepts into certain grades of a Rosicrucian Order, and had been given authority to form a group of Masons in England under the Rosicrucian name – but he also was not renowned for his reliability. However, he had belonged to numerous societies, and had met many of the leading occultists of the day, including Éliphas Lévi (see page 71) in Paris in 1861. Although Mackenzie helped in setting up Soc Ros, he did not actually join until 1872, remaining a member for just three years.

FUNCTIONS OF THE MEMBERS

Unlike many Masonic Orders, Soc Ros – which still exists today, with around 60 colleges (the equivalent of lodges) – is focused on study. The Ordinances of the Order state that members are expected to be 'of sufficient ability to appreciate the studies of the Society, which consider the revelation of philosophy, science and theosophy'. Members are encouraged to write papers and deliver lectures on aspects of their study.

The Zelator embarks on a quest for true wisdom; the Theoricus studies theoretical aspects of divinity; the Practicus studies the spirituality of the art of alchemy; the Philosophus studies the philosophies and scriptures of world religions. After these four 'outer-court' grades, the initiate may, if judged fit, be invited to work towards becoming an adept in the Second Order. The Third Order comprises the rulers of Soc Ros. The eighth degree are the officers of the Order, who form the Electoral College to choose the Supreme Magus; the ninth degree consists of the Supreme Magus and a senior and junior deputy, plus a very small number of honorary members.

Soc Ros was a highly influential society, with many occult luminaries among its members. It claimed the famous novelist and politician Edward George Bulwer-Lytton as its Honorary President, but he was never its Grand Patron as often stated.

According to the 20th-century occultist Israel Regardie (see page 114), the aims of Soc Ros were:

> to afford mutual aid and encouragement in working out the great problems of Life, and in discovering the secrets of nature; to facilitate the study of the systems of philosophy founded upon the Kabbalah and the doctrines of Hermes Trismegistus.

It was a clear link from modern times, probably via the 18th-century Brotherhood of the Golden and Rosy Cross (see pages 70 and 81), to the precepts and principles, the ideas and ideals, of the Hermetic Philosophers, the first real Rosicrucians.

SOC ROS ORDERS

The system of grades of the Societas Rosicruciana in Anglia is:

- **First Order**
  Zelator
  Theoricus
  Practicus
  Philosophus

- **Second Order**
  Adeptus Minor
  Adeptus Major
  Adeptus Exemptus

- **Third Order**
  Magister
  Magus

These grades are identical to those of the 18th-century German Order, the Brotherhood of the Golden and Rosy Cross (see page 70).

Right Edward George Bulwer-Lytton (Baron Lytton) (1803–73) had a serious interest in Rosicrucianism; he met the French occultist Éliphas Lévi when he visited London.

The Golden Dawn emerges

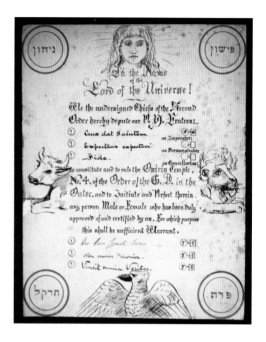

Robert Wentworth Little died in 1878 and was succeeded as Supreme Magus of the Societas Rosicruciana in Anglia by Dr William Robert Woodman (1828–91), a retired physician who had joined Soc Ros a few months after it began. He greatly increased the emphasis of the society on Kabbalah (see pages 50–53). Two other senior members of Soc Ros were William Wynn Westcott (1848–1925), a London coroner, and Samuel Liddell 'MacGregor' Mathers (1854–1918), a self-styled Jacobite supporter (his title of 'Comte MacGregor de Glenstrae' was entirely spurious). These three were the founders of the Hermetic Order of the Golden Dawn.

Above *The official charter establishing the Golden Dawn (1888), signed by Mathers, Westcott and Woodman.*

The actual origins of the Golden Dawn are confused, as much by the deliberate obfuscation of the founders as by anything else. The official story was that Westcott found a manuscript of around 60 pages on a London bookstall; it was written in cipher, and set out the basics of five esoteric rituals. With the manuscript was the address of a German adept. Another version is that the papers containing the enciphered ritual had been sent to Westcott by an elderly clergyman known in esoteric circles, the Rev. A.F.A. Woodford, in 1887.

THE TRIUMVIRATE IS FORMED

It is now considered more probable that the cipher manuscript was among the papers of Kenneth Mackenzie (see page 105), who died in 1886. Mackenzie had been Grand Secretary of the Swedenborgian Rite of Freemasonry, and was also a member of, among others, a small alchemical research group, the Society of Eight. Westcott, as much a magpie collector of secret societies as Mackenzie, had been a member of both, and now took over the Swedenborgian Rite.

Mackenzie's widow passed all his esoteric papers to Westcott. Finding the cipher manuscript, and having little difficulty in deciphering it, Westcott decided that this was an excellent opportunity to start his own occult society.

He recruited William Woodman, the well-respected Supreme Magus of Soc Ros, as one joint leader, and Samuel Mathers as the other, giving Mathers the task of fleshing out the somewhat skeletal ritual into a full working ritual.

The problem, as with all new esoteric societies, was authenticity. Westcott solved this by inventing a German Order, Goldene Dämmerung (Golden Dawn), and had several letters forged in German from its leader, one Fräulein Anna Sprengel, granting authority to form a branch of the Order in Britain. (Most members only saw the English 'translations' of these letters; the 'originals' were clearly written by someone with little knowledge of German.) A final letter, dated 1890, conveniently announced that Fräulein Sprengel had died and that there would be no further contact.

A KERNEL OF TRUTH

In one sense, however, the German heritage of the Golden Dawn is genuine, in that (with the addition of a Neophyte grade below Zelator) Westcott, Woodman and Mathers borrowed the grade structure of Societas Rosicruciana in Anglia, which Robert Wentworth Little and Kenneth Mackenzie had in turn borrowed from the Brotherhood of the Golden and Rosy Cross. The Golden Dawn had positioned itself – in fact as well as fiction – in the line of succession from German Rosicrucianism.

As for the cipher manuscript, it is likely that it contained a draft ritual structure that Mackenzie had written either for a short-lived society that he had founded around 1874, the Hermetic Order of Egypt, or for another Order in which he was involved, the Royal Oriental Order of the Sat B'hai.

In two ways the Hermetic Order of the Golden Dawn was very different from both the Societas Rosicruciana in Anglia and the Brotherhood of the Golden and Rosy Cross: it was open to both non-Masons and women. In this it was following the example of the

Below *Dr William Robert Woodman (1828–91), Supreme Magus of Societas Rosicruciana in Anglia and co-founder of the Golden Dawn, in Masonic regalia.*

Above *A rare and striking portrait of Golden Dawn leader Samuel Liddell 'MacGregor' Mathers (1854–1918) painted by his wife Moina.*

Theosophical Society, founded in 1875 by Helena Petrovna Blavatsky (1831–91). Theosophy was a deliberate blend of Eastern and Western mystical religion, and it is probable that one of the motivations of the Golden Dawn was to offer an alternative that was rooted firmly in European Rosicrucian and Hermetic beliefs – the Western Mystery Tradition. It is probably not a coincidence that Westcott began planning the Golden Dawn in 1887, the same year that Madame Blavatsky moved to London.

The Golden Dawn began in February 1888, with the three founders signing pledges of allegiance to each other (and to Fräulein Sprengel); a year later, despite little publicity, membership had grown to around 60. Many of the early members were also in Soc Ros, but by the end of 1891 about half of those in the London temple were women.

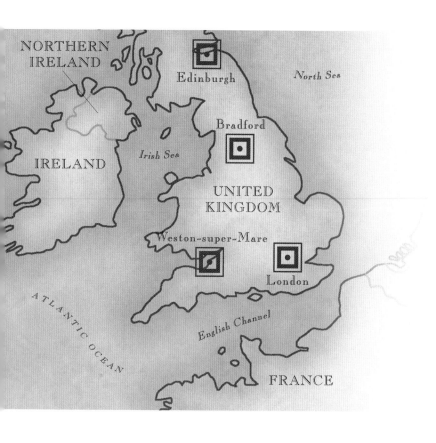

The heyday of the Golden Dawn

Another major difference between the Golden Dawn and its immediate predecessor, the Societas Rosicruciana in Anglia, was that it was not just a study group, learning the theory of Rosicrucian-type teachings. The Outer Order certainly began with theory, but initiates could progress, through examinations, to the Second Order – and this involved practical work.

Initially, however, only the Outer Order actually existed. Westcott, Woodman and Mathers positioned themselves at the lowest level of the Second Order, Adeptus Minor, and said they were under the authority of three Secret Chiefs at Adeptus Exemptus level; in reality these were themselves and 'Fräulein Sprengel'. The Third Order comprised spirits on the astral plane. Secret Chiefs were a similar concept to Unknown Superiors (see pages 32 and 97).

THE 'TRADITIONAL HISTORY' OF THE ORDER

The history given to each new initiate stated that the society was actually a revival of an Order whose members were now deceased; among those named as adepts were Kenneth Mackenzie and Éliphas Lévi, who had died in 1875. Although traditional histories are almost invariably colourful works of fiction and not to be relied upon as being in any way historical, this one actually gave due credit to two of the main sources of the Golden Dawn's teachings. Mackenzie had clearly been a major 'local' influence, while Lévi's writings were substantially plagiarized by Mathers as

Left Éliphas Lévi (Alphonse Louis Constant) (1810–75), the much-esteemed French occultist whose writings influenced the Golden Dawn.

he devised the rituals and teachings of the Golden Dawn.

Woodman died in 1891, and Westcott became Supreme Magus of Soc Ros, remaining in that position until his death. Although Westcott had initially created the Golden Dawn, Mathers now effectively took control of it.

THE RR ET AC

Over time, as more members progressed up the grade levels, it became necessary for Mathers to devise rituals and a body of teachings for the three Adeptus grades of the Second Order, which was called Ordo Rosae Rubeae et Aureae Crucis (RR et AC), the Order of the Rose of Ruby and Cross of Gold. This might have been an echo of the Brotherhood of the Golden and Rosy Cross, of which Mathers and Westcott would certainly have known, but it was certainly a reference to the original Rosicrucian 'foundation myth'. Mathers and his wife designed a highly ornate seven-sided vault based on the description in the first Rosicrucian manifesto of the vault in which the body of Christian Rosenbreuz had been found (see pages 62 and 111); this was used for initiation into the Adeptus Minor grade of the Second Order.

It was in this Order that the real work of the Golden Dawn was done; there was a clear distinction between the preparatory Outer Order and the RR et AC. Progression to the latter was by invitation only (plus examination); some members of the Outer Order did not even know that there was a Second Order.

MEMBERSHIP

The Hermetic Order of the Golden Dawn was never a large society. In addition to its initial Isis-Urania Temple in London, which had around 80 members, it established temples in Weston-super-Mare in the south-west of England, Bradford in the north and Edinburgh in Scotland.

Most members were of the professional class. A number were doctors, and several were writers including, most famously, the Irish poet W.B. Yeats, the supernatural writers

Left An unusual painting recently identified as Mina Bergson (later Moina Mathers, 1865–1928); the artist is Beatrice Offor, who shared a studio with Mina and Annie Horniman, when they were all students at the Slade School of Art in London.

Arthur Machen and Algernon Blackwood and the esoteric historian A.E. Waite. Significant female members included Mathers's wife Moina and the tea heiress Annie Horniman (they were both artists, and had met when students at the Slade School), and the actress Florence Farr (mistress of George Bernard Shaw, among others).

It was Moina Mathers who drew the original Golden Dawn Tarot cards, of which every member had to make their own copies (see page 117). Both Tarot and Kabbalah were taught as a major part of the magical system of the Golden Dawn. Mathers borrowed from Éliphas Lévi and further developed a complex system of 'correspondences' between Tarot, Kabbalah, the astrological planets, colours, gods, animals, plants and much more, to be used in rituals. He also developed Lévi's three laws of magic – the force of the will, the astral medium and the theory of correspondences – and added a fourth, directed imagination. The Golden Dawn's teaching on magic became a thoroughly worked-out and complex system.

In 1892 Mathers, still Chief of the Order, moved to Paris, leaving Westcott in charge in England, using the study material that Mathers was still producing. In fact Annie Horniman, who was an able administrator, was running most things, including the teaching and examination of Outer Order members. The first half of the 1890s were the glory days of the Golden Dawn for both the Outer Order and the RR et AC.

Mathers and his wife designed a highly ornate seven-sided vault based on the description in the first Rosicrucian manifesto of the vault in which the body of Christian Rosenkreuz had been found; this was used for initiation into the Adeptus Minor grade of the Second Order.

Teachings and rituals of the Golden Dawn

The Hermetic Order of the Golden Dawn drew together a host of esoteric teachings that make up what is usually called the Western Mystery Tradition, to provide a comprehensive magical training course. Through a system of instruction, ritual, examination and initiations, members could step up through the grades, becoming knowledgeable in the theory and proficient in the practice of many different spiritual, mystical and magical areas.

Members of the Golden Dawn studied just about everything that natural philosophers, alchemists, Hermeticists, Rosicrucians and other occultists had learned and developed over the previous centuries, right back to ancient times.

RANGE OF STUDIES

They studied the ancient Greek and Egyptian mystery religions, Hermeticism, and the principles of alchemy and astrology. They learned the Hebrew alphabet as a necessary aid to a detailed study of Kabbalah, and they learned an esoteric interpretation of Tarot, linked with Kabbalah, astrology and much more. Tarot and geomancy (a form of divination using random marks on paper) were used not for crude fortune-telling, but to stimulate the powers of the imagination, intuition and clairvoyance. They learned Tattwa Vision, a powerful form of visualization using symbols and colours to create a gateway they could pass through in their imagination. They learned Words of Power, and how to speak or 'vibrate' them. And, from the work of John Dee three hundred years earlier, they learned the Enochian or Angelic language.

Among much else, members of the Second Order were also taught Enochian Chess, a four-handed version of chess using pieces representing Egyptian gods and goddesses; each player had a King, Queen, Knight, Bishop (or Ship) and Rook, and four pawns (represented as canopic jars, used to contain the internal organs of mummified bodies). Devised by William Wynn Westcott, Enochian Chess could be played as a game, or used as an extremely complex form of divination. As Westcott left the Golden Dawn in 1897, and 'MacGregor' Mathers had little interest in Enochian Chess, it seems that, while RR et AC initiates learned the rudiments of the system, few became adept in its use.

Left Dr William Wynn Westcott (1848–1925) originated the idea for the Golden Dawn from the Mysterious Cipher manuscript.

Left A modern full-size replica of the original Golden Dawn Vault of the Adepti.

THE LESSER BANISHING RITUAL

The aim of 'the Great Work' was to purify and gain control of one's inner self, to enable spiritual growth and to unite with the Divine Self. All of this was within a Judeo-Christian framework; as in all Rosicrucian-type groups, Christian symbols were a vital part of all that members did.

In the Outer Order members learned the theory of magic, but did not practise it, except for what is known as the Lesser Banishing Ritual of the Pentagram. This, like most rituals, has more than one purpose. It is used objectively to define and purify the space in which the work is to be done, but perhaps more importantly it has a subjective, psychological purpose – to raise the consciousness of each participant, to prepare *them* for the work ahead.

The Lesser Banishing Ritual begins with the celebrant, or the individual, making the sign of the Cross, specifically as a Kabbalistic Cross, visualizing lines of brilliant white light across the body, while using words of power

related to some of the Sephiroth (see page 50) in saying in Hebrew: 'Thou art the Kingdom, the Power and the Glory, for ever, Amen.' Then, facing first east, then south, west and north, a pentacle (five-pointed star) is drawn in the air and one of the sacred names of God is spoken for each compass point. Finally, again facing each point in turn, the four Archangels are named, each associated with a visualization of one of the four traditional elements. Variations on the Lesser Banishing Ritual are now used in many esoteric groups, including some Wiccan rituals.

THE RITUAL IN THE VAULT OF THE ADEPTI

The initiation rituals for each grade of the Outer Order of the Golden Dawn drew heavily on the structure and content of Masonic initiations – hardly surprising, in the light of both the Golden Dawn's immediate forerunner, the Masonic Rosicrucian group the Societas Rosicruciana in Anglia, and

Freemasonry's own links with Rosicrucianism (see pages 80–81).

By the beginning of 1892 Mathers had completed the rituals and graded teachings for the Second Order, Ordo Rosae Rubeae et Aureae Crucis (RR et AC). Those members who progressed through the Outer Order and were admitted to the RR et AC (never more than about one-third) experienced complex initiation rituals.

Between them 'MacGregor' and Moina Mathers had designed, created and richly decorated a full-sized copy of the tomb of Christian Rosenkreuz (see page 62), which they called the Vault of the Adepti. The vault was seven-sided, around 3.6 m (12 ft) across, with highly colourful symbolic designs on its walls, each 1.5 m (5 ft) wide by 2.4 m (8 ft) high, with a rose on its ceiling. In its centre, under a circular altar, was a coffin, in which lay the Chief Adept of the Order during part of the initiation of the new member. By all accounts it was a tremendously powerful initiatory ritual.

The collapse of the Golden Dawn

The heiress Annie Horniman had been the main source of funding for 'MacGregor' Mathers since 1891; he appears to have had no gainful employment. He and Moina were enjoying their life in Paris to the full. Late in 1896, when Mathers (always imperious) demanded yet more money from Horniman, she cut off her funding. Aware that the senior members in London were beginning to question his authority, Mathers demanded a written pledge of personal loyalty from every member of the Second Order; Horniman refused, and Mathers promptly expelled her from the Order.

In 1897 word leaked to the authorities that William Wynn Westcott, ostensibly a pillar of the community, was running an occult secret society. (It is generally thought that Mathers was responsible for this leak.) Westcott was given an ultimatum by the authorities: if he wanted to continue as a London coroner, he must give up the Golden Dawn. He did so, and Florence Farr took over running it in Britain. She did not have the competence of either Westcott or Horniman; she let the teaching and examinations slide into chaos; and she allowed the Inner Order to get out of control, with members no longer studying, but performing astral travel together in a group called 'the Sphere'. The Order rapidly fell into disorder. Worse was to come.

LIES, REBELLION AND EXPULSION

In early 1900 Florence Farr too began to become tired of Mathers's imperiousness. In an angry exchange, Mathers revealed the truth about Fräulein Sprengel. There was

Right Actress Florence Farr (1860–1917) in the role of Rebecca West in Ibsen's Rosmersholm, 1891. *A dedicated occultist, she was not a skilled administrator.*

uproar in the Golden Dawn, as members realized that their Order was founded on a series of lies. Still worse was to come.

A young poet and mountaineer called Aleister Crowley had joined the Golden Dawn in late 1898. By December 1899 he had shot through the teachings and examinations of the entire Outer Order and, having discovered its existence, demanded initiation into the RR et AC. Farr and other senior members felt he was not a fit person to be accepted into the Inner Order, and refused. (This is a prerogative of most, if not all, secret societies: that advancement up the initiatory ladder depends as much on assessment of the aspirant's character by his or her superiors as on technical proficiency in mastering each level.)

Crowley stormed off to Paris to see Mathers, who, already angry with Farr, promptly initiated Crowley into the RR et AC himself. The London Temple would not accept this, and refused Crowley the papers containing the Adeptus Minor teachings. Furious at this open rebellion against his authority, Mathers authorized Crowley, as his Envoy Extraordinaire, to take possession of the London Temple. In April 1900 Crowley turned up there in full Highland dress, but was repulsed.

This was the last straw. The senior London members of the Golden Dawn expelled both Crowley and Mathers, the last remaining founder, from the Order. W.B. Yeats took control of the Outer Order. Horniman returned, and tried to sort out the mess that Farr had created.

A further crisis was external. An American couple known as Theo and Laura Horos, who had set up their own Order of Theocratic Unity, were in court for (among other things) conspiracy to defraud and the 'procurement for immoral purposes' of three young women. It turned out that they had based their Order in part on the Golden Dawn, having conned Mathers into loaning them some of his ritual books. During their trial in the last quarter of 1901 the Golden Dawn received a lot of lurid publicity.

DISHARMONY AND DIVISION

The Order managed to struggle on for another year or two, but with massive tensions between the senior members it was difficult to repair what had been broken, and it split into three main groups. A few members stayed loyal to Mathers and founded a new Alpha et Omega Order, with temples in London and Edinburgh. This survived Mathers's death in 1918, but not the death of Moina Mathers in 1928.

The esoteric historian A.E. Waite took control of the original Isis-Urania Temple, including its vault, renamed the Hermetic Order as the Holy Order of the Golden Dawn (usually known as the Independent and Rectified Rite) and shifted its emphasis away from ritual magic to esoteric Christianity. This Order continued until 1914; the following year Waite replaced it with a new group called the Fellowship of the Rosy Cross, which included the mystical writer Evelyn Underhill and the occult novelist Charles Williams.

Led by Dr Robert W. Felkin, those who wanted to continue the magical teachings of the original Golden Dawn formed a new Order, Stella Matutina (the Order of the Morning Star). Yeats remained a member of this until 1925. The novelist and occultist Dion Fortune was a member, as was the children's writer E. Nesbit. Stella Matutina eventually faded out by the mid-1930s.

The influence of the Golden Dawn

The Hermetic Order of the Golden Dawn lasted barely 15 years, and for the last few of those it was falling apart. Yet esoteric historians and modern occultists agree that it was the most significant organization of its kind, partly for its very existence and its body of teachings, partly for the astonishing group of people it attracted, but mainly for the influence it has had on esoteric societies throughout the Western world in the century since its messy demise.

Left *Rudolf Steiner (1861–1925), founder of Anthroposophy, influenced many esoteric societies including Max Heindel's Rosicrucian Fellowship.*

The three immediate successors to the Golden Dawn had their own schisms and factions; friends with different esoteric interests ended up in different societies, while people with broadly similar interests might have clashes of personality and also end up in different groups. Add to this the publicity from several other court cases in the first decade of the 20th century, and the spectacular volte-face of one of the chief adepts of Stella Matutina, Christina Stoddart – who became a fundamentalist Christian and denounced her former Order as Satanic – and it is not surprising that many people gave up on the esoteric scene completely. But some stuck it out, and new names appeared.

PUBLICATION OF THE GOLDEN DAWN RITUALS

One of these was Israel Regardie (1907–85). He worked as secretary to Aleister Crowley (see pages 123–131) for about three years from 1928. In 1934 he was invited to join Stella Matutina, the main Golden Dawn successor that had preserved its original emphasis. In 1937–40 he published the entirety of the Golden Dawn teachings and rituals in a four-volume work (now available in one large volume). He received some criticism for breaking his vows of secrecy, but many esotericists were pleased to have all the material available together – and in any case, Crowley had published much of it in his magazine *Equinox* some years earlier (1909–19).

The teachings of the Hermetic Order of the Golden Dawn were now available to anyone who wished to have them. There are now dozens (if not hundreds) of different Golden Dawn societies scattered around the Western world – mainly in Britain, North America and Australasia – performing the rituals much as 'MacGregor' Mathers wrote them more than a century ago. Many of these groups claim a lineage back to the original Golden Dawn. Because it was so schismatic in its final years, some of these claims may have a certain amount of validity; but it would be unwise to say that any specific Golden Dawn organization is today the direct successor of the original.

RUDOLF STEINER

Even shortly after the break-up of the Golden Dawn there were other interconnections between esoteric groups. The leader of Stella Matutina, Dr Robert Felkin, was convinced that there were genuine Rosicrucian adepts in Germany – Fräulein Sprengel's Order, which had supposedly given the Golden Dawn its charter. In his search for them he eventually encountered Rudolf Steiner, who would go on to found Anthroposophy in 1913. At that time (1910) Steiner was still head of the Theosophical Society in Germany. He had also been initiated into the Masonic Rite of Memphis and Misraim, a hugely complex 96-degree fringe Masonic Order founded by the influential English Freemason John Yarker in 1872. In 1906 Steiner was granted a charter to set up this Rite in Berlin. He was, therefore, familiar with two very different types of esoteric group: the personal mystical path of Theosophy and initiatory lodges with grade systems, as in Freemasonry.

He also had, within the Theosophical Society, an inner circle of adepts who practised clairvoyance. Felkin was hugely impressed by Steiner, and sent a member of Stella Matutina to study under him and eventually bring back to England Steiner's techniques. These were incorporated into the secret teachings of the inner order of Stella Matutina.

THE BUILDERS OF THE ADYTUM

One American Order that has very firm roots in the Golden Dawn is the Builders of the Adytum (BOTA), founded by Paul Foster Case (1884–1956). Case became interested in the occult in his teens. He was probably one of the anonymous co-authors of the modern classic Hermetic text, *The Kybalion* (1912). In 1916 he published a series of articles on Tarot that later became *The Book of Tokens* (1934). In 1919 he joined the New York Thoth-Hermes Temple of 'MacGregor' Mathers's Alpha et Omega version of the Golden Dawn, which was run by a close friend, Michael Whitty. Case rose rapidly through the grades, and on Whitty's death was appointed leader of the lodge.

However, he had expressed doubts about some aspects of Golden Dawn teachings, particularly Enochian Magic, and in 1920 Moina Mathers expelled him from the Order. Case had already set up a study group within the lodge, called the Hermetic Order of Atlantis, and when he left Alpha et Omega he took most of its members with him. The Order became the School of Ageless Wisdom in 1923, which in turn became Builders of the Adytum in 1938, having moved its headquarters to Los Angeles.

BOTA is one of the largest and most respected occult orders in America. As students progress up the grade system they can set up a chapter of their own, known as a Pronaos; BOTA now has Pronaoi around the world. It is perhaps best known as a school of Tarot, but also lays a great deal of emphasis on Kabbalah, astrology and meditation.

SOCIETY OF THE INNER LIGHT

The Hermetic Order of the Golden Dawn has spawned numerous other organizations with a range of emphases. Some of these are more related to Aleister Crowley's teachings (see pages 124–125), while others go back to the occult writer Dion Fortune.

Born Violet Mary Firth (1890–1946), Fortune took her name from her Latin motto *Deo non fortuna* when she was a member of the Alpha et Omega Temple run by the novelist J.W. Brodie-Innes, and then of the Stella Matutina lodge. She had previously been a

There are now dozens (if not hundreds) of different Golden Dawn societies scattered around the Western world performing the rituals much as 'MacGregor' Mathers wrote them more than a century ago.

Theosophist, and with the permission of Moina Mathers formed a branch called the Christian Mystic Lodge of the Theosophical Society in 1922. After a spectacular falling out with Moina Mathers, involving psychic warfare between them, she renamed her organization the Fellowship of the Inner Light in 1928. It was later renamed the Society of the Inner Light, after her death.

Dion Fortune is also known for her work, with other occultists, to protect Britain against German invasion during the Second World War, in what has been called the Magical Battle of Britain.

The Society of the Inner Light initially taught a version of the original Golden Dawn grades, with a strong emphasis on Kabbalah and on the power of myth in the Matter of Britain (the body of specifically British mythology, especially the Arthurian stories); but over the years the emphasis changed. In the 1960s, in a sort of echo of Waite's revisioning of the Golden Dawn (see page 113), the Society more or less abandoned the ritual and Hermetic aspects of its work to focus on mystical and philosophical areas. Several senior members left.

Left Dion Fortune (Violet Mary Firth) (1890–1946). In addition to founding the influential Society of the Inner Light she wrote numerous significant esoteric books, both non-fiction and fiction.

Opposite The Rider-Waite Tarot, designed by Pamela Colman Smith under the direction of A.E. Waite, became the standard Tarot pack for most of the 20th century.

SERVANTS OF THE LIGHT

Two of these members, W.E. Butler and Gareth Knight, set up the Helios Course on Practical Kabbalah, a correspondence course based on Knight's book on the subject. The course become so successful that in 1973 it formed the basis of a new school of occult science, the Servants of the Light (SOL), founded by Butler with Dolores and Michael Ashcroft-Nowicki, who have run it since Butler's death in 1978.

Based in the British Channel Islands, SOL now has over 2,500 members in more than 20 countries. Its training in the Western Mystery Tradition is still firmly based on Kabbalah, and it traces its roots back clearly through Fortune's Society of the Inner Light to the Hermetic Order of the Golden Dawn. It believes that 'all who desire to do so should be able to study the Mysteries, the true inner spiritual heritage of the West'. SOL states that it is a 'contacted school', explaining that it is 'in direct psychic contact with the Inner Planes ... the school is firmly and deeply linked to the Inner Hierarchy, where its true Directors reside'. Once more this is an echo of the Secret Chiefs who are a familiar feature of many esoteric societies.

In the 1990s the leadership of the Society of the Inner Light changed, and after 25 years of running his own ritual group Gareth Knight was invited back to advise them on how to restore their old emphasis on the grade system and rituals.

LINKS BETWEEN ESOTERIC TRADITIONS

Although the Western Mystery Tradition with its Rosicrucian heritage is very different from the Theosophical tradition created by Madame Blavatsky, with its blending of mystical Christianity with elements of Hinduism and Buddhism, there have been several times when these two esoteric lines have come into contact, usually through individual people. This is not surprising; many people who pursue an esoteric quest try more than one path along the way. The presence of both Madame Blavatsky and the

The Society of the Inner Light initially taught a version of the original Golden Dawn grades, with a strong emphasis on Kabbalah and on the power of myth.

TAROT DESIGNS

Most of the successors to the Golden Dawn teach Kabbalah, and most also lay great emphasis on Tarot. Connections between Tarot and the Kabbalah were first explored by Éliphas Lévi in his *Dogme et Rituel de la Haute Magie* (1855–56); expanded by Mathers, these ideas formed an important part of Golden Dawn teaching. To make the correspondences between the 22 paths of the Sephiroth and the 22 cards of the Major Arcana match better, the Golden Dawn swapped around the order of two cards, Justice (originally 8) and Strength (originally 11), to 11 and 8 in their own teachings.

Every member of the original Golden Dawn had to make their own copy of Moina Mathers's drawings of the Tarot cards. After the break-up of the Golden Dawn, A.E. Waite was the first to make these designs and interpretations public in 1910, in what became known as the Rider-Waite Tarot (Rider was the publisher). The cards were actually drawn by the artist Pamela Colman Smith to Waite's instructions. Although they were quite crudely drawn and coloured, they became popular largely because they were the first commercially available pack to have illustrations for the Minor Arcana, rather than just pip cards as in the previously popular Marseille Tarot.

The Tarot designed by Paul Foster Case for the Builders of the Adytum is almost identical to the Rider-Waite pack, though much better drawn. As he had belonged to the Alpha et Omega Order run by Moina Mathers, it seems likely that these are very close to her original designs.

In his publication of the Golden Dawn teachings, Israel Regardie described the Tarot cards, and gave their symbolic meanings. His descriptions were incorporated in a pack drawn by Robert Wang, which – though called the Golden Dawn Tarot – is very different in some ways from the Waite and Case packs.

Aleister Crowley designed an extraordinarily different Tarot, painted by Lady Frieda Harris; he called it *The Book of Thoth*, emphasizing the myth propounded by Etteilla in 1783 (see page 71) that Tarot had ancient Egyptian origins, having been conceived by Hermes Trismegistus himself. Interestingly the Tarot of the Brotherhood of Light (see page 130), which had connections with the Ordo Templi Orientis of which Crowley became British head, has a very strong Egyptian look; the usual lightning-struck Tower, for example, is shown as a pyramid.

The Servants of the Light are one of several modern esoteric societies to produce their own distinctive Tarot pack, under the direction of Dolores Ashcroft-Nowicki.

STRENGTH.

THE HERMIT.

WHEEL of FORTUNE.

JUSTICE .

Left Annie Besant
(1847–1933) was
a leading Theosophist,
Co-Mason and
social reformer.

Above Madame Helena
Petrova Blavatsky
(1831–91), author
and founder of the
Theosophical Society.

Hermetic Order of the Golden Dawn in London at the same time means that some connections there were inevitable. One outstanding example of overlap between various esoteric traditions is Rudolf Steiner.

Steiner, who founded the Anthroposophical Society in 1913, had been the head of the Theosophical Society in Germany until he fell out with Madame Blavatsky's successor Annie Besant. Steiner had connections with Max Heindel and the Rosicrucian Fellowship (see page 72), Robert Felkin and Stella Matutina (see page 115), and Theodor Reuss, the founder of the Ordo Templi Orientis (see pages 130–131).

Another link between different esoteric traditions is that senior members of occult organizations are often priests or bishops in small, unorthodox Churches. Bishops in the established Churches claim Apostolic Succession – that they are part of a continuous line going back to the original apostles and thus to Christ. The Apostolic Succession is passed on by the laying on of hands by one or more bishops in the act of consecration of a new bishop.

Over the centuries, Catholic or Orthodox bishops have occasionally left their Churches to become independent or to found other denominations. Having received the

Apostolic Succession, any bishop can then pass it on to others. From the point of view of the Roman Catholic Church, any such consecration, outside its jurisdiction, is illicit, but still valid. Bishops consecrated in this unorthodox way are known as *episcopi vagantes* or wandering bishops (see pages 32–33).

In 1908 Arnold Harris Mathew was consecrated as bishop by the Old Catholic Church in Utrecht, and tried to set up the Old Catholic Church in Britain. In 1914 he consecrated his successor, who in turn consecrated three more bishops in the following two years. By now most of the clergy of the Church were Theosophists; as they had moved substantially away from the continental Old Catholic Church, they changed their name in 1918 to the Liberal Catholic Church. Most leading Theosophists of the 20th century were bishops or priests in the Liberal Catholic Church, as are the founders and leaders of many other esoteric groups today, including Servants of the Light.

THE GNOSTIC CATHOLIC CHURCH

The different versions of the Ordo Templi Orientis (see pages 130–131) also have associated Churches, usually some form of the Gnostic Catholic Church. This originated with a 19th-century French occultist, Jules Doinel (1842–1903), who claimed to have found a manuscript written by an early Cathar martyr who died in 1022 (see page 13). After a series of visions, Doinel supposedly made contact with 40 long-dead Cathar bishops, who urged him to revive Gnostic beliefs and re-establish the Église Gnostique de France. One of the early bishops of this new Church was Gerard Encausse, better known as Papus (1865–1916), a well-known occultist and writer on the Tarot. Papus and another bishop, Jean Bricaud (1881–1934), led a split in the Church, setting up the Gnostic Catholic Church.

In June 1908 Papus organized an 'International Masonic Conference', actually focused solely on esoteric and 'fringe' Rites, in Paris. Here, Theodor Reuss, founder of the OTO, conferred a Masonic charter and degrees on Papus, who in return made him a patriarch of the Gnostic Catholic Church. Reuss then set up his own branch of the Church. In 1913 Bricaud received legitimate consecration from a wandering bishop, and in 1919 he reconsecrated Reuss, establishing his legitimacy in the Apostolic Succession.

Through Reuss, Aleister Crowley and all his successors as leaders of the various versions of OTO are also (competing) patriarchs of the Gnostic Catholic Church, with Apostolic Succession. The Gnostic Catholic Church uses a Gnostic Mass written by Crowley in 1913.

Below The French occult writer Papus (Gerard Encausse), co-founder of the Gnostic Catholic Church, who received a valid consecration as a bishop from Jean Bricaud around 1913.

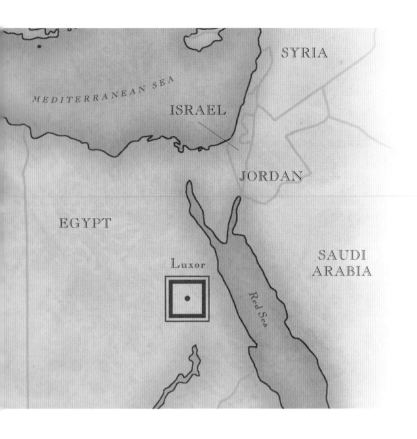

Karnak

For many people in the esoteric world ancient Egypt was one of the most important sources of spiritual wisdom. In fact, many of the Golden Dawn's temples in Britain were named after Egyptian gods: the Isis-Urania Temple in London, the Horus Temple in Bradford, and the Amun-Ra temple in Edinburgh.

The so-called Temple of Karnak, situated about 3 km (1¾ miles) north of Luxor in Egypt, is actually several temples – three major ones and numerous smaller ones – all on the same site. A place of pilgrimage for nearly four thousand years, this is probably the largest temple complex in the world, covering 100 hectares (247 acres), and developed over more than 1,300 years. Karnak is a relatively new name for the complex; its name in antiquity was Ipet-isut, meaning 'the most select of places'. There are three separate precincts, each enclosed by high mud-brick walls, dedicated to different gods.

PRECINCT OF AMUN

The Precinct of Amun, pictured here, is the largest and most spectacular part of the whole temple complex. Amun was originally the god of Thebes, but when he was merged with the sun-god Ra as Amun-Ra he became the most important god in Egypt. First he was represented as a goose, and then as a ram; later he was shown as a man with a feathered headdress, a remnant of the goose imagery. The name Amun is believed to come from an ancient Egyptian name Imn, meaning the Hidden One or the Secret One – hidden or unknown because he represented absolute holiness as the creator god.

PRECINCT OF MONTU

To the north of the Precinct of Amun lies the smallest of the three walled areas, the Precinct of Montu. Montu was the hawk-headed god of war and sport, and was at one time the supreme deity of Upper Egypt. This precinct also contains temples to the gods Harpra and Ma'at.

PRECINCT OF MUT

To the south of the Precinct of Amun is the Precinct of Mut, the consort of Amun-Ra. She was known as the Queen of the Gods, and was the mother of the moon god Khonsu. The Temple of Mut is enclosed on three sides by a bow-shaped sacred lake.

① THE CRYOSPHINXES

Outside the walls of the Precinct of Amun is an avenue of cryosphinxes, ram's-headed sphinxes, symbolizing Amun, each one holding a statue of King Rameses II (c.1303–c.1213 BCE) between its paws.

② FIRST PYLON

The First Pylon is the main entrance to the whole complex. Dating to the 7th century BCE, it originally stood more than 40 m (130 ft) high. It is thought that this pylon was unfinished, as the height is uneven and a mud-brick building ramp is still in place on the inside. The First Pylon leads into the first courtyard of the Precinct of Amun – at 837 sq m (9000 sq ft) the largest courtyard of any Egyptian temple.

③ TEMPLE OF RAMESES III

Leading off from this courtyard is a barque chapel built by Rameses III (c.1212–c.1155 BCE), originally a copy of his mortuary temple at Medinet Habu. A small pylon opens into a court lined with statues of him, leading to a hypostyle hall and sanctuary.

④ SECOND PYLON

The Second Pylon is the gateway into the Hypostyle Hall. It was built by Rameses II. Just before this pylon there once stood two massive statues of Rameses II; the feet of one of them can still be seen.

⑤ GREAT HYPOSTYLE HALL

Millennia after it was built, the Hypostyle Hall is still the largest religious room in the world, measuring around 91 x 48 m (300 x 158 ft). It contains 134 huge columns, most of them 15 m (50 ft) high, although the 12 central ones are an astonishing 21 m (70 ft) high.

⑥ THE MIDDLE KINGDOM COURT

After six pylons in all, at the very heart of the main walled enclosure is the Middle Kingdom Court and Inner Sanctuary, where the earliest temple to Amun, with an image of the god, once stood.

⑦ THE FESTIVAL TEMPLE

Beyond the Middle Kingdom Court is the oldest remaining part of the temple, the Festival Hall built by Tuthmosis III (1479–1425 BCE). He called it the Most Splendid of Monuments.

⑧ SACRED LAKE

The sacred lake at Karnak is the largest at any Egyptian temple. In rituals and festivals, golden barges bearing images of the gods would sail across it. More mundanely, the lake also supplied water for the priests' ritual ablutions. A stone tunnel at the south of the lake enabled access for a flock of geese dedicated to Amun.

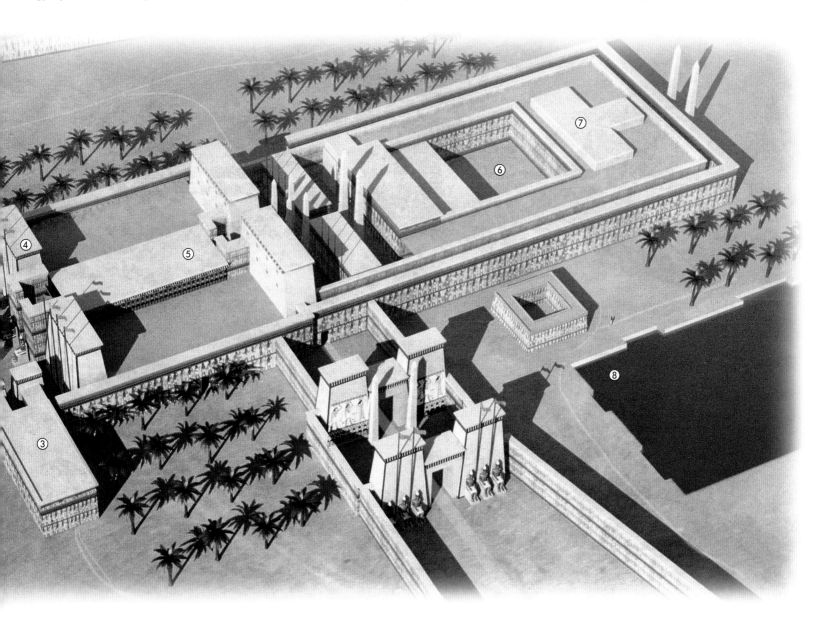

CHAPTER 9

ALEISTER CROWLEY AND THE ORDO TEMPLI ORIENTIS

Aleister Crowley, known as 'the Great Beast 666' and 'the wickedest man in the world', might not be someone who is immediately associated with spirituality. Yet he was a member of the Hermetic Order of the Golden Dawn, was the British head of the Ordo Templi Orientis (OTO), wrote *The Book of the Law* (which some people consider as scripture), re-established Thelema as a spiritual philosophy and was the patriarch of a Gnostic Church. Whatever his at times outrageous reputation, he has left a body of work – in his writings, various competing movements and in a powerful Tarot pack – that esotericists today rate very highly.

Crowley after the Golden Dawn

Aleister Crowley (1875–1947) was thrown out of the Hermetic Order of the Golden Dawn, along with its last-remaining founder, in 1900; he had been a member for less than 18 months. He remained an ally of 'MacGregor' Mathers for some four years, until the inevitable falling out between two magical adepts with equally massive egos.

Born Edward Alexander Crowley, he grew up in an Exclusive Brethren ('Plymouth Brethren') home – a strict upbringing that he spent the rest of his life rebelling against. On attaining his majority he inherited a substantial amount from his father, who had died when he was five, enabling him to live a somewhat sybaritic life with a variety of sexual partners, as well as self-publishing volumes of poetry, producing some startling paintings and becoming a very accomplished mountaineer, but it is for his occult life that Crowley became famous, or infamous.

EVENTS LEADING TO THE A∴A∴

In 1903 he married Rose Kelly, sister of the artist Gerald Kelly (who would go on to be knighted and become President of the Royal Academy). While on their honeymoon they spent a night in the King's Chamber of the Great Pyramid, and Crowley performed a ritual there. A few months later in Cairo, Rose felt drawn to the Egyptian god Horus;

when Crowley invoked him, he was visited by a spirit being called Aiwass, apparently his Holy Guardian Angel, who dictated to him *The Book of the Law* or *Liber Legis*, probably his most important occult work.

On his return to Europe, Crowley told Mathers that he had been in direct contact with the Secret Chiefs, and must therefore be made head of the (Alpha et Omega) Golden Dawn. Instead, Mathers expelled him.

In 1909 Crowley set up a very expensively produced occult journal called *The Equinox* as 'the official organ of the A∴A∴'; this was a new Order he had founded, the Argenteum Astrum (Silver Star). The journal was subtitled 'The Review of Scientific Illuminism' and had the motto 'The Method of Science – the Aim of Religion' – this was a

Right *A young-looking Aleister Crowley as 'The Magician'. This is dated 1911 in Crowley's* Confessions, *making him 36.*

combination of ideas reminiscent of earlier esotericists such as the Rosicrucians and the Hermetic Philosophers.

In the A∴A∴ Crowley taught that the way to advancement through the grades of the Order was through personal enlightenment and experience, not through performing a series of rituals with others in a lodge. *The Book of the Law* had said that he should take what was worth using from previous systems, and purge the rest. Consequently, to the fury of Mathers, who took out an injunction to try to stop him, Crowley published some of the rituals of the Golden Dawn in *The Equinox*.

The A∴A∴ never had many members, but many of today's schools of occult science follow Crowley's adaptation of the Golden Dawn system, emphasizing personal growth rather than levels in a lodge.

THELEMA

Crowley's main esoteric legacy is known as Thelema (Greek for 'will'). The term Thelemite is used loosely to describe people following his teachings, but it has a specific origin. In 1920 Crowley and a few followers set up a short-lived esoteric community in the small port of Cefalù, on the north coast of Sicily. He called it the Abbey of Thelema, after a fictional abbey in the 16th-century

Left Rose Edith Kelly (1874–1932) with Aleister Crowley and their daughter Lola Zaza. Crowley divorced Rose and committed her to an asylum for her alcoholism. She later remarried.

classic parody *Gargantua and Pantagruel* by François Rabelais. Normally monks commit themselves to poverty, chastity and obedience, but in Rabelais's Abbey of Thelema the dictum was 'Do as thou wilt shall be the whole of the Law'. Crowley adopted this, and many people (because of his hedonistic lifestyle) see it as a recipe for licence. In fact it is anything but.

Rabelais had borrowed the idea from St Augustine, who intended it to mean that those whose will was completely in line with

God's will would perform only virtuous actions, and so would need no law to compel them to do good.

As with much else from 19th- and 20th-century esotericism, this saying has been adopted by present-day Pagans, especially Wiccans – but they, as with today's Thelemites, always follow it with the second part of the saying, 'Love is the Law, Love under Will', which gives it a far more profound meaning.

A MIXED LEGACY

Crowley had a bad press throughout his life, and still has a very dubious reputation. There is no doubt he led a dissolute life. He was self-centred and a massive self-publicist, revelling even in the worst bad publicity. He delighted in labels like 'the wickedest man in the world', but he was never a Satanist. He loathed Christianity, but his life was a genuine search for union with God; many of today's esotericists rate his work very highly.

Crowley had an influence on much of modern Paganism, particularly Wicca. Gerald Gardner, the founder of Wicca, met Crowley in 1946, and Crowley made him an honorary member of the OTO. Wicca, being an initiatory esoteric religion, has similarities to aspects of the structure, ritual and teachings of the OTO, the Golden Dawn and even Freemasonry.

Aleister Crowley was self-centred and a massive self-publicist, revelling even in the worst bad publicity. He delighted in labels like 'the wickedest man in the world', although he was never a Satanist. He loathed Christianity, but his life was a genuine search for union with God; many of today's esotericists rate his work very highly.

The Book of Thoth

Crowley's own esoteric organization, Argentium Astrum, was based on the second order of the Golden Dawn, Ordo Rosae Rubeae et Aureae Crucis (RR et AC), which, like much of the Western Mystery Tradition, has a Judeo-Christian basis. It also has a strong basis in Hermeticism, which was originally the magical philosophy of Greek-inspired Egypt in the first few centuries CE. Egyptian mythology with its own complexity of gods and goddesses contributed another element.

In 1781 a French Freemason, Antoine Court de Gébelin, wrote in one volume of his massive (and somewhat unscholarly) work on myths and legends, *Le Monde Primitif*, that Tarot was an ancient Egyptian work, embodying all the wisdom of the ancients in symbolic form. In 1783 the Paris fortune-teller Etteilla picked up on this, stating that Tarot was actually *The Book of Thoth*; it was planned by Hermes Trismegistus (see page 17) and took 17 mages four years to create. This may have been pure invention, but it influenced the more serious and far more influential French occultist Éliphas Lévi, who in his *Dogme et Rituel de la Haute Magie* (1855–56) called Tarot 'of all books the most primitive'. Lévi drew correspondences between the 22 Major Trumps, the 22 Hebrew letters and the 22 paths between the Sephiroth of the Kabbalistic Tree of Life. In his own book on Tarot in 1896, Papus

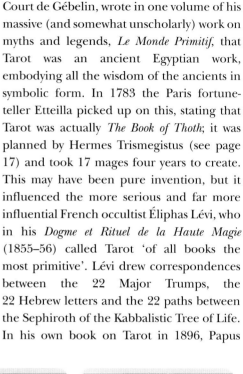

Crowley received his most vital work, *The Book of the Law*, in Egypt, and clearly felt a strong affinity with its religious heritage and symbolism.

Many centuries before Carl Jung wrote about mythological archetypes, the similarities between the gods of different cultures were noted. So, for example, the Greek god Zeus was seen as equivalent to the Roman god Jove or Jupiter; the Greek god Kronos was equivalent to the Roman Saturn; and so on.

THOTH AND THE TAROT

The Egyptian god Thoth equated with the Roman god Mercury and the Greek god Hermes. This was the messenger god, the god of communication, the traditional founder of the Arts and Sciences. Thoth was the god of wisdom and of writing, the scribe to the gods.

The Fool

Queen of Wands

The Moon

Right *The striking colours, imagery and movement found within these cards make* The Book of Thoth *an unusual and powerful Tarot pack.*

The Star

The Tower

Princess of Disks

Right *Hermes Trismegistus, in a floor mosaic by Giovanni di Stefano, Siena Cathedral, 1488. In 1614 the scholar Isaac Casaubon showed the* Corpus Hermeticum *was not as ancient as earlier believed, dating it to c.300 CE.*

(Gérard Encausse) wrote that the symbols on Tarot cards 'at once prove that the Tarot of Marseille is really the exact representation of the primitive Egyptian Tarot, slightly altered to the epoch denoted by the costumes'. So when Crowley planned his own Tarot and called it *The Book of Thoth*, he was simply following an already established esoteric tradition (see pages 70–71).

UNUSUAL IMAGES

The images in *The Book of Thoth* were painted by his close friend Lady Frieda Harris (1877–1962) and were first exhibited in 1942, five years before Crowley's death. They appeared as illustrations in Crowley's limited-edition book of the same title in 1944, but were not published as a Tarot pack until 1969.

The pictures are startling in their style, which is quite unlike that of more traditional Tarots. There are undoubted Egyptian influences on some of the cards; for example, the Hanged Man hangs from an *ankh* (the Egyptian symbol representing life), and the Moon card shows the jackal god Anubis. The three creatures on the Wheel of Fortune are the Sphinx with a sword, Hermanubis (a combination of Hermes and Anubis), and Typhon, a storm giant in Greek mythology, though, as these three creatures appeared in many earlier Tarots, they are not unique to Crowley's (or Harris's) interpretation.

There are also influences from other mythologies and esoteric cultures as well. Lady Frieda Harris was a member of Co-Masonry, a form of Freemasonry that admitted women as well as men, and so was familiar with esoteric symbolism. There also appear to be some Pagan influences on some of the images; the Fool is both a Green Man and a horned-god figure.

THE MAGUS'S THREE STAGES?

The Book of Thoth is unusual in having three Magician or Magus cards, though for divination only one of these should be used. Lady Frieda Harris painted several versions of a number of the cards, striving to capture the essence of each one perfectly, and it may be that the extra cards were alternative versions, which were included simply to fill up space on the printed sheets, and as a bonus to enable personal choice. It has been suggested, however, that the three Magician or Magus cards celebrate Hermes Trismegistus (Thrice-Great Hermes), and that they illustrate three stages in the development of a magus from child to adult to shaman. Alternatively, some believe that the three cards are a symbolic portrayal of stages of a practical work of magic.

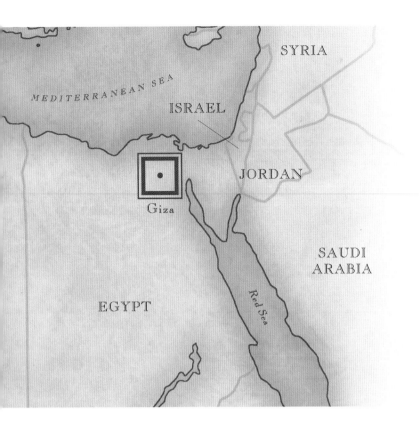

The pyramids

The pyramids of Giza, just south-west of Cairo, are the only one of the Seven Wonders of the World to survive into modern times. The three main pyramids at Giza are: the Great Pyramid, or Pyramid of Khufu or Cheops; the slightly smaller Pyramid of Khafre; and the much smaller Pyramid of Menkaure. In the same complex lie the Sphinx and numerous smaller constructions. The pyramids exerted a powerful influence over Aleister Crowley and the Golden Dawn movement.

Controversy still surrounds both why and how the pyramids were built. Scholarly Egyptologists have always believed they were the tombs of the pharaohs who built them, but there is a strong view that this was never their purpose – though there is no consensus on what, in that case, the pyramids were for.

METHOD OF CONSTRUCTION

Most theories concerning *how* they were constructed rely on ramps. The idea that the stone blocks, weighing many tonnes, were hauled up a long, straight ramp has fallen out of favour; such a ramp would take at least as much rock to build as each pyramid itself. Most theories now suggest some sort of spiral ramp, either around or inside the pyramid. Two recent theories – that kites were used to help lift the blocks into place, or that the 'stone' blocks were actually concrete poured into moulds *in situ* – have found little scholarly support.

Several popular writers have claimed that the positioning of the three pyramids at Giza mirrors exactly the three stars in Orion's Belt, though scholars tend to dismiss this. Whether or not it is so, any further claimed correlations between the pattern of other Egyptian pyramids and the whole constellation of Orion have no validity.

The three well-known pyramids and the Sphinx are only part of a huge complex of monuments known as the Giza complex or necropolis. There are also funerary temples, causeways and many smaller pyramids.

As we have seen (see page 124), in 1903 Crowley married Rose Kelly, and the couple spent a night in the King's Chamber of the Great Pyramid. Later, Rose felt inexplicably guided to an image of Horus in a museum in Cairo; and when Crowley invoked Horus in their Cairo apartment he was given the text of *The Book of the Law* or *Liber Legis*.

The pyramids have been not just an interest but an obsession for many researchers over the centuries. Sir Isaac Newton (see page 47) incorporated detailed measurements of the Great Pyramid in his work on gravity. Millennialist Christians have studied the pyramids to help them calculate the date of the Second Coming. Modern Rosicrucians including Harvey Spencer Lewis (see page 73) have based esoteric theories on their own interpretations of the pyramids.

① THE GREAT PYRAMID

The Pyramid of Khufu (pharaoh 2589–2566 BCE) is the largest of the three, originally 280 Egyptian royal cubits (147 m/481 ft) tall, though erosion and other damage – including the loss of its pyramidion capstone – have reduced its height to 139 m (455½ ft). Each side was originally nearly 231 m (758 ft) long at the base. The pyramid contains three chambers connected by passages: an unfinished one below ground level; above it the Queen's Chamber; and above that the King's Chamber with its granite sarcophagus.

② THE PYRAMID OF KHAFRE

Khufu's son Khafre was pharaoh from 2558 to 2532 BCE. Because his pyramid has a more elevated position and its sides are steeper, it actually looks higher than that of Khufu, though in fact at 138 m (454¾ ft) high – originally 146 m (478½ ft) – it is slightly lower. It contains two chambers, one (possibly a storeroom for treasure) entirely cut into the bedrock of the plateau, the other (containing a sarcophagus) with its base cut into the bedrock, but rising into the body of the pyramid. At its apex, Khafre's Pyramid still has some of the smooth white casing stones that originally covered all the pyramids. Near the end of the long causeway leading from the pyramid's mortuary temple of the Valley Temple lies the Great Sphinx.

③ THE PYRAMID OF MENKAURE

The pyramid of Khafre's son Menkaure (pharoah 2532–2503 BCE) is much smaller than the other two, but has an intricate series of corridors and chambers within it. It is now only 62 m (204 ft) high – originally 73 m (240 ft) – and its sides are 109 m (357 ft) long at the base. Although Menkaure ruled as pharaoh for nearly 30 years, his pyramid was not complete when he died; it was finished by his son Shepsekaf.

④ THE SPHINX

There are many sphinxes in Europe, some with a human head and others with a ram's head, but there is only one Great Sphinx: the largest stone sculpture in the world, at 46 m (150 ft) long. Estimates of its age differ widely, the traditional belief being that it was built by Khafre, or his father Khufu, while others claim it is much older than any of the pyramids. Much of the detail of the original carving has been lost over the centuries through weathering.

⑤ THE KHUFU SHIP

In 1954 a disassembled ship was discovered, carefully buried in a pit next to the Great Pyramid. The 44 m (143 ft) long ship has been reconstructed from its 1,200 pieces, largely of cedar planking, and is now on display in its own museum on the site. It is thought the ship, a solar barge, was buried with Khufu for his journey into the afterlife; it would carry him across the sky with the sun god Ra.

The Ordo Templi Orientis

Aleister Crowley is also closely associated with the Ordo Templi Orientis (OTO), an esoteric group founded in Germany in 1906 by Theodor Reuss (1855–1923), a journalist and opera singer. Reuss had previously attempted to set up a revived version of the Bavarian Illuminati (see pages 96–97). He then obtained a charter to form a German branch of the Rite of Memphis and Misraim (see page 115).

Above *A 1911 charter from Theodor Reuss granting Aleister Crowley membership in one of Reuss's many Orders.*

The OTO probably drew some of its ideas from both of these groups. It was also almost certainly influenced by the Hermetic Brotherhood of Light, of which a friend of Reuss, the wealthy industrialist Carl Kellner, was an initiate. Founded in 1895, this taught a system of sex-magic devised by Paschal Beverly Randolph, whose various occult societies had ended up, among other things, spawning the Fraternitas Rosae Crucis (see page 72). The Brotherhood of Light, under the leadership of C.C. Zain, became the Church of Light in 1932, and now offers correspondence courses mainly in astrology and Tarot. The interconnections between late 19th- and early 20th-century esoteric Orders were highly complicated.

CROWLEY V. REUSS

The OTO had nine degrees (with a tenth only for the head of the Order in each country); the ninth degree contained the main secrets of sex-magic. The probably apocryphal story goes that Reuss read something that Crowley had published on sex-magic (Crowley always spelt it sex-magick) and accused him of stealing the secret information of the ninth

degree of the OTO; when he realized that Crowley had come up with the material independently, he was so impressed that he initiated Crowley into the OTO immediately. In 1912 he made Crowley head of the (already existing) OTO in Britain, and Crowley took the impressive title 'Supreme and Holy King of Ireland, Iona and all the Britains within the Sanctuary of the Gnosis'.

Crowley immediately turned the British OTO Thelemic, insisting that his own *Liber Legis* or *Book of the Law* should be the volume of Sacred Law in every lodge (see page 87). Many members objected; Crowley expelled some of them. Unsurprisingly, Crowley and Reuss fell out with each other. Crowley later appointed a North American head of the OTO. In response Reuss initiated H. Spencer Lewis (who was later to found AMORC; see page 73), granting him a charter to form a lodge.

Reuss died in 1923, and Crowley appointed himself head of the OTO worldwide. Many members ignored this. At a secret conference of occultists in Germany in 1925, Crowley proclaimed that he was the sole head of all Rosicrucian-type groups in

Germany; most of the German occultists refused to accept him, though one group did accept his value as an occult teacher and translated some of his works into German. Even that was too much for some, and Germany split into pro- and anti-Crowley factions for many years.

Crowley was never successful in gaining worldwide control of the OTO or in building it up as a viable occult Order. Various fragments of the OTO continued to exist, with or without him, throughout his life and after his death in 1947; the Crowleyite groups were Thelemite (see page 125).

WORLDWIDE OTO VARIANTS

In 1969 an American, Grady McMurtry (1918–85), announced that in 1943 Crowley had appointed him his Caliph or successor; McMurtry incorporated the OTO in California with himself as its head. The 'Caliphate' OTO is now the largest version of OTO in the world, but its legitimacy is challenged by several other groups. These include the 'Typhonian' OTO, headed by British occultist Kenneth Grant (born 1924), who had actually worked with Crowley; the 'Society' OTO in America and Spain; and the Albion OTO in Britain. In an echo of the legal battles in 1928 between Fraternitas

Rosae Crucis and AMORC (both of which, like the OTO, can trace back their influences ultimately to Paschal Beverly Randolph), McMurtry's Caliphate OTO went to court to assert its legitimacy as the true successor to Crowley's OTO. OTO leaders are also patriarchs of the Gnostic Catholic Church (see page 119).

Today the OTO, in its several versions worldwide, is the successor to Crowley's Thelemic adaptation, rather than to Reuss's original OTO – and technically Crowley was

only granted jurisdiction over the British OTO. However, as we have seen throughout, legitimacy and authority are largely a matter of assertion and imaginative charters rather than of genuine lines of personal or organizational succession. Simply through existing, esoteric Orders create their own validity. Many esotericists think it regrettable that so many organizations insist on claiming a unique position and denigrating their competitors, instead of celebrating the diversity within the world of esoteric societies.

Left Aleister Crowley in highland dress with his Scarlet Woman, Leah Hirsig, at the Abbey of Thelema at Cefalú, Sicily, in 1920. Leah is holding their baby, Anna Leah (nicknamed Poupée), who died shortly afterwards aged 8 months.

Left Theodor Reuss (1855–1923), who drew on several esoteric traditions in founding the Ordo Templi Orientis.

CHAPTER 10

OPUS DEI AND THE PRIORY OF SION

In 2003 Dan Brown's thriller *The Da Vinci Code*, as well as introducing millions of new readers to ideas that had appeared 21 years earlier in *The Holy Blood and the Holy Grail* by Michael Baigent, Richard Leigh and Henry Lincoln, presented as fact a large amount of intriguing information about two organizations: Opus Dei, with its albino killer-monk Silas, and the Priory of Sion, a centuries-old protector of deeply heretical spiritual secrets. Enmeshed in the theory was the intriguing story of Abbé Bérenger Saunière and Rennes-le-Château. But was this fact or fantasy? This chapter briefly sets the record straight.

Opus Dei

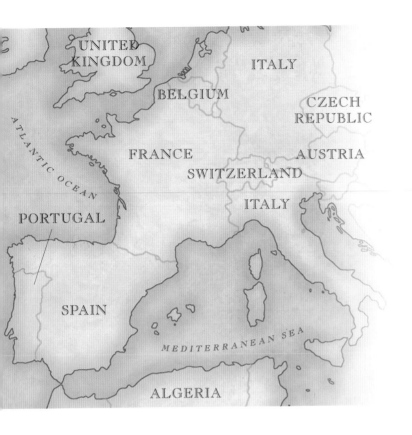

Opus Dei does not have any albino killer-monks; in fact, it does not have any monks at all. It is a lay Order, with members in many different professions. Opus Dei, meaning 'the Work of God', was founded in 1928 by a Spanish priest, Monsignor Josemaria Escrivá de Balaguer (1902–75), who was made a saint by Pope John Paul II in 2002. The aim of the organization is to encourage Catholics to make God the centre of every aspect of their lives: they dedicate themselves and all their actions to God. The message of Opus Dei is that everyone is called to holiness.

There are more than 80,000 members worldwide, over half of these in continental Europe and maybe a quarter in South America – traditional Catholic countries. The USA has around 5,000 members, while the UK has only around 500.

CRITICISM OF OPUS DEI

Pope John Paul II made Opus Dei a 'personal prelature' in 1982. This means that the Order is responsible only to the Pope, and lies completely outside the normal structures of the Roman Catholic Church. Normally a prelate, such as a bishop or archbishop, is responsible for a geographical area – a diocese or archdiocese. The prelate of Opus Dei is responsible for all the people in Opus Dei, wherever they are. This can sometimes create difficulties in parishes, when Opus Dei members give more loyalty

Left Mgr Josemaria Escrivá de Balaguer, the controversial founder of Opus Dei, was fast-tracked to sainthood.

Right A typical cilice, worn by dedicated Opus Dei members; the token pain reminds them of Christ's suffering.

to the organization than to their parish priest and bishop.

Because of this dedication, the communal living of many members and their utter commitment to the cause, Opus Dei has come in for much criticism. It has been accused of being a secret society within the Catholic Church. In the time of Pope John Paul II, who greatly admired the organization, it gained considerable power and influence within the Church. There are persistent rumours of antagonism between Opus Dei and the Jesuits, who, with their open loyalty to the Pope, used to hold much the same power.

Opus Dei has also received some criticism because of its very conservative nature. Escrivá himself supported Franco in the Spanish Civil War, and the organization has had connections with several ultra-right-wing regimes. It has also been censured because it aims particularly for professional people, for high-pressure recruitment of students and even Catholic high-school pupils. Although he was careful not to criticize the organization directly, in 1981 the then-Archbishop of Westminster, Cardinal Basil Hume, set out strict guidelines for Opus Dei's recruitment of young people.

OPUS DEI'S RESPONSE

Many non-Opus Dei Catholics felt that the canonization of Escrivá was pushed through with unseemly haste, just 27 years after his death, and that serious concerns about both Escrivá himself and the organization he founded had been ignored. In response, Opus Dei points to its aim: spreading the message of universal holiness.

It is debatable whether *The Da Vinci Code* has done Opus Dei more harm than good. It has misled many people about the nature of the organization, but the resultant publicity has also provided an opportunity for Opus Dei to explain what it really is.

MEMBERSHIP

There are three main levels of membership. Nearly one-third of all members are called numeraries. They live in single-sex residences, take a commitment to celibacy and give most of their income to support work done by Opus Dei members. Around one-fifth are associates; they do not live in residences, but otherwise make similar commitments to the numeraries. Around half of all members are called supernumeraries; they live in the wider community and may be married with families. Opus Dei tends to attract well-educated (and well-off) professionals – engineers, lawyers, teachers, businesspeople and those who have some influence in the world – even a former British Cabinet minister is a member. Although it is overwhelmingly a lay organization, around 2 per cent of Opus Dei's members are priests.

In Dan Brown's novel, Silas flagellates himself with a scourge until his back is running with blood. A minority of dedicated Catholics have performed this sort of action over the centuries, partly as a penance for their sin, and partly in order to 'share' the pain of Christ on the Cross. The cilice, which Silas also uses, is a metal chain bracelet worn around the upper thigh; sharp points on the inside prick painfully into the skin, though usually without drawing blood. Those members of Opus Dei who use the cilice might wear it for an hour or so a day as a form of corporal mortification.

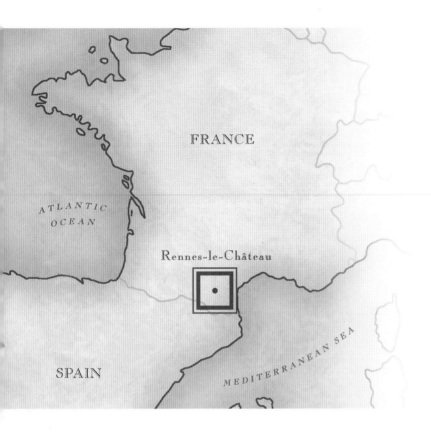

The mystery of Rennes-le-Château

In 1885 a young priest, Abbé Bérenger Saunière (1852–1917), took up his post at the church of Sainte Marie-Madeleine in Rennes-le-Château, a remote hilltop village in the French Pyrenees. A few years later Saunière suddenly started spending money on repairing and redecorating the church, building a new home, entertaining lavishly, and improving the village itself.

Where did the money for this largesse come from? What was Abbé Saunière's secret?

In 1982 *The Holy Blood and the Holy Grail* exploded on the scene, with its complex series of historical speculations about the bloodline of Jesus and the Priory of Sion. Written by Michael Baigent, Richard Leigh and Henry Lincoln, the book devoted a lot of attention to Bérenger Saunière and his supposed discoveries at Rennes-le-Château.

THE ABBÉ'S STORY

At its simplest, the story is that Saunière, having borrowed a little money, was doing some much-needed renovations to the church. While repairing the altar he found that one of the stone pillars supporting it was hollow, and concealed within it were four parchments. Saunière took these to Paris to be evaluated by scholars at Saint-Sulpice.

The documents, it is said, contained evidence that – if made public – could have caused the vast edifice of Christianity to crumble into dust. Evidence, perhaps, that Jesus had survived the crucifixion, or that he had fathered a line of descendants that

continued to the present day. Whatever the secret was, it must be suppressed; and so Saunière was paid (by the Vatican?) to keep his mouth shut.

In the 1960s copies of these supposed parchments surfaced. Two contained detailed genealogies; the other two contained Latin texts, but with the words run together and with anomalies in the lettering. One included a simple but enigmatic statement about the Merovingian King Dagobert II of France (c.650–79); the other, after very complex decryption, contained a puzzling text about a shepherdess, the painter Poussin and blue apples. Geometric analysis of this, and of various paintings by Poussin, has led some authors to claim that it reveals where Jesus's body is buried, among other things.

Saunière repaired and redecorated the church, supposedly including heterodox imagery. He built the Villa Bethania, and the Tour Magdala for his library; he paid for a new road to the village. There are also reports that he would go out at night, on his own, digging in the graveyard. The mystery grew and grew. He would make secret trips away

from Rennes-le-Château, but nobody knew where he went. One visitor to the little mountaintop village was Archduke Johann von Habsburg, a cousin of Emperor Franz Joseph of Austria. Another was Emma Calvé, the renowned opera singer, who had a serious interest in the occult; some have speculated that Saunière had a relationship with her.

Or did he have a relationship with his maid, Marie Denarnaud (1868–1953), a girl 16 years his junior? After all, he placed the Villa Bethania in her name, and she lived there for 35 years after his death. She apparently told people in Rennes-le-Château that they were walking on gold; she promised to reveal the truth before she died, but a stroke left her without speech, so Saunière's secrets went with Marie to her grave.

Saunière's own death is shrouded in mystery. Marie apparently ordered his coffin five days before he had the stroke that killed him. He is said to have died unshriven, because the priest who came to give him the Last Rites refused to absolve him of his sins – and was so horrified by what he had been told that he never smiled again.

AN ELABORATE HOAX

The problem with the entire story of Bérenger Saunière is that there was no mystery at all about him before the mid-1950s. Noël Corbu, who bought the Villa Bethania from Marie Denarnaud, turned it into a restaurant and hotel. Because of its remote location it was unsuccessful, so to drum up trade Corbu told a local newspaper that Saunière had discovered treasure in Rennes-le-Château – and the whole story began to develop. Gérard de Sède wrote it up as a book in *L'Or de Rennes* (1967), later retitled *Le Trésor Maudit* (The Cursed Treasure). Pierre Plantard incorporated the story of Saunière's mysterious parchments and unexplained wealth into the *Dossiers Secrets* of the Priory of Sion. Next Baigent, Leigh and Lincoln brought the story to the attention of the world outside France.

The enciphered 'parchments' are modern forgeries. Saunière made his money by selling private Masses, for which he was disciplined by the Church. Nevertheless the mystery of Rennes-le-Château refuses to go away, with frequent new revelations and refutations. Perhaps the full truth will never be known.

Above *The Tour Magdala on the hilltop at Rennes-le-Château. Saunière built it as his library and study.*

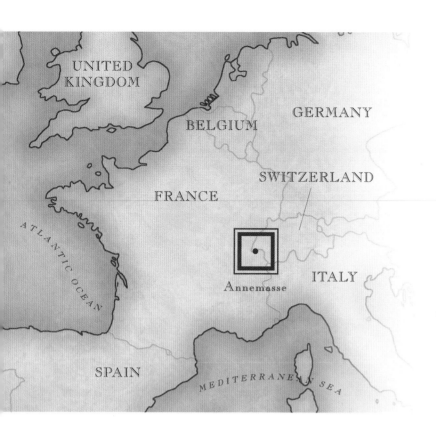

The Priory of Sion

According to the list of 'facts' at the beginning of The Da Vinci Code, *'The Priory of Sion – a European secret society founded in 1099 – is a real organization'. It then mentions 'parchments known as Les Dossiers Secrets' found in the Bibliothèque Nationale in Paris in 1975, listing leaders of the Priory of Sion including Leonardo da Vinci. The documents existed, but were not parchments; they were ordinary typed sheets of paper, and had been deposited at the Bibliothèque Nationale in the 1960s.*

Although Michael Baigent and Richard Leigh, two of the authors of *The Holy Blood and the Holy Grail*, lost their breach-of-copyright case, the judge ruled that significant portions of Dan Brown's novel – specifically the Leigh Teabing 'lectures' – had clearly been based on the book by Baigent, Leigh and Lincoln

THE STORY OF JESUS' BLOODLINE

The story, as now believed by many thousands (if not millions) of people, is that the Priory of Sion is the ultimate secret society. It was founded, we are told, in 1099, and the Knights Templar were set up as its military and administrative arm. Its purpose was to protect the explosive secret that Jesus was married to Mary Magdalene and had a child by her. After the crucifixion (which Jesus may or may not have survived, depending on the version), the Magdalene fled to the south of France with her child. Over the centuries the bloodline of Jesus married into the French royal line of the Merovingians.

When the Knights Templar were founded, their first task was to dig tunnels under

Left The Da Vinci Code *made numerous factual errors about Leonardo da Vinci, including calling him by his birthplace instead of his name. There is no evidence that Leonardo had any heretical beliefs, let alone that he was Grand Master of a fictional secret society.*

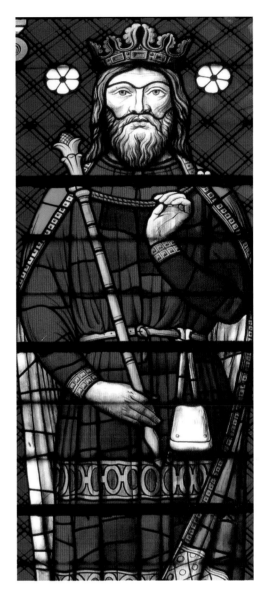

The Priory of Sion is a completely modern creation that has nothing to do with the Merovingians, the Knights Templar, Leonardo or Sir Isaac Newton.

Temple Mount in Jerusalem (see pages 30–31); there they found proof of the holy bloodline, the family tree of Jesus, perhaps the bones of Mary Magdalene and even treasure. In Dan Brown's version, the documents about Jesus filled 'four enormous trunks'.

The Templars went to Scotland and became the Freemasons (see page 76), filling Rosslyn Chapel with their symbolism (see pages 31, 79 and 140); but behind the scenes, the Priory of Sion – with Leonardo da Vinci, Victor Hugo, Claude Debussy and Jean Cocteau among its Grand Masters – held on to their secrets. Other Grand Masters were luminaries among the Hermetic Philosophers, Rosicrucians, early Freemasons and the founders of the Royal Society: Robert Fludd, Johann Valentin Andreae, Robert Boyle and Sir Isaac Newton (see pages 64, 66 and 69). The Grand Master in the 1980s was Pierre Plantard.

PLANTARD'S IMAGININGS
In fact Pierre Plantard, who had a somewhat chequered past, created the Priory of Sion with three friends in 1956, in the French town of Annemasse. Initially, the Priory of Sion appears to have been little more than a tiny right-wing Catholic group that was focused on chivalric ideas and involved in local politics; it was named after a nearby hill, the Col du Mt Sion.

Like several people in genuine secret societies, including the Chevalier Ramsay (see pages 76–77) and 'MacGregor' Mathers (see pages 106–107), Plantard was an ardent royalist. He wanted to re-establish the French monarchy, specifically the Merovingian dynasty that was ousted by the Carolingians in 751 CE. He also believed, or at least claimed, that he was a descendant of the Merovingian line. When he came across the now well-known story of Abbé Bérenger Saunière and Rennes-le-Château (see pages 136–137), he incorporated it into his own fantasies of self-importance, and the Priory of Sion was reborn.

DEBUNKING THE MYTH
Whether there is any genuine mystery about Saunière and Rennes-le-Château is open to legitimate debate. However, the Priory of Sion – as first written about by Baigent, Leigh and Lincoln and then by Dan Brown – is a completely modern creation that has nothing to do with the Merovingians, or with the Knights Templar, Leonardo or Sir Isaac Newton. Plantard was clearly knowledgeable about the esoteric history of Europe, and inserted a lot of 'validating' details into his creation, just as many secret societies create an 'authenticating' lineage (see pages 72, 84 and 104). Interestingly, Plantard claimed that in his youth he knew Georges Monti, who had been secretary to Joséphan Péladan, founder of the Kabbalistic Order of the Rosy Cross and the Catholic Order of the Rose+Cross (see page 71). Among the ideas Plantard borrowed from earlier societies was an unusual detail from the Brotherhood of the Golden and Rosy Cross (see pages 70 and 81), that the Grand Masters were all known as 'John' with an identifying number.

As for *The Da Vinci Code*'s claim that the Priory of Sion 'had another, more important duty as well – to protect the bloodline itself', this had nothing to do with Plantard's fantasies, but was entirely the invention of Baigent, Leigh and Lincoln in *The Holy Blood and the Holy Grail*. However, because of Dan Brown's novel, the Priory of Sion has taken on a completely spurious reality in many people's minds, in a similar way to the Illuminati (see pages 95–101).

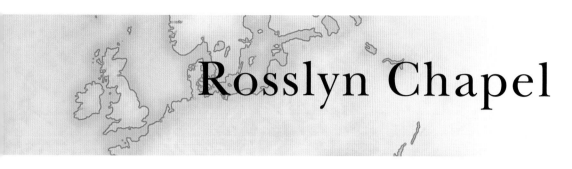

Rosslyn Chapel

Rosslyn Chapel is a small church with a mystery greatly out of proportion to its size. Some call it an esoteric art gallery, others a treasure house of Templar or Masonic imagery. Some believe that it holds the secret of the Holy Grail. Since its inclusion in The Da Vinci Code, *speculation about the chapel has reached new heights, and careless or deliberate misinformation is rife.*

Rosslyn Chapel is situated near the small Scottish village of Roslin, a few miles south of Edinburgh. The barons of Roslin – and later the Earls of Caithness – were an important family in the 15th and 16th centuries; their family name was Sinclair or St Clair (see pages 78–79). Sir William Sinclair (one of several with that name) commissioned the church, and it was built in 1440–46.

SHAPE, SIZE AND NAME OF THE CHURCH

There is an argument over whether the church was always meant to be its present shape and size, or whether it comprises just the choir and sanctuary of what was intended to be a larger church. Speculative 'historians' who argue for the former claim (with no evidence) that the chapel's layout is a copy of Herod's Temple in Jerusalem, with the large end wall supposedly copying the Wailing Wall. In contrast, genuine historians believe it is the chancel of what was originally intended to be a larger church; they point to the evidence of foundations for the unbuilt nave and transept, and show that the end wall is simply one side of the transept. In fact, Rosslyn Chapel was one of 42 'collegiate churches' built in Scotland in the mid-13th to mid-16th centuries, half of them (like Rosslyn) in the 15th century. They were private family churches where the dead could

be laid, and a small 'college' of priests would pray for the repose of their souls.

Even the name Rosslyn has been subject to misinterpretation, with some claiming erroneously that it refers to the Rose Line, a meridian line supposedly passing through the chapel. Neither does it mean 'ancient knowledge through the ages', as some writers have claimed. In fact Rosslyn and Roslin come from the Celtic words *ros*, meaning a promontory or point, and *lyn*, which means a waterfall.

CARVINGS

Rosslyn Chapel is full of carvings, many of which can be interpreted symbolically. This is true of carvings in any church; in fact the only difference is that there are so many of them in Rosslyn Chapel, representing characters and events from the Bible. Any supposedly Templar or Masonic symbolism arises simply because the Templars and Masons adopted existing Christian symbolism.

A carving of a head with a gash on the forehead is said to represent both the slain apprentice Mason who carved the pillar and Hiram Abiff, the legendary Mason of Solomon's Temple, whose story is re-enacted in the third-degree ritual of Freemasonry (see page 87). However, this head has been greatly altered over the years to make it represent the apprentice of the legend. The

gash is not original; even in the mid-19th century it was only a daub of paint. Originally the head was bearded; the beard has been crudely chiselled away to make the head look like that of a young man, the apprentice.

One carving of a man with horns holding a stone tablet has been interpreted as the Devil recording lost souls – a strange image for a church. In fact it is Moses with the Ten Commandments, based on a mistranslation of Exodus 34:29–30 in pre-Reformation bibles, stating that Moses had horns when he came down from Mount Sinai. (The correct translation is that his face shone.)

① THE APPRENTICE PILLAR

The legend says that the Master Mason, commissioned to carve a complex pillar from a drawing, went to Italy to study the original. On his return he found that his apprentice had carved a beautiful and intricate pillar. He was so consumed with envy that he struck his apprentice on the head, killing him. However, detailed documentation of the Sinclair family and Rosslyn Chapel in the late 17th century does not mention this legend, which can only be traced back to the late 18th century, and which can also be found in other churches.

② PILLARS AND ARCHES

There is a total of 14 pillars in the Rosslyn chapel, forming an arcade of 12 pointed arches on three sides of the nave. Each pillar is heavily decorated with intricate carvings.

③ GREEN MEN

The chapel features more than 110 carvings of Green Men, with one excellent example on the east wall. Some writers claim that these show Pagan symbolism and that Rosslyn was therefore heretical, or even not a Christian church. But the Green Man, who is often found in old churches, is a good example of the Christianizing of a Pagan symbol; instead of representing nature and fertility, it now symbolizes immortality, and Christ taking on human form.

④ MUSICAL CEILING

The stone arched roof is covered in squares, many showing stars or flowers. Two researchers, father and son, believe that the different patterns on the stones encode a piece of music using certain harmonic intervals, such as the augmented fourth, which the Church had banned as 'the Devil's chord'.

CHAPTER 11

HELL-FIRE CLUBS

Satanic rituals, with young women lying naked on black-clad altars and defrocked priests performing black Masses over them ... One member, the MP John Wilkes, once smuggled in a baboon dressed in a black cloak and released it during a ceremony; it leaped on to the shoulder of Lord Sandwich, who cried out in fear, thinking it was the Devil come to claim him ... Such are the fictional stories told about the infamous Hell-Fire Club. The reality is just as colourful.

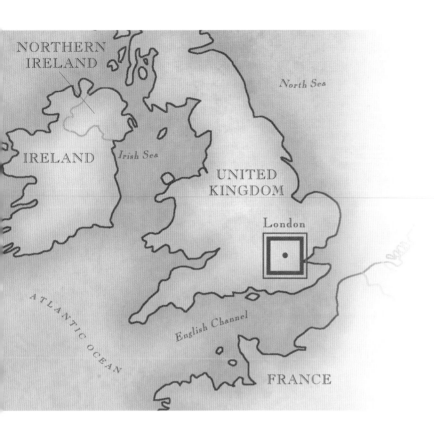

The original Hell-Fire Club

In the middle of the 18th century, it is said, there was a special club for high-born gentlemen. They would meet and indulge in Satanic rituals and sexual licentiousness. They were the Hell-Fire Club, and their wicked leader was Sir Francis Dashwood of Medmenham Abbey. But this standard telling of the story is factually incorrect in several details.

Sir Francis Dashwood's group was never called the Hell-Fire Club, but was the Friars of St Francis of Wycombe, or the Monks of Medmenham, and it was just one of many such clubs, not only in Britain, but around Europe – and almost certainly none of them was actually Satanic.

London was full of clubs, some meeting in the fashionable coffee houses, others in taverns. Some were political, admitting only Whigs or Tories; others were literary; still others were clearly for fun. Some of the clubs established in the early 18th century are still the most exclusive gentlemen's clubs in London today, guarding their membership partly by the sheer cost of belonging to them, and partly by the process of either accepting or 'blackballing' potential members – existing members voting on their admission by putting white or black balls in a ballot box.

Francis Dashwood had nothing to do with the actual Hell-Fire Club; he was only 11 years old when it was founded in London around 1719 by Philip, Duke of Wharton (1698–1731), but Dashwood must later have been influenced by a club condemned in the *London Gazette* as 'impious and blasphemous'.

Opposite Somerset House, between the Strand and the River Thames, London, at the time of its use for meetings of the Hell-Fire Club. Illustrated by Jan Kip for John Strype's 1720 revision of Stow's Survey of London.

Left Philip, Duke of Wharton (1698–1731), prominent politician, notorious womanizer, gambler and drinker, who founded the original Hell-Fire Club in London in 1719.

WHARTON'S CLUB

Wharton was a strong Jacobite supporter; indeed, the Old Pretender James Stuart, son of James II, made him (Jacobite) Duke of Northumberland in 1716. King George I made him first Duke of Wharton in 1718, probably to try to gain his allegiance and support for the Hanoverian monarchy. Wharton was a prominent, influential and very outspoken politician; in a House of Lords debate on investment in the South Sea Company in 1721 he insulted the Earl Stanhope so strongly that Stanhope burst a blood vessel and died the next day. Wharton himself lost £120,000 in the South Sea Bubble – a vast amount at the time.

Although he was a lord, Wharton was in every way anti-establishment; he was an atheist and a liberal freethinker, a libertarian, a womanizer, a gambler and a very heavy drinker. He set out to shock 'respectable' society by mocking the established Churches in his Hell-Fire Club, originally in the George and Vulture tavern near the Bank of England in the City of London.

Very unusually, his club's membership of about 40 included women as well as men, including Wharton's mistress, Lady Mary Wortley Montagu, a leading feminist intellectual and one of the greatest society beauties of her day. The meals included Breast of Venus (poussin, or young chicken, topped with a cherry to look like a nipple), Devil's Loins, Holy Ghost Pie and a drink called Hell-Fire Punch.

There were other similar clubs, including at least two Hell-Fire Clubs in Ireland. The main activities were eating thoroughly good meals and drinking very large amounts of alcohol; some clubs also used the privacy of closed doors and a very select membership to indulge in sexual licence.

Wharton's club, which met in several establishments in central London, including the prestigious Somerset House off the Strand, achieved its aim of upsetting the right people; it was roundly condemned by both the Lord Chancellor and King George I, who issued an Order in Council to suppress 'immorality and profaneness'.

THE ANTIENT NOBLE ORDER OF THE GORMOGONS

Wharton closed his club shortly afterwards, when he went on to become Grand Master of the Grand Lodge of Freemasonry for a year (see page 85). When it was made clear that he would not be allowed to promote the Jacobite cause within Freemasonry, he left not only the post, but the society itself. He then set up a Jacobite equivalent of the Freemasons, the Antient Noble Order of the Gormogons, which held its Grand Chapter in a tavern in London's Fleet Street and lasted from 1724 until Wharton's death in 1731.

Following in the tradition of the Hell-Fire Club mocking the Christian Church, its main purpose appears to have been to ridicule Freemasonry; for example, members coming to it from Freemasonry had to burn their Masonic apron and gloves before being initiated. In a further mocking gesture, the foundation legend of the Order of the Gormogons asserted that it had been created by the first emperor of China; it also claimed that the Czar of Russia was a member.

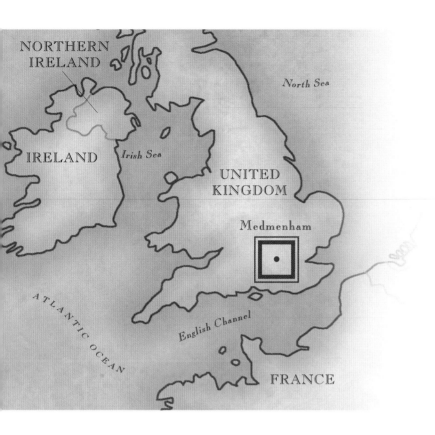

The monks of Medmenham

When Sir Francis Dashwood (1708–81) founded his own club sometime between 1742 and 1752, initially in a central London tavern (probably the George and Vulture again, but possibly the George, an old coaching inn that still stands near London Bridge railway station), it had the same essential qualities as the Duke of Wharton's Hell-Fire Club.

Again, this was a high-class club for 'society' gentlemen; Dashwood's co-founder was John Montagu, Earl of Sandwich (1718–92), after whom both the humble sandwich and the Sandwich Islands (the original name of Hawaii) were named.

Around 1752–53 Dashwood moved his club to Medmenham Abbey, near West Wycombe, west of London. It had originally been a Cistercian abbey, built around 1200, but was closed down by Henry VIII and passed into private ownership; Dashwood leased it from its owners in 1751.

PAGAN INFLUENCES

He had visited the early excavations of the House of Mysteries at Pompeii in 1748, and now set about re-creating what might be called 'brothel art' in frescoes at the abbey. Following the currently fashionable Gothic style, he built a ruined tower, a cloister and what were euphemistically called 'hermits' cells'. In the grounds he erected phallic and voluptuous female statuary in classic Greco-Roman style, celebrating the Pagan deities and their freedoms, and clearly acknowledging the sacredness of sexuality.

Dashwood was deeply interested in the Pagan religions. The Eleusinian Mysteries, one of the ancient Greek Mystery Religions (see page 16), had held secret ceremonies in caves, probably symbolizing and celebrating fertility, for selected initiates. It is known that the 'monks' of Medmenham were visited by 'nuns'; at least one authority has suggested that the 'chapter room', to which only the inner circle of the group were admitted, was used for some form of sex-magic rituals. Nobody knows for certain, because (like initiates of most secret societies) the 'monks' were sworn to secrecy – and, again like most, they kept their secrets.

MEMBERS IN HIGH PLACES

What is perhaps most surprising to present-day observers of the monks of Medmenham is their high position in society. Sir Francis Dashwood himself was elected a Member of Parliament in 1741, and was appointed Chancellor of the Exchequer in 1762. He was elevated to the House of Lords as Lord le Despenser in 1763, and later became Postmaster-General. In all, Dashwood spent 40 years of his life in Parliament. Other

'DO WHAT THOU WILT'

Above a doorway at Medmenham Abbey was inscribed *Fay Ce Que Voudras*, 'Do what thou wilt', the quotation from François Rabelais's *Gargantua and Pantagruel* that would later be used by Aleister Crowley (see page 125). Dashwood wrote:

Man has a natural right to be free ... by Freedom is not nor can be meant that every individual should act as he lists, and according as he is swayed by his own Passions, Vices or Infirmities: but freedom is a right every man has to do what he will with his own.

Right '*Sir Francis Dashwood at his Devotions*', *William Hogarth, late 1750s. This parodic painting shows the famous libertine dressed as a monk, making his devotions before a nude female figure.*

Dragoons. In London 'she' dressed as a woman, but took an active role as a diplomat at the end of the Seven Years War. London society laid down bets totalling £120,000 on what sex D'Eon was. 'She' spent the last 33 years of 'her' long life as a woman – but was discovered to be a man when she died.

Benjamin Franklin was another close friend of Dashwood and a frequent visitor to Medmenham Abbey. Dashwood was elected to the Royal Society (see page 69) in 1746, and Franklin in 1757. Perhaps the ultimate irony is that Dashwood (forever incorrectly associated with the licentious Hell-Fire Club) and Franklin together wrote a revised edition of the *Book of Common Prayer*, which became widely used in Episcopalian churches in America.

Below The Temple of Music on an island in the lake at West Wycombe Park was inspired by the Temple of Vesta in Rome, and used as a theatre for Sir Francis Dashwood's entertainments.

members of Dashwood's society included: John Montagu, the Earl of Sandwich; his rival, the controversial John Wilkes, MP; George Bubb Dodington, MP, who became Lord Melcombe; and John Stuart, the Earl of Bute (son-in-law of Lady Mary Wortley Montagu), who became Prime Minister. For a while, Britain was actually governed by the Friars of St Francis – another good reason for keeping their oath of secrecy.

Probably not actually a member, but certainly a close friend of Dashwood and the Earl of Sandwich and others in their circle, was the Chevalier D'Eon (1728–1810), one of the most confusing cross-dressers in history. Was he Charles D'Eon or was she Charlotte Genevieve D'Eon Beaumont? As a member of the French Secret Service, 'she' undertook espionage in Russia, fooling the Empress; back in France, 'he' was a captain in the

CHAPTER 12

SECRET SOCIETIES OF THE EAST

Some secret societies move very far from their origins. This chapter explores the ancient antecedents of four Eastern secret societies. The Triads of China were originally monks and freedom-fighters against the oppressive rulers of their country, but are infamous today for organized crime. In Japan the Ninja were fighters who were prepared to flout the usual rules of warfare, to spy, deceive and assassinate, while the Yakuza, according to their own mythology, were formed in the 19th century to defend villages against marauding bandits. In India, the Thuggees were feared throughout the 18th and early 19th centuries, when they waylaid and murdered travellers, killing with a cold efficiency. As with other underground societies, it is often difficult to distinguish between myth and reality in their history; this chapter tries to reveal something of the truth behind the fiction.

The Triads' origins

Like the Freemasons, the Triads have a traditional history. And, like the Freemasons, the factual accuracy of their traditional history should not be assumed. The Triads are thought to have begun formally in China around 1750–60, though the usual story dates back nearly a century earlier. (Other, more fanciful accounts put the origins way back in the mists of time.) Unlike the Freemasons, the Triads began as a grassroots political resistance movement.

Right A fresco painting at the Shaolin Monastery of monks practising kung fu.

The standard Triad legend states that in 1674 troops of the hated Manchu government, which had recently taken over from the Ming dynasty of the native Han people, destroyed a major Shaolin Buddhist monastery. The Shaolin, who traditionally date back to c.500 CE, practised martial arts (specifically kung fu) as an aid to their meditation. They were renowned as fighting monks, and during the Ming dynasty were often in the forefront of battle. Now the Shaolin were outlawed, the temples were closed and the practice of kung fu was punishable by death.

Five monks survived the attack. They endured years of long travels and hardship, banding together as a brotherhood dedicated to ridding China of the Manchu-led Qing (Ch'ing) dynasty. These five taught the members of the resistance movement against the Qing the fighting techniques of kung fu. Their rallying cry was 'Subvert the Qing, Restore the Ming'. They were what would be known today as a popular liberation front. The Shaolin temples were allowed to reopen in the early 19th century, but only for religious purposes; the teaching and practice of kung fu in the temples were illegal.

THE WHITE LOTUS SOCIETY

Whether their origin legend is true or not, the organization was certainly active from around 1760 right through the 19th century, leading insurrections against the Manchu overlords. Other similar groups sprang up, sometimes known by the generic term of Triads, but more usually as Tongs, which simply means halls or meeting places, the equivalent of Masonic lodges. Some Tongs, indeed, were much older than the kung-fu-fighting Shaolin monks; the White Lotus Society, another Buddhist group, fought to liberate China from the Kublai Khan's Mongols as far back as the 14th century. They came from a heterodox Buddhist sect influenced both by Daoism and by Manicheism (see page 13) – a dualist Gnostic religion that sprang up in Persia in the 3rd century CE, and retained a small but strong presence in the Middle East for some centuries; there were Manicheans in China from the 6th century right up to the early 20th century.

The White Lotus Society resurfaced in the late 18th and early 19th centuries in rebellion against the Manchu dynasty, alongside the Illustrious Worthies and the White Cloud. Other similar groups through the centuries include the Red (or Carnation-Painted) Eyebrows Society, the Copper Horses, the Iron Shins, the Yellow Turbans, the Three Incense Sticks and the White Feather.

These were politically inspired secret societies, capable of raising insurgence against the government throughout China. They were disciplined, well led and strongly motivated, partly because their leaders were often failed candidates for the Chinese civil service; they would thus be well educated, but have a deep grudge against authority. In far-flung rural areas where government authority did not quite reach, they were often the effective government.

THE BOXER REBELLION

Resistance against the governing powers culminated in the Boxer Rebellion of November 1899 to September 1901. This was led by the Fist for Righteous Harmony Society; several other groups were involved,

Above *An execution during the failed Boxer Rebellion, from* Le Petit Parisien, *January 1901.*

including the Triads. Next, through subtle manipulation by the Empress Dowager Cixi (the last ruler of the Manchu dynasty), the various secret societies – formerly enemies of the Manchu – turned their attention to the even more hated Westerners, particularly the British, who were seeking to impose their will on the Chinese in trade, technology, politics and religion. It was called the Boxer Rebellion by the British, as a loose description of the ferocious kung-fu-style fighting.

When the Boxer Rebellion failed, it meant the end of the Manchu dynasty, but also the end of the Triads and all the other secret societies; their members scattered – only to surface in a different form a few years later.

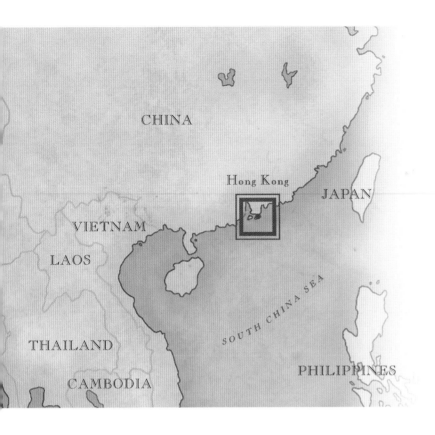

The Triads today

After the fall of the Qing dynasty in 1911, the original purpose of the various Triad societies had been achieved. During the war between the Republicans and the Communists, both sides made use of Triad fighters, but after the Communists took control in 1949 all secret societies were outlawed. The Triads went underground. They were de facto criminals; now they began to indulge in criminal activity.

Many members moved to Hong Kong, which had been a British colony from the mid-19th century, and by the 1950s and 1960s organized crime in Hong Kong was largely under the control of the Triads – probably with the active cooperation of some elements of the police. Despite the Triads being outlawed in mainland China, many trading ports became centres of Triad activity.

TRIAD AND TONG MEMBERSHIP

From the late 19th century onwards, with the freer flow of many peoples around the world, numbers of Chinese emigrated to the West. They took the Triads with them – not as a fighting force, but more as a sort of fraternal society, a way of sticking together and of protecting ordinary people.

That is one of several reasons why they are often compared to the Freemasons. The Triads have highly complex initiation ceremonies based on esoteric religious beliefs, in which new members are given the traditional history of the movement and various secrets, including recognition signs; they swear to obey the rules of the lodge (or Tong) and to give mutual support to other

members; and they are sworn to secrecy. There are said to be strong resemblances between some of the Triad initiation rituals and the Masonic symbolism of third-degree and some side-degree rituals, with a special emphasis on resurrection. Each Tong has a hierarchy of officers from master to messengers, analogous to those of a Masonic lodge. One major difference (in addition, of course, to the criminal nature of the Triads) is that Tongs operate independently of each other; there is no equivalent of a Grand Lodge controlling and coordinating the activities of all the Tongs in a Triad. This means that there can be fierce competition between individual Tongs, sometimes leading to bloody turf wars. Usually these stay within the confines of the Triads themselves, though sometimes the wider Chinese community can be affected.

THE TRIADS IN BRITAIN

Triads have operated in Britain since the 1950s; one group in particular, the Hong Kong 14K Triad, was heavily involved in drug-trafficking in London and several other major cities. When it was clear in the mid-

1980s that Hong Kong would be returned to China, large numbers of Chinese left Hong Kong to come to Britain. With them came several major Triad groups; these included the Wo On Lok and the San Yee On, which brought with them their expertise in gambling and money-laundering. The Wo On Lok is strongest in Manchester, while the 14K is still strong in London and Liverpool.

The Triads exercise a powerful control over Chinese businesses, including the omnipresent Chinese restaurants; like the Mafia, the flipside of looking after your own people is the protection racket, whereby businesses pay the equivalent of a regular insurance premium to ensure that they are not smashed up and closed down.

By 2001 there were around a quarter of a million Chinese in Britain. The Triads recruit mainly from the Chinese population, including second-generation (British-born) Chinese. In the course of the 20th century the Triads spread out from China to other countries of the Far East. Triads in Britain now also include members from Malaysia, Singapore, Vietnam and other countries, in addition to China.

THE TRIADS IN AMERICA

In the USA, while the Mafia has always been strong in industrial cities such as Chicago and on the eastern seaboard, the Triads (usually known as Tongs in America) have traditionally been strong on the west coast, particularly in California. Now, however, they are spreading in chinatown areas of cities throughout the country.

As in Britain, they now include members from other Far Eastern countries. Their criminal activities range from street gangs, through the shady side of the entertainment business (gambling, prostitution, drugs), to sophisticated credit-card fraud and semi-legitimate businesses engaged in money-laundering.

Until recently the Chinese government has, at least publicly, treated the Triads as a troublesome aspect of trading ports, and specifically of Hong Kong. Since the beginning of the 21st century, however, it has admitted that they are a major criminal problem throughout China, dealing in drugs, illegal migrants, prostitution, extortion and murder.

Below Hong Kong c.1890. Hong Kong and other trading ports around China were to become centres of Triad criminal activity throughout the 20th century.

The Forbidden City, Beijing

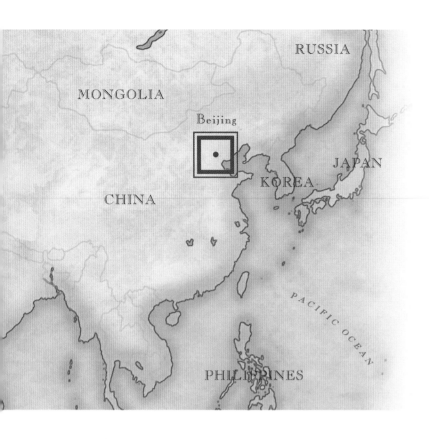

The Triads began in the 1760s in opposition to the Manchu emperors of the Qing dynasty who ruled China from 1644 to 1911. The Qing were aristocrats, seen by most Chinese people (the Han) as oppressive foreigners. Although the Forbidden City was originally built by the Ming emperors, it became the centre of rule of the hated Qing emperors who overthrew them.

Situated in the centre of Beijing, north of Tiananmen Square, the Forbidden City is the largest palace complex in the world. Construction began in 1407, in the fifth year of the third emperor of the Ming dynasty, and was completed in 1420. Legend says that one million workers were needed to construct the city, which is said to have 9,999 rooms in some 980 buildings, within 90 different palaces. Over about 500 years, 24 emperors from the Ming and Qing dynasties ruled over China from here.

Most of the buildings were roofed with yellow glazed tiles, yellow being a royal colour, but the royal library was roofed with black tiles, because of a belief that as black represented water it could extinguish fire.

The emperor was seen as the son of heaven, and so his palace was sacred, and forbidden to ordinary people – hence the name Forbidden City. No trees were allowed to grow within the entire complex, because nothing must be seen as higher than the emperor. A more practical reason might be that assassins could hide in trees. To deter assassins tunnelling under the city, the bricks in the foundations were laid 15 layers deep, with alternate layers lengthwise and crosswise.

TAIHEMEN SQUARE

The entrance at the southern end of the Forbidden City is through the Meridian Gate into a huge courtyard, Taihemen Square (meaning Gate of Supreme Harmony), which has five bridges over the Golden Water River. These symbolize the five Confucian virtues: humanity, duty, wisdom, reliability and ceremonial propriety. Only the Emperor could use the central bridge; the two on either side were used by members of the royal family, while the two outer bridges were for court officials.

① CEREMONIAL HALLS

Within Taihemen Square three halls stand on a three-tiered white marble terrace: the Hall of Preserving Harmony, where imperial ceremonies were rehearsed and banquets were held; the Hall of Central Harmony, where the Emperor would prepare for ceremonies, and rest; and the Hall of Supreme Harmony, where the ceremonies took place.

② HALL OF SUPREME HARMONY

This hall is the largest wooden building in China, and dominates the entire Forbidden City, rising 30 m (98 ft) above the square. Emperors of the Ming and Qing dynasties held their enthronement, wedding and birthday ceremonies in this hall; it was also used at the launch of military expeditions. The current hall dates back to 1695–97; seven previous halls were destroyed by fire.

③ IMPERIAL THRONE

In the centre of the hall the imperial sandalwood throne stands on a 2 m (6½ ft) high platform, and is surrounded by six gold-lacquered pillars showing dragons. There are dragons throughout the hall, including ones carved on the throne itself, and in the middle of the ceiling, where two dragons are playing with pearls.

④ BRONZE LIONS

The main gate of the Outer Court is guarded by two bronze lions symbolizing imperial power. On the eastern side is a male lion; its right front paw is raised and is holding a pomegranate, representing power. On the western side is a female lion; her left front paw rests on a lion cub, symbolizing a thriving and prosperous imperial family.

⑤ INNER COURT

The Inner Court was the home of the Emperor and his family. Apart from ceremonial occasions, the emperors of the Qing dynasty rarely left this court. The Inner Court contained three halls: the Palace of Heavenly Purity, occupied by the Emperor, representing the Heavens and the male principle of Yang; the Hall of Earthly Tranquillity, occupied by the Empress, who represented the Earth and the female principle of Yin; and the Hall of Union and Peace, where the Emperor and Empress, Yang and Yin, would meet and meld harmoniously. In this hall were kept 25 jade seals representing imperial authority, inside gold boxes covered in yellow silk.

The Inner Court also contained the Palace of Tranquil Longevity, built by Hongli, the Qianlong emperor (1711–99), for his retirement. He was the fourth Qing emperor to rule over China. Like a miniaturized Forbidden City, it incorporated an Outer Court and an Inner Court, temples and gardens.

⑥ THE EMPEROR'S AND EMPRESS'S PALACES

The Emperor's palace, the Palace of Heavenly Purity, contained a total of 27 beds in nine rooms on two levels. The Emperor would sleep in a different bed each night, randomly chosen, for security.

The empress's residence, the Hall of Earthly Tranquillity, contained (as well as her personal bedchamber) the bridal chambers that were used by the Emperor and Empress in the days immediately after their wedding. To the east and west of these palaces were smaller palaces and courtyards where the Emperor's concubines and children lived.

⑦ HILL OF ACCUMULATED ELEGANCE

North of the Forbidden City, in the Imperial Gardens, is the Hill of Accumulated Elegance, an artificial mound built on the site of the former Hall of Appreciating Flowers. About 10 m (33 ft), the hill is surmounted by the Pavilion of Imperial Scenery. Once a year, on the ninth day of the ninth lunar month (nine was a sacred number in China), the Emperor, with his Empress and concubines, would climb this hill to survey their land and appreciate the autumnal colours.

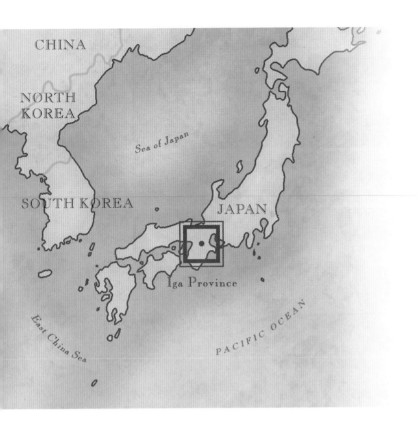

The Ninja

The Ninja are well known from films, manga (Japanese comics) and computer games as black-clad superheroes with amazing fighting skills. In reality they were closer to the Assassins (see pages 35–43): highly skilled professional contract killers; and they did not always wear black. The word ninja comes from the term ninjutsu, *which can be translated as 'the art of stealth'.*

Left Yamabushi *monks in procession, with their distinctive headwear and carrying their conch-shell trumpets, the* horagai *or* jinkai *(war shell) used to signal movements in battle.*

The Ninja are thought to have become a significant fighting force in 14th-century Japan as a way for *daimyo*, or local feudal rulers, to fight between themselves without going to all-out war, but their origins can be traced back five hundred years earlier.

One of the Ninja's functions was to do the dirty work that the prestigious Samurai warriors would not demean themselves and sully their honour by doing. Samurai warriors were highly respected; they fought in a skilful but stylized way, and had a high code of honour. They would certainly not use subterfuge, cheating or dirty tricks in their fighting, part of the stock-in-trade for Ninja warriors. The Ninja were the Special Forces of their day; they were fearless assassins, but they were also spies and

Left *Tokugawa Ieyasu (1542/3–1616), who became Shogun (great leader) of Japan in 1603 and established the Tokugawa shogunate which brought stability to Japan for over 250 years.*

saboteurs. Samurai warriors had absolute loyalty to their political rulers; in contrast the Ninja valued personal freedom and family loyalty before any political power, local or national. They were effectively mercenaries, hiring out their skills.

DUAL INFLUENCES

While most Samurai were Zen Buddhists, the Ninja were strongly influenced by two groups. One was the *yamabushi* or mystical monks skilled in mind–body awareness, who travelled on long and arduous pilgrimages through the mountains from one shrine to another; the *yamabushi* included Chinese warrior monks who had fled to Japan at the end of the Chinese T'ang dynasty around 900 CE. Ninja warriors would sometimes disguise themselves as *yamabushi* (which means 'those who live [or hide or sleep] in the mountains') in order to travel freely and undetected.

The other influence was a secretive initiatory society, the Shingon; this was a heterodox Buddhist sect very different from most forms of Chinese and Japanese Buddhism. The Shingon focused on active,

practical Buddhism rather than abstruse theological theory. Through rituals and meditation they aimed to unite the physical, mental and spiritual in natural harmony.

Both groups, the *yamabushi* and the Shingon, settled mainly in the Iga province of Japan (part of the Mie Prefecture today) and around Mount Koya, south of Osaka. This was also the main home of the Ninja clans, perhaps as many as seventy or eighty altogether. The Iga school of *ninjutsu* was one of the two most important Ninja training schools in Japan. Without question the Ninja absorbed influences from these spiritual sources. It is also probably from them that they gained some of their reputation for magical abilities. To learn to overcome subconscious fear, for example, the *yamabushi* would walk on red-hot coals, chant and meditate under freezing waterfalls, and hang from cliff edges by their feet. It is hardly surprising that legend ascribes their origin (and sometimes that of the Ninja) to *tengu*, crow-men descended from demons.

The Shingon influence on Ninja beliefs meant that they would use complex hand gestures (*mudras*) for channelling and

focusing their energy; their opponents, misinterpreting this as a form of magic used against them, were unnerved by this.

ESPIONAGE AND FIGHTING SKILLS

The Ninja were not exclusively male. Female Ninja were called *Kunoichi*; posing as servants, dancers or entertainers, or even using seduction, they were able to gain access to places where male Ninja could not, and so were highly valued spies.

Living in harmony with nature, the Ninja held all life as sacred. But, because of their lack of loyalty to political rulers, the government was hostile to them, leading the Ninja – almost in self-defence – to become guerrilla fighters. Being highly skilled in 18 martial arts such as karate, bojutsu and kenjutsu, they readily found work fighting for or against different local warlords. The 15th century was their heyday, and it was probably from this period that many of the legends of their fighting skill originated.

In 1603 Tokugawa Ieyasu became the Shogun, or great leader, of Japan. To consolidate his power base he brought all Ninja under his control, using them mainly as his espionage network, known as *Onmitsu*. Their task was secretly to gather information about the *daimyo* around the country and feed it back to Ieyasu. But the Ninja played both sides; the *daimyo* also employed Ninja, illegally, in order to conceal their secrets from the *Onmitsu*. The Tokugawa shogunate lasted until 1867. During this long period of stability there was eventually no need for the specialist skills of the Ninja, and they faded away.

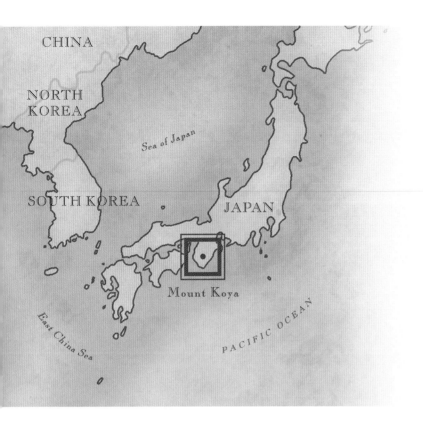

The Shingon sect

The Shingon began as a secretive initiatory society very different from the usual forms of Buddhism in China and Japan. They were founded by a monk called Kukai (774–835 CE), who went to China in 804–806 to study mystical Buddhism; when he returned to Japan after 30 months, he first became abbot of a Kyoto temple, then in 819 he founded a monastery for meditation on Mount Koya, south of Osaka.

Shingon, which means 'the True Word' or 'the Mystical Word', taught how to become a Buddha during one's earthly life; the secret teachings were passed on by word of mouth, as were early Kabbalist teachings (see pages 50–53). They focused on mysticism, magic and healing, which also resonate with the Western Mystery Tradition.

BELIEFS AND CONCEPTS
Kukai wrote the three-volume *Hizoboyaku* or *Jewel Key to the Store of Mysteries*, in which he expressed the belief that the mystical teachings of esoteric Buddhism are superior to the public teachings of any of the paths of exoteric Buddhism as founded and taught by the historical Buddha, Sakyamuni or Siddhartha Gautama. Behind Sakyamuni (and other earthly Buddhas) is the Great Sun Buddha, known as Vairocana or Dainichi – the Adi-Buddha or primordial Buddha, the ultimate cosmic reality. The equivalent in Kabbalism would be Ain Sof, the One behind and beyond everything in existence.

At the heart of Shingon lies the concept that it is possible for the individual to contact and unite with the ineffable now, rather

Right *A small stupa-like pagoda at Garan Temple, the central temple complex on Mt Koya, Japan, where Kukai first taught Shingon Buddhism in 819 CE.*

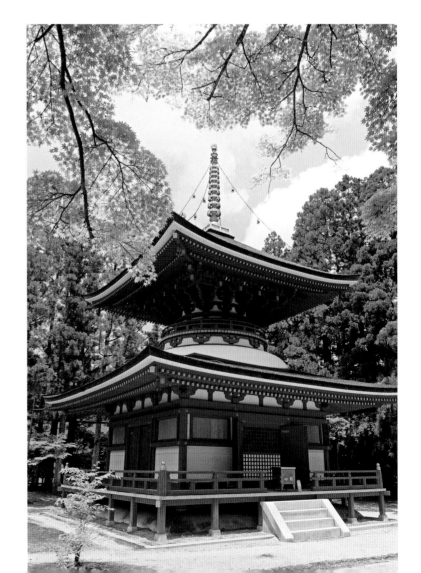

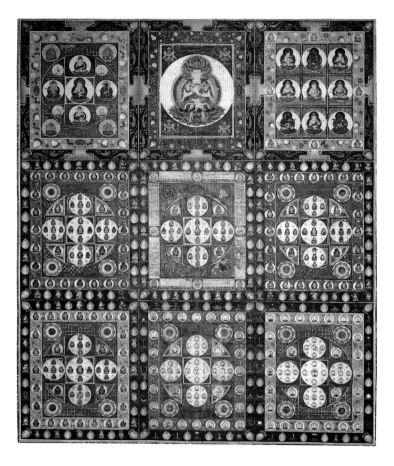

*Left The Kongokai
(Diamond World)
mandala is made
up of nine mandalas
symbolizing different
levels of reality
(9th century).*

than having to go through repeated
reincarnations until one is ready to step off
the Wheel and attain nirvana (a state of peace
and enlightenment). The best known of
Kukai's 50 treatises is the *Sokushin-jobutsugi*
(*The Doctrine of Becoming a Buddha with One's
Body During One's Earthly Existence*).

Each person has an inherent Buddha-
nature within himself or herself. Through
the meditations and rituals of Shingon, it is
possible to realize one's Buddhahood and
identify with the Great Sun Buddha. This is a
very similar belief to that of Gnosticism: that
by knowing the God-within, our immanent
divinity, we can know (and know that we are a
part of) the God-without, the ultimate
transcendent divine One (see page 12).

MUDRAS, MANTRAS AND MANDALAS

Shingon Buddhism in Japan can ultimately
be traced back to Tantric Buddhism in India.
Today, in the West, Tantra is usually thought
of as a mystical form of sex, but that is only a
small part of it. At its heart, the essence of
Tantric Buddhism – and hence of Shingon

Buddhism – is its emphasis on the *practice* of
Buddhism rather than the theory, doctrine or
dogma of it.

As with the Western Mystery Tradition,
ritual plays an important part in Shingon.
The involvement of body, speech and mind is
crucial. The secret teachings (known as
mikkyo) included devotional gestures
(*mudras*), the repeating of sacred words of
power or incantations (*mantras*), the use of
symbolic images (*mandalas*) representing the
secret teachings, and meditation. All of these
were spiritually powerful. Through ritual and
meditation one could achieve self-realization
and attain enlightenment.

There are two main *mandalas*, the Womb
World (or *Taiziukai*) *mandala*, based on
the Dainichikyou Sutra, and the Diamond
(or *Kongokai*) *mandala*, based on the
Kongouchoukyou Sutra. Meditation on the
Womb World *mandala*, which represents the
world of physical phenomena, broadens the
worshipper's attention, while the Diamond
mandala, which represents the cosmic or
transcendental Buddha, concentrates it.

The elaborate ceremonial of Shingon
Buddhism made it popular among all classes
of people in Japan. The educated aristocracy
appreciated not only the beauty but also the
intellectual depth of the *mandalas*, while
simplified forms of the gestures (*mudras*) and
the *mantras* became popular folk charms,
used like talismans and amulets to attract
good fortune or ward off evil.

The different sects of Japanese Buddhism
are heavily intertwined in their history and
influences, their teachings and practices.
Shingon and *mikkyo* are often associated
with Tendai Buddhism, based on the Lotus
Sutra, which was founded by Saicho, a
contemporary of Kukai. Shingon and
Tendai developed alongside each other
for centuries. An offshoot of Tendai
Buddhism, founded by the 13th-century
teacher Nichiren Daishonin, became the
heterodox Buddhist sect of Nichiren Shoshu.
Its present-day lay movement, Soka Gakkai,
has become popular among artists and actors
in the West – just as some modern versions of
Kabbalah have.

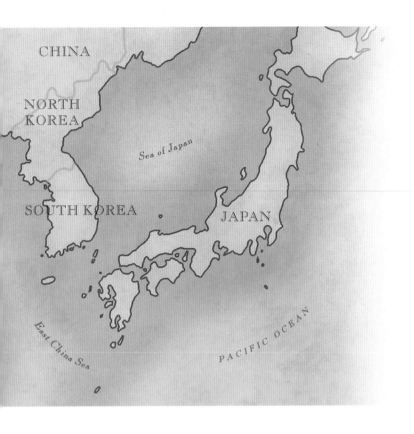

The Yakuza

The Yakuza began at around the same time as the Ninja faded away, and for a related reason: stability under the Tokugawa shogunate. The prestigious Samurai warriors found themselves underemployed, and many of them went rogue and were known as masterless Samurai, ronin *or* kabuki-mono *('crazy ones'). They roamed the countryside, dressed in outlandish costumes, spoke their own incomprehensible slang dialect and wore their long swords openly thrust through their belts; basically they were gangs of street louts who plundered villages and terrified the ordinary Japanese population.*

According to their own mythology, the Yakuza were formed to defend villages and towns against the marauding *kabuki-mono*. They were ordinary people, just like those they were protecting: shopkeepers, innkeepers, tradesmen. They took up weapons to defend the defenceless and took the name *machi-yakko*, meaning 'city servants'. Amateur fighters and ill equipped in comparison with the *kabuki-mono*, they became folk heroes.

CRIMINAL PRACTICES

In reality it is just as likely – perhaps even more so – that the Yakuza themselves descended from the *kabuki-mono*. Alternatively they were simply street thugs, the lowest of the low, social misfits who banded together into a community. The name Yakuza comes from the numbers eight (*ya*), nine (*ku*) and three (*za*), which add up to give the worthless score of 20 in Oicho-Kabu, a Japanese card game similar to Blackjack; the Yakuza were the Unwanted in society. They included gamblers (*bakuto*) and street peddlers (*tekiya*), both terms still in use in the Yakuza today.

In the late 19th century the Yakuza dropped gambling for a while to concentrate on outdoor crime, including the rickshaw business, dock-working and the building trade. In the political turmoil of the early 20th century the Yakuza became involved in politics, providing the muscle for right-wing groups, carrying out assassinations and violent intimidation, including suppressing unions. They were known as *oyoku* ('right wing') and formed several powerful societies, the best known being the Black Dragon Society. These groups were large enough to be involved in opium-smuggling as well as the usual prostitution and gambling.

Following the Second World War, when food was rationed, the Yakuza became heavily involved in the black-market provision of food and alcohol. By the 1960s they had become straightforward gangsters, running organized crime and committing serious street offences; they even wore sharp black suits in imitation of American gangsters. At this point there were nearly 200,000 members throughout Japan, in more than five thousand gangs; crackdowns since then have halved both figures. As with the Mafia

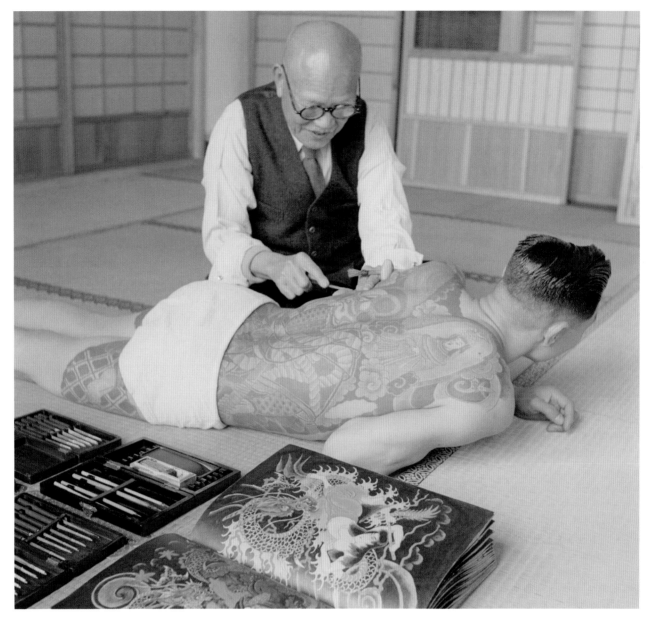

and the Triads, turf wars between these gangs have led to many deaths, including innocent people caught in the crossfire. Today the Yakuza are heavily involved in the distribution of pornography, in prostitution and in the trafficking of girls and young women. They run blackmail, extortion and protection rackets, but as a matter of honour are never involved in simple stealing.

GANG MEMBERSHIP

Unlike the Mafia, the Triads and other organized-crime groups, the Yakuza do not hide their existence or even their individual membership. Many wear distinctive clothing,

or dark glasses; often the headquarters of a Yakuza group will have a sign on the door. Because they still see themselves as protectors of the poor and downtrodden, in some impoverished areas they function almost like local government.

There does not seem to be any spiritual element to the Yakuza, but there is a strong bond between members. Because many of them come from the street poor, being in a Yakuza gang gives them a sense of family, of close brotherhood, of identity – and of order, because the head of a group of gangs is like the strict head of a family; in fact, he has the title of *Oyabun* meaning 'Father', and his

word is law. In the hierarchy below the *Oyabun* are Elder Brothers (*kyodai*) and Younger Brothers (*shatei*) with their own subordinate gangs.

Infringement of the orders of the *Oyabun* by a *kobun* ('foster-child') incurs a physical penance: cutting off the last joint of one little finger, wrapping it neatly in paper and giving it to him. Many members of the Yakuza are missing more than one finger joint. It is also traditional for Yakuza members to be heavily tattooed, sometimes all over their bodies; other Yakuza have a black ring tattooed around their arm for each crime they commit.

The Thuggees

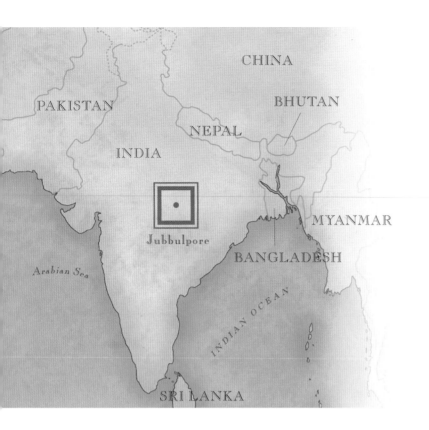

Some sources claim that the Thuggees (pronounced Tuggees and meaning 'deceivers') date as far back as around 1300, but there is little reliable evidence of them before the late 17th century. Although certain sources claim they were responsible for more than two million deaths, a more sober and realistic estimate is around 50,000.

There is a mythological story that the goddess Devi Durga – a consort of Shiva and closely related to Kali, another consort of Shiva – commissioned the Thuggees to murder people, to counter the positive creativity of Brahma in populating the Earth. They would be able to kill with impunity; she would protect them from the authorities; she would even dispose of the bodies. One night, after killing their victims, a group of Thuggees hid, to see how Devi Durga would dispose of them. The goddess spotted them and told them that, because they had disobeyed her, she would remove her protection from them – from now on they would have to get rid of the bodies themselves. However, one version of the story tells that she gave one of her teeth to be the Thuggees' magical pickaxe, used to dig the graves of their victims and treated with great

Left *Ram Luckun Sein, a hereditary thuggee of Bengal, with his guard, 1858.*

respect in their rituals. She also gave them the hem of her garment to be the yellow scarf or *rumal* that the Thuggees used to strangle their victims.

The Thuggees were devotees of the Hindu goddess Kali. Although popularly seen as the goddess of destruction, Kali is also regarded as the Divine Mother by many Hindus, being responsible for life, death and creation. Most Kali devotees had nothing to do with the Thuggees. Strangely, as they were devoted to Kali, Thuggees included Sikhs and Muslims, as well as Hindus.

MODE OF OPERATION

The way the Thuggees usually worked was to befriend a group of travellers, offering to share their journey with them for company and mutual protection; sometimes they claimed to be pilgrims, merchants or soldiers. At some point, preferably at pre-arranged places, they would kill their victims by strangling them with the *rumal*; this was to avoid shedding their blood, which was prohibited to them. The attacks were always well coordinated with, if possible, as many as three Thuggees to each victim:

one to do the strangling, the other two to pin the unfortunate person to the ground. After the dead had been plundered of their goods, they would be buried, with complex ritual, sometimes in mass graves, which had been used for this purpose for decades.

The apparently brazen brutality of the Thuggees led to the word's incorporation into English as 'thug'. This is a misconception in two ways. First, Thuggees were not thug-like bandits. Most of them lived normal lives with normal jobs; some of them were professionals, including doctors, nurses and even policemen. Second, simple theft was not the purpose of their killings; anything they gained was a bonus. They were killing for their goddess; they even believed that their victims would go to Paradise because they had been sacrificed as an offering to Kali and, by performing this duty for her, they would also go to Paradise.

SUPPRESSION OF THE THUGGEES

The English rulers of India knew that travellers sometimes disappeared, but did not become aware of the Thuggees until the 1820s, when William Henry Sleeman, a magistrate in Jubbulpore, spotted a group of travellers who appeared to be carrying stolen goods; he spoke to one of them, then followed the group and tricked them into returning to Jubbulpore. Another member then revealed to Sleeman the recently buried bodies of three men and a boy; all had been strangled. Sleeman investigated further, and began to uncover the true extent of the Thuggees' killings. When he reported what he had discovered, the East India Company was initially reluctant to become involved because of the Thuggees' devotion to Kali; to crack down on them might be interpreted as religious persecution. Considering the general level of ignorance among the British

Above The goddess Devi Durga on her tiger, slaying the buffalo demon Raktabij, and Kali catching the demon's blood on her tongue to stop it touching the ground.

about Indian religious practices, this was remarkably perceptive.

Sleeman continued to present his evidence and pursue groups of Thuggees, and was eventually appointed General Superintendent for the Suppression of the Thuggees; more than 1,400 Thuggees were hanged or transported in the next two or three decades, and by about 1850 they had effectively been wiped out.

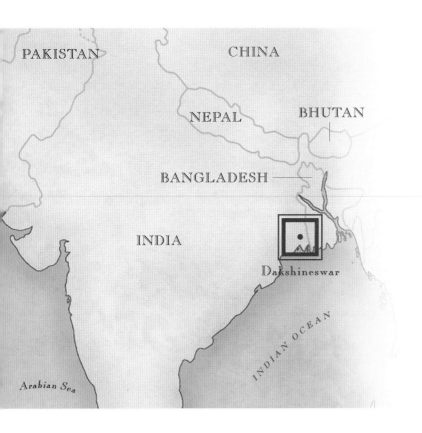

Dakshineswar Kali Temple

As we have seen, the Thuggees were devoted to the Hindu goddess Kali, who is often seen as the goddess of destruction and annihilation, a dark and dangerous goddess, renowned for her violence on the battlefield; but she also has a benevolent maternal aspect and is seen by many Hindus as the Divine Mother. Although she inspires fear in her enemies, for her followers she takes away the fear of death.

A famous temple to the goddess Kali is situated at Dakshineswar, about 6.5 km (4 miles) north of Kolkata (formerly Calcutta) in West Bengal, eastern India. It is next to the Vivekananda Bridge on the eastern bank of the Hooghli River, which is the westernmost branch of the River Ganges.

ORIGIN OF THE TEMPLE

According to legend, in 1847 a pious and wealthy widow, Rani Rasmani, was about to set out on a long pilgrimage from Calcutta to the sacred city of Benares (now Varanasi) to offer her devotion to Kali. There was no train service between the cities, so she was going to travel by boat – her convoy consisting of 24 boats conveying her relatives, servants and supplies.

The night before she was due to leave, the Divine Mother appeared to Rani Rasmani in the form of the goddess Kali and told her that she had no need to travel to Benares. Instead she should build a temple to Kali on the banks of the River Ganges so that the goddess could be worshipped there. Construction began in 1847 and the temple complex was complete by 1855.

RAMAKRISHNA

On consecration of the temple in 1855, an elderly and very scholarly sage was appointed head priest. He died within a year, and his younger brother Ramakrishna took his place. Ramakrishna became filled with an overwhelming love of god, known in Hinduism as *maha-bhava*. In this state he would fall to the ground, completely immersed in a deep spiritual trance and insensate to the outside world. He did not restrict himself to the gods of Hinduism, such as Kali, Shiva and Krishna, but would also express his devotion to Christ and other deities. They would appear to him in physical form and merge into him, making Ramakrishna himself an avatar of the gods.

Ramakrishna was so often intoxicated with the love of god that he was relieved of his duties as temple priest, but he continued to live in the temple complex, in a room in the north-west corner of the temple compound, until his death in 1886 at the age of 50. The intensity of his spiritual practices and his realization of the divine inspired many followers and helped make the temple a place of pilgrimage and devotion.

TEMPLE COMPLEX

Dakshineswar is a vast complex, comprising orchards, flower gardens and two reservoirs as well as the many temples and other buildings. These include a large music hall or *natmandir*, two music towers or *nahabats*, and a smaller temple dedicated to Radhakanta or Krishna. There is a group of ancient trees, the *panchavati*, under which Ramakrishna would meditate.

DAKSHINESWAR TODAY

Today the complex also houses orphanages, schools and homes for the elderly. This work is an expression of Kali as the Divine Mother, caring for and protecting her children. Pilgrims bring their personal anxieties and family problems to Kali in their individual personal prayers, or in puja, a formal ceremony of prayers, songs and rituals, showing humility, giving reverence and thanks and making offerings to the god.

① MAIN TEMPLE

The whitewashed main temple, which houses the idol of Kali, is set on a platform in the middle of a huge, paved rectangular courtyard running north–south, which is bounded by a band of blood-red paint. Although the temple looks fabulous and exotic, it is actually an ornamental variation of a typical Bengali hut.

Within the temple, set on the marble floor, is a basalt image of Kali. Dressed richly in gold brocade, she exemplifies the contradictions of the goddess, the bringer of both tenderness and terror; she is both the giver and the taker of life: the womb and the tomb. She has four arms. With her lower left hand she holds a severed human head; her upper left hand holds a blood-stained sabre. But her right hands dispense boons to her children, and allay their fears. She is shown with three eyes, the third symbolizing divine wisdom.

② *CHHATRIS*

The curved roof is topped by nine *chhatris*, or dome-shaped canopies. This architectural feature is fundamental to both Hindu and Moghul architecture.

③ HOOGHLI RIVER

The temple is situated on a tributary of the Ganges called the Hooghli. Although it is just a branch of the River Ganges, the Hooghli nevertheless takes on all of that river's sacred significance.

④ BATHING *GHAT*

Pilgrims bathe together in the sacred river at the edge of the temple complex. *Ghats*, which are steps leading to bathing platforms, are an important feature of many Indian temples.

⑤ *CHANDNI*

The *chandni* or porch is the riverside entrance to the temple complex. Traditionally, the temple watchmen lived in the *chandni*.

⑥ TEMPLES TO SIVA

Twelve temples to Siva, six on either side of the *chandni*, line the riverside edge of the complex. Siva was the consort of Kali and, according to mythology, Siva – as destroyer of the world – uses Kali's energy.

Glossary

ALCHEMY

Alchemy has been called 'the science of magic'. The medieval and Renaissance alchemists performed complex chemical operations attempting to create the Philosopher's Stone, a reddish powder or tincture supposedly conferring long life. Some alchemists received patronage from kings who hoped they could turn base metals such as lead into gold, but alchemy is primarily about the transformation of the soul. See pages 48–49.

ANTHROPOSOPHY

A religious philosophy, a form of esoteric Christianity, founded by Rudolf Steiner (1861–1925), formerly the leader of the Theosophical Society in Germany. Anthroposophy had many practical outcomes including systems of biodynamic agriculture, the forerunner of organic farming, and of education, the Steiner or Waldorf Schools. See pages 72, 115 and 118.

APOSTOLIC SUCCESSION

A symbolic power transmitted in the consecration of bishops through the laying on of hands in a supposedly unbroken line going back to the apostles. It is a feature of the Catholic, Orthodox and Anglican/Episcopalian Churches, and of many smaller offshoot Churches such as the Old Catholics and the Liberal Catholics, and individual 'Wandering Bishops' (*episcopi vagantes*), some connected to esoteric societies. See pages 32–33 and 118–119.

THE ASSASSINS

A sect of Ismaeli Shi'ite Islam founded in Persia in 1090 CE, famous for its targeted murders of political and religious leaders in the Middle East, particularly Syria, over the next two centuries. See pages 35–43.

CATHARISM

A Gnostic Christian sect which flourished in the Languedoc, now southern France, in the 12th century. They were wiped out by the Catholic Church in the Albigensian Crusade in the early- to mid-13th century. See page 13.

CORRESPONDENCES

A complex system of symbolic links between astrological signs, Hebrew letters/numbers, the Sephiroth of the Kabbalistic Tree of Life, Tarot cards, Egyptian, Hindu and other gods, musical notes, precious stones, colours, scents, plants, animals and much more. In magical rituals the relevant symbols, colours, sounds, etc. are used together. See page 109.

CROWLEY, ALEISTER

Known as 'the Great Beast 666', Crowley (1875–1947) was a colourful and controversial figure in British occultism. Briefly a member of the Hermetic Order of the Golden Dawn, he founded his own society, Argenteum Astrum, and became British leader of the Ordo Templi Orientis. Among much else he was responsible for creating the Thoth Tarot. See pages 123–131 and 168.

DEGREE (FREEMASONRY)

Basic Craft Freemasonry has three degrees, or initiatory levels of advancement: Entered Apprentice, Fellow Craft and Master Mason. It is necessary to be a Master Mason to join any of Freemasonry's many other Orders, each of which has its own system of degrees, some of them very complex. The Scottish Rite in American Freemasonry and the Ancient and Accepted Rite, or Rose Croix, in British Freemasonry have 33 degrees. See pages 86–89.

DRUIDRY

A Neo-Pagan religion based in part on an ancient British religion, modern Druidry is strongly nature-based. Like Wicca it celebrates Beltaine (roughly May Day), Lughnasad (Lammas), Samhain (Hallowe'en), Imbolg (Candlemas) and the Solstices and Equinoxes. Some Druids are bards – poets and storytellers; others are environmental activists.

DUALISM

Loosely, this is the belief that there are opposed forces of Good and Evil in the universe. More specifically, many dualist religions believe that the world was created by an Evil God, that spirit is good and matter is evil, and that we as humans have sparks of the Divine trapped within our material bodies. The Abrahamic religions, while monotheistic, have a dualist element in that they believe that God is opposed by Satan. See page 13.

ESOTERIC

Deriving from the Greek for 'inner' or 'within', this term refers to beliefs and teachings given only to initiated members of a religion or organization.

EXOTERIC

Deriving from the Greek for 'outside' or 'outward form', this term refers to beliefs and teachings openly available to anyone, not just the initiated.

THE EXPERIENTIAL

That which is known through direct personal experience, rather than accepted on the basis of someone else's authority. Esoteric religions and secret societies usually lay a great emphasis on the importance of personal spiritual experience and knowledge, in contrast to mainstream exoteric religions which tell their members what to believe.

FREEMASONRY

Calling itself 'a society with secrets' rather than a secret society, Freemasonry's origins are unclear, but certainly predate its formal organization under a Grand Lodge in London in 1717. The subject of much speculation, and often criticized for its symbolic 'histories' and its colourful rituals, Freemasonry today is largely philanthropic in nature. See pages 75–91.

FREETHINKERS

Those who deliberately choose their own beliefs, especially in the field of religion, rather than mutely accepting what they are told to believe by figures of authority. The alchemists and Hermetic Philosophers of the 16th and 17th centuries were Freethinkers; so were the Rosicrucians of both allegory and reality. Putting their beliefs into action, many Freethinkers of the 18th and 19th centuries, who in terms of religion were Deists, Unitarians or Quakers, were social reformers, with liberal attitudes to established views on slavery, race, women's position in society, the poor, health reform, education for all, freedom of speech, freedom of religion, etc. Often lambasted in their own time, they were the creators of today's liberal democracies in the western world. See page 55.

GEMATRIA

A highly complex system of numerological analysis of written text, usually in Hebrew, to find deeper spiritual meanings. In Hebrew every letter is also a number, so words can easily be given a numerical equivalent. If two words reduce to the same number they are believed to be linked. See pages 50–51.

GNOSTICISM

A broad label covering a number of religions and religious beliefs which focus on believers receiving personal knowledge (Greek: *gnosis*) of the divine, rather than just accepting what a priest tells them. See pages 12–14.

HELL-FIRE CLUB

Popularly, a supposedly 'Satanic' club run by Sir Francis Dashwood at Medmenham Abbey in the mid-18th century. In reality, a drinking and sex club in London founded by Philip, Duke of Wharton 20 years earlier. See pages 143–147.

HERMES TRISMEGISTUS

Hermes Trismegistus was a mythical semi-divine spiritual philosopher, supposedly the author of several highly influential Greek-Egyptian esoteric texts actually written c.150–400 CE, which were translated into Latin by Marsilio Ficino in the 15th century. See pages 17 and 54–55.

HERMETIC ORDER OF THE GOLDEN DAWN

Short-lived but extremely influential occult society founded in London in 1888. See pages 103–119.

HERMETIC PHILOSOPHERS

In the 16th and 17th centuries, a number of loosely linked but independent esoteric thinkers including scientists, alchemists, astrologers, doctors, etc. They were the 'real' Rosicrucians, and the forerunners of both Freemasonry and the Royal Society. See pages 54–55 and 68–69.

HOLY OF HOLIES

The most sacred room in the Temple in Jerusalem which only the Jewish High Priest could enter once a year. See pages 92–93.

ILLUMINATI

A Bavarian society whose interests were political as well as esoteric. Although short-lived in reality, the Illuminati live on in hundreds of wild conspiracy theories. See pages 95–101.

KABBALAH

Originally a Jewish mystical system, Kabbalah was adopted by 16th-century Christian Hermetic Philosophers, and thus by post-Rosicrucian groups such as the Golden Dawn. See pages 50–53.

KNIGHTS HOSPITALLER

Founded in 1080 to care for sick pilgrims in the Holy Land, it became a military Order shortly afterwards. Following the demise of the Knights Templar, the Knights Hospitaller took over much of their property and some of their members. See page 20.

KNIGHTS TEMPLAR

Founded in 1119 to protect pilgrims to the Holy Land, the Knights Templar became not just a superb fighting force but also very efficient bankers. Their downfall still fuels conspiracy theories today. See pages 19–33.

LÉVI, ÉLIPHAS

Originally trained to be a Catholic priest, Alphonse Louis Constant (1810–75) hebraicized his name as Éliphas Lévi and became one of the most influential occultists of the 19th century. See pages 71 and 108.

MACKENZIE, KENNETH

Kenneth Mackenzie (1833–86) was instrumental in the founding of Societas Rosicruciana in Anglia, and was a member of several occult societies. It is considered likely that rituals he wrote for one of these were the Cipher Manuscript behind the founding of the Golden Dawn. See pages 105, 106 and 108.

MAJOR ARCANA

The 22 highly symbolic cards in a Tarot pack, including the Fool, the Magician, the Wheel of Fortune, the Hanged Man, Judgement, etc. See pages 71 and 117.

MANICHEISM

A dualist religion founded by the 3rd-century Persian prophet Mani. It continued for many centuries, and was the probable source of several other dualist religions including Catharism. See page 13.

MATHERS, 'MACGREGOR'

Samuel Liddell 'MacGregor' Mathers (1854–1918) was one of the three founder members of the Hermetic Order of the Golden Dawn. Albeit eccentric and autocratic, he was an important translator of esoteric texts and creator of rituals. See pages 106–113.

METEMPSYCHOSIS

A Greek term for the transmigration of souls, the passing of the soul after death from one body to another, human or animal: reincarnation. This concept was believed in by Gnostics, Neo-Platonists and many early Christians.

MINOR ARCANA

The 56 Tarot cards similar to playing cards with one extra Court card: the pip cards 1–10, and in most packs King, Queen, Knight and Page, in the suits Cups, Swords, Wands and Coins (or similar). In some packs the pip cards are illustrated to help show their esoteric meaning. See page 117.

MITHRAISM

A mystery religion focused on the (probably) Persian saviour-god Mithra or Mithras, which was very popular with Roman soldiers in the first four centuries CE. There are several similarities between Roman Mithraism and Christianity in this period, but it is not always clear which religion influenced the other. See page 16.

MONOTHEISM

Belief that there is one God, as found in Zoroastrianism, Judaism, Christianity, Islam, the Bahá'í Faith, etc.

NEO-PAGANISM

The development from the mid-20th century of several related new nature-respecting religions in the Western world which draw inspiration from pre-Christian religions. These include Witchcraft/Wicca, Druidry, Heathenry/the Northern Tradition and others. They are usually initiatory and involve magic. None of them has any connection with Satanism.

NEOPLATONISM

Neoplatonism was a school of philosophy which developed in the first few centuries CE. Emphasizing the importance of the experiential, it was influential on both exoteric and especially esoteric religious beliefs throughout the centuries. See pages 14–15.

NEO-PYTHAGORIANISM

Linked to Neoplatonism, Neo-Pythagorian ideas are a development of the teachings of Pythagorus, especially on the spiritual symbolism of numbers as expressed in areas as diverse as music and architecture. See page 15.

NINJA

The Ninja were highly skilled professional fighters and killers in 14th–18th-century Japan. They were strongly influenced by the Shingon sect of Buddhism, putting their esoteric spirituality into practical action. See pages 156–159.

OPUS DEI

Opus Dei ('the Work of God') is a controversial lay order within the Roman Catholic Church, founded by Josemaria Escrivá de Balaguer in 1928. See pages 134–135.

ORDER (RELIGIOUS/MASONIC)

An Order is a structured organization with a specific, often spiritual emphasis. It is usually initiatory, requiring vows of commitment from members, such as poverty, chastity and obedience for religious Orders, or secrecy, study and mutual aid for esoteric Orders. It may take years of dedication to progress up the hierarchical levels within an Order.

ORDO TEMPLI ORIENTIS (OTO)

The Ordo Templi Orientis is an esoteric Order (actually several competing Orders) with a lineage, real or assumed, going back to Aleister Crowley. Crowley changed the spiritual emphasis of Theodor Reuss's original OTO to make it Thelemic (see opposite, and pages 124–131).

PALLADISM

A wholly fictional creation of Leo Taxil in the late 19th century, Palladism was supposedly a secret Masonic Order for men and women, devoted to Satanism and sex. See pages 90–91.

PHILOSOPHER'S STONE

Actually a red powder or a tincture rather than a stone, this was the ultimate physical goal for alchemists. It had the attributes of granting longevity and of turning base metals into gold. See pages 48–49.

POLYTHEISM

A belief in many gods, as opposed to one God. Historically the Greek pantheon, and the Babylonian, Egyptian, Roman, Norse and other religious cultures, were all polytheistic. Most of the many versions of Hinduism are polytheistic.

PRIORY OF SION

Despite Dan Brown's *The Da Vinci Code* and numerous other books, the Priory of Sion is not a secret society dating back to the time of the Knights Templar, formed to protect the sacred bloodline of Jesus. It was founded in 1956 in France as a small right-wing local political group. Its supposed history and its list of famous Grand Masters are entirely spurious. See pages 138–139.

ROSENKREUZ, CHRISTIAN

Christian Rosenkreuz (Rosy Cross) was the myth upon whom the Rosicrucians were founded. The first Rosicrucian Manifesto (1614) told the allegorical story of his life and the discovery of his tomb. Some modern Rosicrucian Orders treat the story as factually true. See pages 62–63.

ROSICRUCIAN BROTHERHOOD

The Brotherhood of the Rosy Cross described in the Rosicrucian Manifestos (1614–16) almost certainly never existed, but 'Rosicrucian' groups began to form from the 17th century onwards. One of the most influential was the Brotherhood of the Golden and Rosy Cross, first known of in 1710, then in 1777. See pages 61–73.

RR ET AC

The Ordo Rosae Rubeae et Aureae Crucis (RR et AC), the Order of the Rose of Ruby and Cross of Gold, was the Inner or Second Order of the Hermetic Order of the Golden Dawn, in which the theoretical lessons of the Outer Order were put into practice. See pages 108–113.

SEPHIROTH

The Sephiroth (singular: Sephira) represent ten aspects of God, such as Kether (Crown), Chokmah (Wisdom), Chesed (Mercy) and Tiphareth (Beauty). They are connected by 22 paths on the Kabbalistic Tree of Life (see right and pages 50–51). Sometimes the Tree of Life shows an additional 'hidden' Sephira, Da'at, below the top three.

SHARI'AH LAW

Shari'ah law is the Islamic code of law and morality, based on the Koran and the Hadith (Sayings of Muhammad). Although often perceived by non-Muslims as harsh and inflexible, Shari'ah is intended to be a workable system of justice and mercy covering every aspect of life.

STEINER, RUDOLF

Rudolf Steiner (1861–1925) was the founder of Anthroposophy, and before that the head of the Theosophical Society in Germany. Like many Hermetic Philosophers, he drew together science and spirituality. Max Heindel (1865–1919), founder of the Rosicrucian Fellowship, was greatly impressed by him and probably influenced by him, as was Dr Robert Felkin of Stella Matutina. See pages 72, 114–115 and 118.

TAROT

Tarot packs consist of a Minor Arcana, similar to a normal pack of cards with four extra Court cards, and a Major Arcana consisting of 22 cards such as the Fool, the Magician, the Wheel of Fortune, Temperance and the Hanged Man. As well as divination, Tarot can be used for meditation, storytelling and ritual work. Tarot's origins are unclear, but its esoteric interpretation is relatively modern. See pages 70–71 and 117.

TETRAGRAMMATON

The tetragrammaton is the four-consonant Hebrew name for God, YHWH. Jews will not say the sacred name, substituting *Adonai* (Lord) instead. Non-Jews usually pronounce YHWH as Yahveh. The name Jehovah is a medieval scholarly error caused by inserting the vowels from *Adonai* into YHWH. Because of its power the tetragrammaton is often used in magical ritual.

THELEMITE

A Thelemite is a follower of Thelema, the spiritual teachings of Aleister Crowley, which include sex-magick. Thelema's famous maxims are 'Do as thou Wilt shall be the whole of the Law' and 'Love is the Law, Love under Will'. Today Thelemites include members of the OTO (see opposite) and the Argenteum Astrum. See pages 124–125.

THEODICY

Theodicy refers to all attempts by different religions to explain why there is pain and evil in a world created by a good God. See pages 13–14.

THEOSOPHY/THEOSOPHICAL SOCIETY

The Theosophical Society was founded by Madame Helena Petrovna Blavatsky (1831–91) in 1875. Loosely speaking, Theosophy is a blend of mystical and theologically liberal Christianity with esoteric teachings drawn from Hinduism and Buddhism. Theosophy had a strong influence on many esoteric and New Age movements. Its second leader, Annie Besant, was a prominent freethinking social campaigner. See pages 107 and 116–119.

THOTH

Thoth was the Egyptian equivalent of the Greek Hermes, the Roman Mercury and to some extent the Norse Odin; he was the god of writing and communication. Because of the importance and mystery of writing in early cultures, Thoth was credited with the invention of all sciences, religion and magic. Aleister Crowley entitled his Tarot *The Book of Thoth*. See pages 126–127.

THUGGEES

The Thuggees were a religious sect in India in the 17th to 19th centuries, who believed it was their duty to kill travellers for Kali, the goddess of life, death and creation. See pages 162–163.

TREE OF LIFE

The Tree of Life is a diagrammatic model of God's relationship with the cosmos, and man's relationship with God. It includes the ten Sephiroth (see left) connected by 22 paths. The Hermetic Order of the Golden Dawn taught that there was a relationship between the 22 paths and the 22 cards of the Major Arcana of Tarot. See pages 50–51.

TRIADS

The Triads or Tongs are secret societies found mainly in the Chinese communities of Western cities. They are the Chinese equivalent of the Mafia, involved in drugs, prostitution, gambling, money laundering, protection rackets and other crimes. See pages 150–153.

WESTERN MYSTERY TRADITION

The Western Mystery Tradition is an overall term for esoteric spirituality in the Western world. Depending on the emphasis in different societies, it can include teachings on Tarot, Kabbalah, alchemy, astrology, mythology (including the Arthurian/Grail myths) and more.

YAKUZA

The Yakuza are a major part of criminal society in Japan. As with the Mafia and the Triads, they are often involved in prostitution, blackmail and protection rackets, but unlike them they are readily identifiable. As with many secret societies, whether spiritual, political or criminal, there is an internal hierarchy, and there is a strict code of conduct for members. See pages 160–161.

Bibliography

Access to Western Esotericism, Antoine Faivre, State University of New York 1994

Alchemy: The Medieval Alchemists and their Royal Art, Johannes Fabricius, Aquarian 1989 edn

Alchemy: The Secret Art, Stanislas Klossowski de Rola, Thames & Hudson 1973

The Aleister Crowley Scrapbook, Sandy Robertson, Foulsham 1988

American Freemasons: Three Centuries of Building Communities, Mark A Tabbert, New York University Press 2005

The Arcana of Freemasonry: A History of Masonic Signs & Symbols, Albert Churchward, 1915, Weiser 2005 edn

The Art of Memory, Frances A Yates, Routledge & Kegan Paul 1986

Beyond the Craft, Keith B Jackson, Lewis Masonic, 4th edn 1994

The Book of Ceremonial Magic, AE Waite, William Rider & Son 1911

The Book of Tokens: Tarot Meditations, Paul Foster Case, Builders of the Adytum 1934, 1989 edn

A Brief History of Secret Societies, David V Barrett, Constable & Robinson 2007

The Brotherhood of the Rosy Cross: A History of the Rosicrucians, AE Waite, Rider 1924

Brotherhoods of Fear: A History of Violent Organisations, Paul Elliot, Blandford 1998

Chambers Dictionary of Beliefs and Religions, Rosemary Goring, ed, Chambers 1992

Chambers Dictionary of the Unexplained, Una McGovern, ed, Chambers 2007

Cracking the Freemason's Code: The Truth about Solomon's Key and the Brotherhood, Robert LD Cooper, Rider 2006

The Craft: A History of English Freemasonry, John Hamill, Aquarian/Crucible 1986

The Dawn of Astrology: A Cultural History of Western Astrology, Vol 1: The Ancient and Classical Worlds, Nicholas Campion, Continuum 2008

Devil-Worship in France, with Diana Vaughan and the Question of Modern Palladism, AE Waite, 1896, Weiser Books 2003 edn

A Dictionary of Freemasonry, Robert A Macoy, Bell 1989, originally *General History, Cyclopedia and Dictionary of Freemasonry*, Masonic Publishing Co 1850

The Element Encyclopedia of Secret Societies and Hidden History, John Michael Greer, HarperElement 2006

The Elements of Mysticism, RA Gilbert, Element 1991

The Encyclopedia of Heresies and Heretics, Leonard George, Robson Books 1995

Encyclopedia of Mystical and Paranormal Experience, Rosemary Ellen Guiley, HarperCollins 1991

Encyclopedia of the Unexplained, Richard Cavendish, Routledge & Kegan Paul 1984

Fortean Times, periodical, Dennis Publishing

Freemasonry: A Journey through Ritual and Symbol, W Kirk MacNulty, Thames & Hudson 1991

Freemasonry on Both Sides of the Atlantic, William R Weisberger, ed, Columbia University Press 2002

Freemasonry – The Reality, Tobias Churton, Lewis Masonic 2007

Freemasonry Today, periodical, Grand Lodge Publications

Gnosticism: Its History and Influence, Benjamin Walker, Aquarian Press 1983

The Gnostics, Tobias Churton, Weidenfeld & Nicolson 1987

The Gnostics: The First Christian Heretics, Sean Martin, Pocket Essentials 2006

The Golden Builders: Alchemists, Rosicrucians and the First Free Masons, Tobias Churton, Signal 2002

The Golden Dawn, Israel Regardie, one-vol 6th edn, Llewellyn 1989

The Hell-Fire Friars: Sex, Politics and Religion, Gerald Suster, Robson Books 2000

Hermetica, Vols 1–4, ed & trs by Walter Scott, 1924, Shambhala 1985 edn

Hermetica, ed & trs by Walter Scott, Foreword by Adrian G Gilbert, Solos Press 1997

Hidden Symbolism of Alchemy and the Occult Arts, Herbert Silberer, 1917, Dover 1971

A History of Magic, Richard Cavendish, Weidenfeld & Nicholson 1987

The History of Magic and the Occult, Kurt Seligmann, Pantheon Books 1948

A History of Magic, Witchcraft and Occultism, WB Crow, Aquarian Press 1968

A History of White Magic, Gareth Knight, AR Mowbray 1978

Kabbalah: Tradition of Hidden Knowledge, Z'ev Ben Shimon Halevi, Thames & Hudson 1979

Lost Christianities: The Battles for Scripture and the Faiths We Never Knew, Bart D Ehrman, OUP 2003

The Lure and Romance of Alchemy: A history of the secret link between magic and science, CJS Thompson, 1932, Bell 1990

Magick in Theory and Practice, Aleister Crowley, 1929, Castle Books 1991

Magic: The Western Tradition, Francis King, Thames & Hudson 1975

The Magical Arts: Western Occultism and Occultists, Richard Cavendish, Arkana 1984

The Magus, or Celestial Intelligencer; being a complete system of Occult Philosophy, Francis Barrett, 1801, Aquarian Press 1989 facsimile

A New Encyclopedia of Freemasonry, AE Waite, 1921, University Books 1970

The New Believers: A Survey of Sects, "Cults" & Alternative Religions, David V Barrett, Cassell 2001

Nobly Born: An Illustrated History of the Knights Templar, Stephen Dafoe, Lewis Masonic 2007

The Occult Philosophy in the Elizabethan Age, Frances A Yates, Routledge & Kegan Paul 1979

The Other God: Dualist Religions from Antiquity to the Cathar Heresy, Yuri Stoyanov, Yale Nota Bene 2000

The Penguin Dictionary of Religions, John R Hinnells, Penguin 1984

The Perennial Dictionary of World Religions, Keith Crim, ed, Harper and Row 1989

The Perfect Heresy: The Life and Death of the Cathars, Stephen O'Shea, Profile Books 2000

The Real History Behind the Templars, Sharan Newman, Berkley 2007

Religions of the World: A comprehensive encyclopedia of beliefs and practices, J Gordon Melton & Martin Baumann, eds, 4 vols, ABC–CLIO 2002

Revelations of the Golden Dawn: The Rise & Fall of a Magical Order, RA Gilbert, Quantum 1997

The Rosicrucian Enlightenment, Frances A Yates, Routledge 1972

The Rosicrucian Enlightenment Revisited, Ralph White, ed, Lindisfarne Books 1999

Rosslyn Chapel Revealed, Michael TRB Turnbull, Sutton Publishing 2007

The Rosslyn Hoax? – Viewing Rosslyn Chapel from a new perspective, Robert LD Cooper, Lewis Masonic 2006

Secret Societies, Norman MacKenzie, ed, Aldus 1967

The Social Impact of Freemasonry on the Modern Western World: The Canonbury Papers Vol 1, MDJ Scanlan, ed, Canonbury Masonic Research Centre 2002

The Spirit of Masonry, Foster Bailey, Lucis Press 1957

Symbolism in Craft Freemasonry, Colin Dyer, 1976, Lewis Masonic 2003 edn

The Tarot of the Bohemians, Papus, George Redway 1896, trs AP Morton, Studio Editions 1994

The Templars: Knights of God, Edward Burman, Aquarian Press 1986

The Theatre of the World: Alchemy, Astrology and Magic in Renaissance Prague, Peter Marshall, Harvill Secker 2006

Warrior Cults: A History of Magical, Mystical and Murderous Organisations, Paul Elliott, Blandford 1995

The Way of Hermes: Corpus Hermeticum, Duckworth 1999

The Way of the Craftsman: A Search for the Spiritual Essence of Freemasonry, W Kirk MacNulty, Arkana 1988

The Western Way: A Practical Guide to the Western Mystery Tradition. Vol 2 The Hermetic Tradition, Caitlín & John Matthews, Arkana 1986

Who's Afraid of Freemasons?, Alexander Piatigorsky, Harvill 1997

World Freemasonry: An Illustrated History, John Hamill & RA Gilbert, Aquarian Press 1991

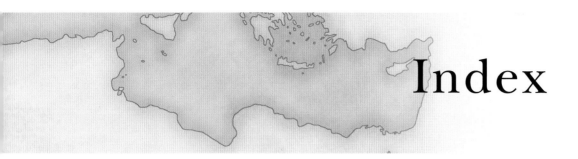

Index

Acknowledgements

The author would like to thank all those who have shared their knowledge over the years. Especial thanks to Geraldine Beskin of Atlantis Bookshop, London, for her friendship and wisdom, for allowing use of her painting of MacGregor Mathers by Moina Mathers, and for her identification of the painting of Mina Bergson by Beatrice Offor.

PICTURE ACKNOWLEDGEMENTS

akg-images 23, 32, 39, 160, 62; /Elie Bernager 86; /British Library 29, 77; /Jean-Paul Dumontier 139; /Alfio Garozzo 16. **Alamy**/Bertrand Boysset, Visual Art Library 82; /Andrew Butler, The National Trust Photolibrary 147 bottom; /David Cairns 1, 79, 141; /Frank Chmura 59; /Classic Image 64, 84, 144; /Damon Coulter 156; /EmmePi Images 15; /Robert Estall Photo Agency 142; /Eddie Gerald 53; /Golden Gate Images 158; /Lebrecht Music and Arts Photo Library 105; /Londonstills.com 83; /Francisco Martinez 122; /Mary Evans Picture Library 97, 98, 157; /Miguel A. Munoz Pellicer 137; /The Print Collector 68; /Benjamin Redeleit, Imagebroker 67; /Judith Tewson 31; /Trip 38; /Bob Turner 102; /Visual Arts Library (London) 104; /VISUM Foto GmbH 60; /Julia Waterlow, Eye Ubiquitous 148. **The Art Archive** 14; Archaeological Museum, Venice, Alfredo Dagli Orti 17; /Bodleian Library Oxford, Add A287 folio 12v 49. **Supplied courtesy of David Barrett** 126. **Bridgeman Art Library**/Bibliotheque Nationale, Paris, Archives Charmet 37; /Boston Athenaeum 80; /Hamah, Syria, Bildarchiv Steffens 34; /Louvre, Paris 99; /Private Collection 51, 73 top, 106, 107 right, 147 top; /Private Collection, The Stapleton Collection 52. **British Library** 13. **Bruce Castle Museum** (Haringey Culture, Libraries & Learning) 109. **Chic and Tabatha Cicero** 111. **Corbis**/118 right, 153; /ANSA/ANSA 100; /Niall Benvie 21; /Bettmann 69, 113, 118 left, 138; /Stefano Bianchetti 96; /Christophe Boisvieux 150; /Bojan Brecelj 8; /Horace Bristol 161; /Brooklyn Museum 163; /Pascal Deloche, Godong 43; /Orjan F. Ellingvag 135; /Fine Art Photographic Library 65; /Origlia Franco, Sygma 22; /Historical Picture Archive 145; /Hulton-Deutsch Collection 125; /Phillipe Lissac, Godong 7; /William Manning, www.williammanning.com 46; /Vittoriano Rastelli 101 right; /Lee Snider, Photo Images 81; /Stapleton Collection 42, 54, 55, 57; /Jacques Torregano, JT0212 25; /Steven Vidler, Eurasia Press 44. **Getty Images** 112, 114, 124, 134; /AFP 101 left; /Doug Armand 94; /Martin Gray 5, 164; /Andrew Ward/Life File 74. **Supplied courtesy of Robert Gilbert** 107 left, 110. **Jupiterimages** 10. **P. R. Koenig**, http://www.cyberlink.ch/~koenig 130, 131 bottom left;. **The Library and Museum of Freemasonry** 88. **Mary Evans Picture Library** 28, 30, 47, 70, 71, 87, 89, 90, 91, 108, 151, 162; /Harry Price 9. **Robert McLean** 132. **Scala**, Florence, Photo Opera Metropolitana Siena 127. **TopFoto**/Fortean 66; /Roger-Viollet 63 bottom, 119; /Topham Picturepoint 33 left, 63 top, 116, 131 centre; /Charles Walker 18, 73 bottom, 78, 115, 117

The publishers would also like to thank Geraldine Beskin for her kind assistance in sourcing photographs and illustrations.

Executive Editor Sandra Rigby
Senior Editor Charlotte Macey
Executive Art Editor Sally Bond
Designers Annika Skoog, Shane Whiting & Claire Dale for Cobalt ID
Illustrator Lee Gibbons
Senior Production Controller Simone Nauerth
Picture Researcher Vickie Walters